MARVEL

Purdue Studies in Romance Literatures

Editorial Board

Íñigo Sánchez Llama, Series Editor
Elena Coda
Paul B. Dixon
Patricia Hart

Deborah Houk Schocket
Gwen Kirkpatrick
Allen G. Wood

Howard Mancing, Consulting Editor
Floyd Merrell, Consulting Editor
Joyce L. Detzner, Production Editor
Susan Y. Clawson, Consulting Production Editor

Associate Editors

French
Jeanette Beer
Paul Benhamou
Willard Bohn
Thomas Broden
Gerard J. Brault
Mary Ann Caws
Glyn P. Norton
Allan H. Pasco
Gerald Prince
Roseann Runte
Ursula Tidd

Italian
Fiora A. Bassanese
Peter Carravetta
Benjamin Lawton
Franco Masciandaro
Anthony Julian Tamburri

Luso-Brazilian
Fred M. Clark
Marta Peixoto
Ricardo da Silveira Lobo Sternberg

Spanish and Spanish American
Maryellen Bieder
Catherine Connor
Ivy A. Corfis
Frederick A. de Armas
Edward Friedman
Charles Ganelin
David T. Gies
Roberto González Echevarría
David K. Herzberger
Emily Hicks
Djelal Kadir
Amy Kaminsky
Lucille Kerr
Howard Mancing
Floyd Merrell
Alberto Moreiras
Randolph D. Pope
Elżbieta Skłodowska
Marcia Stephenson
Mario Valdés

 volume 70

MARVELOUS BODIES
Italy's New Migrant Cinema

Vetri Nathan

Purdue University Press
West Lafayette, Indiana

Copyright ©2017 by Purdue University. All rights reserved.

♾ The paper used in this book meets the minimum requirements of American National Standard for Information Sciences—Permanence of Paper for Printed Library Materials, ANSI Z39.48-1992.

Printed in the United States of America
Template for interior design by Anita Noble;
template for cover by Heidi Branham.
Cover photo:
from the motion picture *Terraferma* directed by Emanuele Crialese, director of photography Fabio Cianchetti, copyright Cattleya Srl, Babe Films SAS, France 2 Cinéma, by kind permission of Cattleya.

Cataloging-in-Publication Data on file at the Library of Congress

Contents

vii Preface
ix Acknowledgments
1 **Introduction**
   Detourism: Italy's New Migrant Cinema
   8 The Immigration Question
   11 The Cultural Economy of Detourist Films
   14 Multiculturalism vs. Hybridity
   21 Framing Hybridity
27 **Chapter One**
   Cultural Hybridity in Italy
   27 Postcolonial Studies: A Search for Discrepant Experiences
   30 Bhabha's Hybridity
   32 Italy's Chronic Ambivalence—The Ghosts of Crises Past
   38 The Centrality of Ambivalence
   39 The Stereotype-as-Fetish
   40 Stereotype-as-Fetish: The Importance of the Visible and of Repetition
   42 Mimicry
   45 The Menace of Mimicry and the Reinscription of the Stereotype (or, Of Ministers and Orangutans)
   48 The Marvelous: Locating Hybridity on Screen
   52 Postcolonial Studies and Italy— A Few Paths Forward
55 **Chapter Two**
   Beyond Neorealism: The Cinematic Body-as-Nation
   57 The Body-as-Nation
   60 Neorealism Is Dead, Long Live Neorealism!
   62 Containing Neorealism
   71 The Centrality of Chronic Ambivalence in Post-Neorealist Film
   79 The Realist and Humoristic Modes of Representation
85 **Chapter Three**
   Ambivalent Geographies
   86 Oneiric Spaces in Matteo Garrone's *Terra di mezzo*

Contents

- **103** Meditalamerica: *Lamerica* and the Recuperation of Embodied History
- **111** The Politics of Sentimentality: *Quando sei nato non puoi più nasconderti*
- **120** The Haptical Mediterranean: Crialese's *Terraferma*

131 Chapter Four
Ambivalent Desires: Desiring Gazes: Bhabha and Mulvey
- **135** The Volatile Sexual Politics of the Gaze: *Pummarò* and *Lettere dal Sahara*
- **148** Guess Who's Coming for an Italian Dinner?— The Palatable Immigrant in *Bianco e nero*
- **157** Marriage, Bengali-Style: Vittorio Moroni's *Le ferie di Licu*
- **167** Immigrant-as-Masquerade: Sugar-Coated Fantasy in *Lezioni di cioccolato*

175 Chapter Five
Ambivalent Moralities
- **178** Ambivalent Affect: Double-Visions in *La sconosciuta* and *La doppia ora*
- **191** Those Damn Earrings: Latent (?) Orientalism in Francesco Munzi's *Il resto della notte*
- **205** Radio as Koran: The War on Terror in Mohsen Melliti's *Io, l'altro*

213 Conclusion
Inside the Paradise of Marvelous Bodies

229 Notes

233 Bibliography

243 Filmography

245 Index

Preface

With a penetrating gaze, a frail Sicilian grandmother studied my 25-year-old grinning, sun-darkened Indian face. She was ageless, who knows how far beyond ninety. She asked me in perfect Sicilian dialect if, when I took a shower, the water in the bathtub turned brown.

I pretended not to understand her question as I tried to formulate an answer. A man standing next to her repeated her words—with a very apologetic look on his face—into standard Italian. I replied that that could indeed happen if I didn't bathe for a week, but fortunately I showered every day. She then asked me if I was a soldier. I couldn't understand why she could possibly think of me as one, although I took it as a wonderful compliment and glad that at least a practically blind person thought that I had a fit physique. The puzzled man witnessing this conversation asked her what she meant by that question. She promptly answered with another question, asking if I had come to liberate Sicily.

This brief and random interaction personally represented for me the marvelous coming together of colonial and postcolonial spaces, times, and bodies. The shriveled grandmother was not all that senile, or perhaps, her senility had allowed her to be brilliantly lucid and honest. She had mistaken me for an Indian soldier enlisted in the frontlines in one of the British companies that landed on the shores of Sicily in World War II. Her seemingly unambiguously racist question about the color of my skin could also be interpreted as a curious questioning of epidermal difference (if it is not even skin-deep, then perhaps it can indeed be washed away?). The postcolonial irruption of my non-white body had somehow instigated a psychological journey back to a time within this woman, a time when a Sicilian such as herself would have experienced the sight of such a body not in the context of contemporary immigration from the global South to Italy, but in that of the liberation of the Italian peninsula by the Allies. The lady's question led me to discover and explore a part of Indian, Italian, and indeed, *world* history that has been mostly repressed or forgotten, including by myself: that of the role of innumerable Indian soldiers that shouldered a significant portion of the Allied war effort against the Axis powers throughout the world stage, often bearing the first brunt of the casualties.

Preface

Convinced that I was indeed a bonafide Allied soldier, and satisfied in her conviction, the nonagenarian smiled a wide toothless grin. She asked me if I was hungry, and insisted that I eat a double portion of the *crostata* that she had just baked.

* * *

Marvelous Bodies: Italy's New Migrant Cinema explores liminal identities and their cinematic representations of both Italians and immigrants in contemporary Italy.

It is characters such as this Sicilian grandmother—fictional, real, or halfway in-between—who inspired me to write it.

Acknowledgments

This book traces its origins to my work in graduate school at Stanford University. Any expressions of gratitude must therefore begin with my dissertation advisor, Laura Wittman, who always demonstrated complete commitment to the project. Three other fabulous women advised me on my Ph.D. committee. In neighboring UC Berkeley, Barbara Spackman "adopted" me as one of her own right from the start. She was, and will be, a primary inspiration for much of my scholarly work. Elisabeth Mudimbe-Boyi urged me to not be afraid of coining new terms and owning my words, and Carolyn Springer constantly provided discerning reflections on my writing.

I am most grateful to my Editor, Elena Coda, for possessing that prized combination of scholarly acumen and collegiality, and for believing in this project right from the start. Several other scholars have helped me with insightful commentary and advice: Graziella Parati, Anthony Tamburri, Áine O'Healy, Derek Duncan, Christina Lombardi-Diop, Dana Renga, Fulvio Orsitto, Shelleen Greene, and Patrick Barron are some of the generous persons who assisted me in rethinking and refining during different stages of writing. My colleagues David Lummus and Sabrina Ferri deserve a shout-out not only for their professional support on how to survive in academia, but also for their steady friendship. In my current institution, I have been blessed by wonderful mentors in the Department of Modern Languages, Literatures and Cultures: Pratima Prasad, Alex Des Forges, and Claudia Esposito have all helped keep this project on track in many different ways. Fiora Bassanese assisted me continually by being such an outstanding colleague and guide.

The next round of thanks goes a little far back in time, but celebrates people who were no less influential in the creation of this book. During my schooling in India, Brother Anish John urged us to read books, dream, and think critically in a school system that actively dissuades and deadens all creativity. My English teacher during high school at the United World College of the Adriatic in Italy, Henry Thomas, taught me how to "stick to the words" in the text while analyzing literature—a seemingly simple piece of advice for which I am still grateful. My undergraduate advisor at Connecticut College, Paola Sica, slowly but

Acknowledgments

surely urged me to build a career in what I truly loved doing rather than taking the "safer" path of a degree in science or management.

My brother, Pramod, has been a loving and constant presence, something not to be taken for granted. My parents, Janak and Shamim, have always challenged me to welcome different opinions and cultural hybridity rather than be afraid or uncertain about them. Their lesson—to be open to "in-between" identities that do not easily fit into usual categories of all kinds is the main inspiration of this project and my life. In many ways they mirror their own parents' thirst for knowledge and social betterment. My maternal grandfather, Abdulgani Attar, began life as a buffalo herder in a (then) small village—Satara—in India, ended up at the University of Birmingham to study Shakespeare, but then returned to India to help open schools for farmers' children. My paternal grandmother, Arama Nathan, was a pioneering female educator and an embodiment of guts and discipline.

A portion of my article "Mimic-Nation, Mimic-Men: Contextualizing Italy's Migration Culture through Bhabha," from *National Belongings: Hybridity in Italian Colonial and Postcolonial Studies,* was reproduced in Chapter 2 of this volume by permission of Peter Lang International Academic Publishers. Thanks also to Grace Russo Bullaro, editor of *From Terrone to Extracomunitario: New Manifestations of Racism in Contemporary Italian Cinema: Shifting Demographics and Changing Images in a Multi-Cultural Globalized Society* for allowing me to re-publish a portion of my article "Nuovo Cinema Inferno: The Affect of Ambivalence in Giuseppe Tornatore's *La sconosciuta,*" in Chapter 5.

And finally—Angelo. I cannot properly express my gratitude for his love, fortitude, compassion for others, innocence, stubbornness, intelligence, and unquenchable humor. Both he and his family in Italy have accepted me as one of their own—and that is a truly marvelous thing.

Introduction

Detourism:
Italy's New Migrant Cinema

Terra di mezzo (*In-Between Land*, Matteo Garrone, 1996) and *Io, l'altro* (*I, The Other*, Mohsen Melliti, 2006) do not feature on most "must-see" movie lists. The first film explores the lives of immigrant communities from Nigeria, Albania, and Egypt in Rome while the latter is a taut maritime drama/thriller/bromance-gone-wrong set in a tense post–9/11 world. Both films remain largely unnoticed partly because they do not meet the criteria of what constitutes a lucrative Italian product, especially for international release—they are neither art house masterpieces nor one of those emotionally/romantically riveting Italian "pretty" films set in stereotypically touristic landscapes. Indeed, a majority of Italian films that have a global presence tend to be either romantic melodramas such as *Il postino* (*The Postman*, Michael Radford, 1994) and *Cinema Paradiso* (Giuseppe Tornatore, 1988), or occasional film festival circuit and auteur-driven "art-house" productions such as the works by Rossellini, Antonioni, and Fellini, or more recently, films such as Paolo Sorrentino's Academy Award winner *La grande bellezza* (*The Great Beauty*, 2013) and Matteo Garrone's *Gomorra* (*Gomorrah*, 2008). This book investigates films like *Terra di mezzo* and *Io, l'altro* despite their relative inconspicuousness at a global distribution level because they represent both an exciting development in the long and rich trajectory of Italy's filmmaking tradition, as well as pose challenging questions about the study of transnational and globalized cinema and culture. They are examples of Italy's "New Migrant Cinema"—films that explore the nation's dramatic contemporary social and cultural phenomenon of immigration into Italy from the global South.

The United Nations Secretary General's special representative on migration Peter Sutherland declared global trends of human flows to be "one of the great issues of our time" (Ní Chonghaile),

Introduction

pointing to the fact that immigration has most certainly become a major issue for Italy and Europe. The choice of a slim majority of British citizens to leave the European Union by voting for "Brexit" in June 2016 and the election of Donald Trump as President of the United States in November of the same year on a deeply anti-immigrant platform highlight this increasingly polarized global political and cultural reaction to immigration. At the time of writing, the Old Continent's refugee crisis due to instability in the Middle East was making headlines across the world in 2015 and 2016, and yet it is a social and cultural situation that is neither new nor unprecedented for Italy. Indeed, much can be learned by contextualizing today's events through Italy's experience of immigration from the global South that began in the 1980s. Cinematic responses in Italy to this important societal change present an astonishing variety of approaches. One such response is *Terra di mezzo*—a low-budget film by Matteo Garrone, who would go on to gain international fame with his slick crime exposé *Gomorra*. It represents a day in the life of three different groups of immigrants in Rome's periphery with a hybrid documentaristic/dramatic/comedic style. While even Italian audiences may not have easy access to this interesting work, it represents an encouraging trend in Italian cinema of innovative and thought-provoking productions that tackle the nation's complicated birthing of a globalized, "multi-ethnic" society. I would even venture to declare that immigration is one of the prime social catalysts that have stimulated the renewal of Italian cinema after its relative decline in the last two decades of the twentieth century.

Initial new migrant cinema tends to resemble forms of *cinema di impegno* (*cinema engagé*) in the tradition of neorealism one would expect from a socially important subject such as immigration: *Pummarò* (*Tomato*, 1990) and *Lamerica* (1990) have been categorized roughly within this type of "neo-neorealistic" drama. Yet, the most recent scholarship has begun to note that new migrant cinema has evolved from its first initial tendencies toward neo-neorealistic melodramas to a far greater variety of genres:

> At the same time, today's cinema of migration is more subject than genre; beside traditional narratives like those of illegality and crime, deracination and abscondence, the Italian cinema

> of migration takes on an increasingly wider spectrum of topics, layers, and spaces of the most diverse streams and realities of migratory life [...] playing with the genre or the audience's genre expectations is a central feature. (Schrader and Winkler)

Marvelous Bodies parses the degrees of cultural and stylistic hybridity present in even relatively familiar new migrant cinema produced roughly between the two decades 1990 and 2010, and seeks to expose how even in films labeled as neo-neorealistic, such as *Pummarò*, tensions both evident and more subtle rise up to haunt seemingly established dichotomies of a stable Italian/European Self and the displaced Immigrant/Oriental Other. This book attempts first to resolve theoretical definitions of cultural hybridity in order to tackle questions of how race, gender, and national identity are negotiated in Italy today through representations of bodies on screen.

With regard to the formal qualities of this cinematic corpus, it can be said that a general trajectory is that of increasing experimentation with respect to genre from the initial films of the early 1990s to the later films of the late 2000s. However, this trend is not consistent. As I will attempt to demonstrate, many early films already contained complex representations, whereas some later films have maintained more traditional Self/Other dichotomies in their representations of the encounters between Italians and immigrants. For instance, *Terra di mezzo* preempts the evolutionary arc of new migrant cinema released roughly between the two decades explored in this book as it already features many of the hybrid thematic and stylistic elements that have emerged in the later films of the period which show relatively more experimentation beyond the neo-neorealistic and a resulting questioning of Manichean identities. Indeed, as I hope to show in the following chapters, more recent films have flirted with more popular genres of Italian cinema in favor with domestic audiences such as comedies (in the tradition of the *commedia all'italiana*) and crime thrillers (*i gialli*).[1] Regardless of genre, I would like to contend that the specters of past traditions such as neorealism, the *commedia all'italiana*, or the "auteur" film tend to cast shadows over these contemporary films, thus revealing how the stylistic choices of directors in Italy are still connected to ideological and cultural positions. It is my hope to be able to tease apart some of these historical connections, as well as to provide a fruitful critical framework that will contextualize new migrant cinema for further study of other films that have appeared and will undoubtedly continue to emerge in the coming years. The overarching aim of this book is to provide a theoretical framework in order to understand how and why these films voluntarily or involuntarily represent liminal identities.

In this introduction, I first describe how the new migrant films explored in this book are "detourist"—in that they use the dramatic cultural situation of immigration to explore the contours of the Italian nation-state. This section also launches the discussion of cultural hybridity that will then be analyzed in detail in the first chapter. Italy's sharp, often racist, yet ultimately divided response to its postcolonial immigration question might tempt scholars to inferentially connect its negative reactions to its role as a colonizer in the Liberal and Fascist eras, and, at the same time, describe the immigration situation as an unprecedented cultural situation. I would like to move away from the temptation to interpret today's immigration situation as an extraordinary first-time event and illustrate the nation's more complex connections to the nation's history of colonization, unification, and post-war social change. For example, it is important to note that Italy's cruel yet relatively unsuccessful colonial enterprises, which were dominated by discourses and practices of racial and civilizational superiority over the colonized populations, did not arise from a firm belief in a stable national identity but from its perceived insecurities as a hybrid nation. As Jacqueline Andall and Derek Duncan explain, the fear of hybridity characterized Italy's fears of racial contamination in the colonial eras:

> Mussolini, in his Ascension Day Speech (1927) embraced the discourse of public hygiene intent on purging Italy of all its impurities, and imagined himself a surgeon responsible for excising the nation's infected parts. After Empire had been declared in 1936, this fear of contamination gnawed at the sense of Italy's entitlement to its hard-won colonial bounty. Legislation was introduced in Italian East Africa to prohibit contact between colonizers and colonized. (Andall and Duncan 9)

Contemporary Italian society's postcolonial fears of immigration, encouraged by political and social organizations for electoral gain, often echo similar colonial racial and cultural anxieties and thus inadvertently recall a colonial history that has been repressed and disavowed for decades.[2] Yet, as this book will demonstrate, the various cultural and political responses that seek to reduce or delimit migrants and criticize supranational European Union or Schengen-area immigration policies as well as local and national attempts to embrace the social and cultural changes, only further underline the nation's complex positioning as a hybrid entity rather than affirm its status as a Western European/Colonizer nation vis-à-vis the Colonizer/Colonized dichotomy. Indeed, *Marvelous Bodies* intends to illustrate how Italian cinema's responses to immigrant subjects uncover this ambivalent and complicated positioning.

For the reasons mentioned above, this introduction initiates the discussion of cultural hybridity, while the first chapter closely tracks the evolution of understanding of hybridity in the field of postcolonial studies in order to describe my concept of "marvelous bodies." I map hybridity as it moves away from fixity to movement, and from describing specificities for a single (often British/Indian) example of colonial rule to multiple uses, in order to underline the importance of incorporating this change in the study of Italian immigration and its cinematic representations.[3] I argue that Italy sees itself as possessing the unique qualification as being the quintessential internal Other in Western Europe, and this perception directly influences its cinematic response to immigrants—Europe's external Others. This permanent crisis—the contradiction of being both European and ... yet not quite—has caused a situation of what I term as "chronic ambivalence"[4] with regard to its national identity vis-à-vis this dominant cultural dichotomy. My concept of chronic ambivalence is based upon Homi Bhabha's descriptions of the stereotype and cultural hybridity in *The Location of Culture*.[5] Italy's national chronic ambivalence is a central premise to an analysis of the thirteen Italian films of immigration in the following chapters.

The investigation of the formal elements of the films through an understanding of the nation's chronic ambivalence illustrates how the cinematic bodies of immigration on the Italian screen are often what I call "Marvelous," i.e., antithetical to the stereotype produced by mass-consumed images of immigrants that dominate the Italian television and other mass-media, popular

Introduction

imagination, and political discourse. Instead of a disavowal of chronic ambivalence through the application of ethnic or national stereotypes, these cinematic marvelous bodies create a *temporary suspension* of identities, thereby engaging the viewer with an experiential alternative to a Manichean perspective of "Us" versus "Them" and arousing stupor, wonder, or astonishment rather than recognition in the viewer. The "marvelous bodies" of this book's title is therefore, simply put, my term to label the thematic or audiovisual presences of hybridity in cinematic texts and may be applied to "migrant" as well as "Italian" bodies. For example, in *Terra di mezzo*, which is studied in more detail in Chapter 3, Matteo Garrone deliberately plays with the lighting and framing of his bodies within liminal landscapes in Rome's periphery in order to "suspend" their identities. Rather than a safe "documentaristic" recognition of race, nationality, class, and language, he creates an embodied diegetic world that is uniquely destabilizing and marvelous. Visually, he suspends characters' ethnicity and nationality through a variety of stylistic techniques, including an expressive use of lighting and framing of bodies. Figure 1 shows one such resultant Marvelous body—that of Ahmed/Amedeo—a gas station night attendant of Egyptian origin. Ahmed/Amedeo becomes a hybrid body due to a variety of formal and thematic devices that will be discussed in detail in Chapter 3.

Figure 1: Ahmed/Amedeo, the gas station attendant, awaiting customers. *Terra di mezzo*

If Italy is chronically ambivalent as described in my first chapter, then Italy's national cinema, a privileged national art form, should reflect the inherent tensions generated by this ambivalence. The second chapter, "Beyond Neorealism: The

Cinematic Body-as-Nation," demonstrates how this is indeed the case and argues that the study of new migrant film can gain complexity and depth through the contextual lens provided by Italy's post-war cinematic history. By defining and describing the central stylistic, and therefore, ideological tensions in post-war Italian cinema, I reinforce the critical framework with which the contemporary films of immigration will be analyzed in the following chapters. In order to better illustrate hybrid forms that contain elements of both the intellectual self-reflexivity of the filmmakers in neorealism and the self-reflexivity imposed upon the audience by post-neorealist traditions such as the *commedia all'italiana*, I introduce the terms "realist mode" and "humoristic mode" which reflect general stylistic and thematic tendencies in a film to bend toward the traditions of neorealism and post-neorealism respectively. These two modes represent strategies employed within the films explored in the next three chapters.

The analysis of how the films studied in this book fit into the very curious historical context of hybridity in Italy's national cinema in the first two chapters leads to a study of the films themselves. The first of these chapters (Chapter 3, "Ambivalent Geographies") looks at the embodied landscapes explored in four major films and describes the various ways in which filmmakers begin to emphasize representations of interstitial or liminal cultural spaces in contemporary Italy. The fourth chapter ("Ambivalent Desires") examines five films that are preoccupied with complex representations of gender, desire, and sexuality in a rapidly changing Italian society. The fifth and final chapter ("Ambivalent Moralities") analyzes four films that focus on the stereotype of the immigrant-as-criminal and explores ethical and psychological ambivalence through various stylistic innovations.

All films studied in each of the chapters inherently explore a myriad of themes and concerns beyond the basic theme under which they have been placed, but my ordering of the films into these three broad categories serves to use the main thematic focus as a "trigger" or entry-point into the film. Therefore, connections between the three main themes naturally occur more often than not, and it is my hope that the reader will note these echoes of films located in different chapters. Such cross-pollination between the three main themes, I believe, actually serves to bring out some of the most interesting aspects of these films in relief. So, for

Introduction

example, while the analysis of Giuseppe Tornatore's *La sconosciuta* (*The Unknown Woman*, 2006) primarily addresses questions of ambivalent moral/criminal intentions of its main protagonist, it nevertheless presents reflections on the other important aspect, i.e., its focus in the immigrant woman's body as erotic and reproductive object of desire.

Marvelous Bodies does not claim to survey an exhaustive list of films on Italian immigration produced in the last few decades.[6] For example, it leaves out the large category of documentary films, although I have included examples of hybrid genres that play with the boundaries of documentary and fiction. This is a study of some of the most familiar and representative works of new migrant cinema that can be used to understand the multitude of strategies being used by the Italian cinematic industry to represent a changing society while seeking to provide a valid theoretical framework to understanding these strategies. I sincerely hope that this book, which principally looks at films from 1990 to 2010, will provide any reader with further curiosity to explore the wide variety of other even more recent films that explore Italy's hybrid contemporary culture.

To summarize: the central questions I would like to answer by exploring these films placed in three broad thematic groups, through the lens of selected postcolonial and cinematic theories, are: At a psychical level, how do these films mirror an ordering of society in the face of the vital crisis of immigration? How is this ordering in cinema carried out through each film's formal elements? How do stereotypes of nation, race, gender, and culture intersect in creating a coherent national cinematic body that includes or excludes immigrants? How does the ideological and formal ordering of films about immigration compare or contrast with historical precedents in Italy's illustrious cinematic tradition?

The Immigration Question

Italy is experiencing a vital crisis of extensive immigration from the East and South of the world that has major socio-political and cultural implications. What differentiates Italy when compared to other more dominant Western European former colonial nations is the relatively recent boom in its immigrant population after decades of comparative isolation.[7] As immigrant bodies became

Introduction

a familiar sight in Italian public spaces over a short amount of time, it grew to become one of the most important and contentious issues throughout the two decades studied in this book, climaxing during the 2008 national elections, when the Popolo delle libertà (PDL—People of Freedoms), Italy's center-right coalition led by then incumbent prime-minister Silvio Berlusconi, with major support from Umberto Bossi's anti-immigrant Lega Nord (Northern League), were handed a convincing victory. The mayoral race in Rome is an example of how immigration also greatly influenced local politics during the Berlusconi years. Home to a traditionally center-left constituency, Roman voters decisively chose to elect a mayor with faultless neo-fascist credentials,[8] Gianni Alemanno, leaving his opponent and two-time center-left mayor, Francesco Rutelli, to ruefully explain, "Ho perso sulla sicurezza" (I lost on the security [agenda]) (Vitali). The ability to demonstrate a hard line towards immigrants and rising crime (issues that were often conflated) was considered key to winning the mayoral contest in Rome, so much so that during a televised debate on the eve of the elections, even Rutelli accused Berlusconi's coalition, then called the Casa delle libertà, of being too "soft" on immigrants during his five years in power (Foschi). For the first time since the founding of the First Republic, the generally immigrant-friendly parties on the far left were completely left out of parliament. Multiple political and socio-economic factors influenced the mighty swing toward the Right that began with the rise of Berlusconi in the early 1990s, but successful instrumentalization of the fears of rampant immigration was undoubtedly a principal factor for their continued success. The success of the Northern League party in the 1990s and 2000s is an important precursor to the more recent European trend of fringe "Euro-skeptic" migrant-phobic and/or populist right-wing parties gaining wide-spread mainstream support, such as Marine Le Pen's Front National in France, the United Kingdom Independence Party (UKIP), the Dutch Party for Freedom (PVV), Greece's Golden Dawn, Germany's Patriotic Europeans Against the Islamization of the West (Pegida) and Alternative für Deutschland, Hungary's Fidesz, and Poland's Law and Justice Party, among others. The results of the 2008 election in Italy resulted in the continuation of a conservative stamp on social policy in relation to immigration through an accelerated state-sponsored securitization of the immigration question, such as the implementation of the "Bossi-Fini" law in 2002 that criminalized illegal immigration.⁹ Only the Euro-zone economic crisis that gained full-fledged emergency status by 2010, causing the resignation of the Berlusconi government and the one-year technical government of Mario Monti in 2012 caused a temporary distraction from what was undoubtedly the central issue facing the electorate. The installation of a fragile grand-coalition government under Gianni Letta in April 2013, leading to the appointment of Italy's first black minister, the Congolese-Italian Cécile Kyenge as Minister of Equal Opportunity and Integration, once again served as a reminder that the immigration question would always be in the forefront of contemporary Italy's cultural wars. Since 2012, increased instability in the southern and eastern Mediterranean coasts from various failed "Arab Spring" movements, the continued consequences of the Iraq war, the ongoing Syrian war, the rapid development of radical movements such as ISIS, etc., has led to increased pressures on Italy from "boat-people" making tragic attempts to cross the Mediterranean to safety. For example, in 2014, primarily under the new Prime Minister Matteo Renzi from the Partito democratico (PD—Democratic Party), the Italian navy rescued roughly half of the 170,000 immigrants that were in danger of drowning in the Mediterranean through an operation called Mare Nostrum. This initiative has since been disbanded due to lack of funds and replaced by a much-reduced European Frontex Operation Triton (Kingsley). Such pressures on the Mediterranean front have only exacerbated that nation's troubled approach to the question of immigration. The tragic everyday news stories in 2015 of masses of living and dead migrant bodies arriving at Europe's eastern borders and in the Mediterranean, best exemplified at its most extreme by the images of the dead body of three-year-old Syrian refugee Aylan Kurdi,¹⁰ demonstrate the global dimensions of this migration, which was until this moment considered to be primarily a domestic problem of a few Southern European nations such as Italy, Spain, Greece, and Turkey.¹¹ Europe's leaders finally woke up to the urgency of the migrant crisis during this predicament due to it being affected wholly, including at its centers of power, rather than just on its Southern and Eastern peripheries. Even as the E.U. tries to come up with a coherent answer as individual member-states unilaterally put up previously dissolved borders, the very different push-and-pull factors that influence this very heterogeneous mass of bodies trying to enter Europe called "migrants" have been consistently confused and conflated. There is an important distinction to be made between economic migrants, refugees fleeing war, political asylum seekers, and terrorists, but throughout the crisis, media, heads of state, local politicians, and many citizens have continued to deliberately or unconsciously confuse these groups. The tragic attacks in Paris in November 2015 and in Brussels in March 2016 have been and will be used by different powers both in the mainstream and the Muslim minority groups to urge for better integration of the Islamic community in mainstream Europe, or more likely, to polarize the population by perpetuating cultural stereotypes. What remains certain, despite these twists and turns of dramatic events, is the fact that the future of what the entire European project represents will be decided by how the European Union responds to its immigration question.

The Cultural Economy of Detourist Films

Benedict Anderson suggested that all nations are imagined communities. He clarifies that while the entity of the nation is not a falsity or fabrication, it is not an objective and eternal entity but a product of cultural discourse and imagination. Expanding upon this idea of a mechanism of nation-building and identity-creation through cultural products, I would like to posit as a central premise that the new migrant cinema studied in this book is not only an artistic excursion into the world of immigrants—the "Other" or outsiders to the imagined entity of the Italian nation—but is also an indirect cultural (re)appraisal of the "Self," the nation itself. The ideological (side)effects of these films allow them to be examined as particularly rich examples of nation-building through cinema and, in this way, form the latest iteration of a long tradition of cinema as a privileged mass-medium for the creation of Italian-ness. Understood in this perspective, the films studied here are similar to travel literature, in that they create and structure meaning during wandering through which the "home culture" can be secured, stabilized, and then understood. Due to this similarity, I would like to use the concept of *oikos* to better reveal the cultural

Introduction

work of nation-building carried out in these films. This term is coined by Georges Van Den Abbeele to define the traveler's point of reference and stability in the economy of travel:

> The economy of travel requires an *oikos* (the Greek word for "home" from which is derived "economy") in relation to which any wandering can be *comprehended* (enclosed as well as understood). In other words, a home(land) must be posited from which one leaves on the journey and to which one hopes to return—whether one actually makes it back home changes nothing, from this perspective. The positioning of an *oikos*, or *domus* (the Latin translation of *oikos*) is what *domesticates* the voyage by ascribing certain limits to it. (Van Den Abbeele xvii–xviii)

The Italian films that explore the bodies, lifestyles, and landscapes of immigrants as their explicitly declared subject are therefore also implicit and indirect forays into the understanding of the cultural geography that shapes the imagined community of the Italian nation itself. What is particularly of interest to me in these films is not only how these films represent immigrants in Italy, but what they tell us about the Italians themselves.

Due to the presence of these indirect sorties into the exploration of the Italian cultural economy, these films can be termed as "detourist" films, in that they configure a thematic swerve that fulfills the specific ideological function of securing the identity of the Italian *oikos*. In an essay on nineteenth-century traveler Amalia Nizzoli, Barbara Spackman describes the writer's journal about her experiences in Egypt as a "detourist" text, i.e., an indirect construction of an Italian nation through the touristic descriptions of what it is *not* (Spackman 35–54). Inventing a term that is a play on words that utilizes the citationary nature of Orientalism/tourism and the metaphor of a detour, Spackman highlights how Nizzoli's travel narrative of Egyptian life functions as the author's self–nationalization as a European (and therefore Italian) by the process of orientalization of Muslims and the mediation of nationality through her identification with other Europeans in Egypt. It is important to remind the reader here that the films of immigration explored in this book are principally Italian productions hiring the creative powers of vast teams of mostly Italian artists, or even in the rare cases where they are not helmed by an

Italian director (such as Mohsen Melliti's film *Io, l'altro*), are most certainly directed toward Italian audiences. These films therefore do not exactly constitute an "accented cinema," if one is to use the term that Hamid Naficy coined to describe works created by filmmakers that contain translations of their own personal experience of postcoloniality, diaspora, exile, or other displacements (Naficy). Indeed, *Marvelous Bodies* reveals just how slippery the exact locations of such "accents" are in new migrant cinema, and how often hybridity creates situations where there are rapid oscillations and/or dislocations of the "accent" that Naficy's project intends to map in cinematic productions.

New migrant cinema is detourist in that it is consciously or unconsciously concerned with the creation or re-negotiation of Italian-ness as much as it presents testimonials of immigrant reality. In doing so, it fulfills two interesting cultural functions that can be represented by adding and then displacing a hyphen within the term "detourism": so first, this cinema is *de*-tourist—i.e., an antithesis of touristic, in that it explores cultural landscapes, bodies, and rules that displace representations of canonical touristic settings that cinematic audiences associate with Italy and Italians. For example, *Terra di mezzo*, set in Rome, studiously avoids the ubiquitous touristic markers of the Eternal City, concentrating instead on rigorously mundane settings in the urban periphery. In addition to shifting the emphasis to the nation-state's liminal physical and cultural identities through such *de*-tourism, new migrant films are also often "*detour*-ist," in that they intentionally or unintentionally embark on alternative paths that thematically swerve away from their declared subject of exploration (immigrants) into a mostly undeclared exploration of Italy's own cultural identity. To go back to the film I am using as an example: it would be only partly true to call it a film about immigration. As the analysis of *Terra di mezzo* in Chapter 3 demonstrates, migrants are a conduit that allow the filmmakers to simultaneously detour into an exploration of the foibles and strengths of a gamut of Roman citizens that interact with them on a daily basis.

In addition to this double-detourist nature of the films explored in this book, a further, extra layer of richness and complexity is offered by the instability of the supposed *oikos* of the Italian nation that underpins these cinematic wanderings, a situation that will

Introduction

be further explored in the next chapter. When the starting point of reference for the "travel" into otherness is itself in question, when "accents" are sometimes inconveniently present even within the very center of the national cinematic corpus, a rich and complicated series of negotiations around the creation of a national economy of cinematic travel becomes inevitable.

Multiculturalism vs. Hybridity

At this point, scholars are faced with some urgent questions about the appropriate methodology to analyze a complex cultural situation presented by immigration in contemporary Italy, both within the context of the Italian national cultural environment and in its comparative dimensions in relation to other historical and contemporary migratory or globalized cultures. I propose to demonstrate through the analysis of some of the most familiar examples of detourist new migrant cinema that this crisis has the potential of revealing nagging ambivalences not only in contemporary Italian culture, but also in Italy's historical relationships with its own internal South and the South of the world, particularly culturally disavowed or repressed ties such as its problematic unification and its colonial enterprise. Postcolonial theory has traditionally focused on the major former colonial powers such as England and France, but Italy's immigration crisis has finally provoked a long-overdue exploration of what I would like to call the "Italian case." Much needs to be done to recuperate this dearth of analysis and understanding of Italy's location on the map of postcolonial cultures.

Pioneers such as Graziella Parati and Armando Gnisci have done some excellent work to raise the profile of the new field of Italian-immigration studies—mainly within the field of literary studies.[12] Parati, specifically, has been responsible for almost single-handedly acknowledging Italy's immigration question in American scholarship about Italy and bringing the field of Italian immigration to the forefront. Yet, I believe that far more must be done to firmly establish some of the basic premises of the Italian case of postcoloniality (such as the repercussions of its unstable *oikos*). As scholars examine Italy's encounter with the global South, there is an urgent need to take a step back and ask some more basic questions that do not have obvious or easy answers: *Who* exactly is the subaltern in Italy? Does Italy's own partial subalternity not color its response to its newest subalterns?

An example of some productive yet problematic framing of Italy's immigration crisis shows the need to first answer the basic questions above: Armando Gnisci, in his extensive anthology of immigrant literature, commendably sets out to canonize the more familiar texts of new migrant literature, connecting the works of the pioneers such as Salah Methnani and Saidou Moussa-Ba to the tradition of what he calls the literary greats of the "Grande Migrazione," such as Salman Rushdie, Enzenberger, Brodskij, and Walcott (Gnisci 21). In his introduction to the anthology, Gnisci repeatedly calls the current Italian immigration crisis "la Grande Migrazione attuale" (27) and subsumes the Italian crisis under the greater global historical and contemporary migratory phenomena:

> Per concludere, sostengo che la Grande Migrazione attuale, insieme a quella del passaggio tra i due secoli precedenti, rappresenti l'orizzonte degli avventi e delle apparizioni dentro il quale si configurano e vengono compresi alcuni fenomeni inauditi. Dal punto di vista che ci interessa, quello dell'inizio di una vera e propria coevoluzione delle relazioni culturali planetarie, possiamo segnalarne almeno due, sui quali insisto da tempo: la necessità della creazione ex novo di un discorso interculturale, pacifico e amorevole, dentro la civiltà europea, che non ne conosce ancora il principio e l'uso; il manifestarsi di una arte letteraria, e non solo letteraria, della migrazione mondiale. (27–28)
>
> To conclude, I maintain that the contemporary Great Migration, along with that which occurred between the two previous centuries, represent the horizon of the advent and the appearance within which various novel phenomena will be configured and included. From our point of view, that which interests us in the beginning of a true and proper co-evolution of global cultural relations, are at least two things, which I have insisted upon for a long time: the necessity of a new peaceful and loving inter-cultural discourse within the European civilization, which does not yet exist; the appearance of a literary, and not only literary art of global migration.

This approach, though well-intended and not without many merits, presents some important limitations that must be addressed. First, it overlooks the complexity of the Italian

Introduction

encounter with migrants by placing Italy within a "European civilization." This betrays the presence of an unfortunately still quite dominant notion of multiculturalism that presumes a recent contact between previously distinct blocs of culture or civilizations. Second, Gnisci's anthology is also therefore preoccupied with a scientific classification of the various migrant writers on the basis of their cultural origin, leading to awkward pairings, such as the Roma (gypsy communities, referred to in Italy as the *Rom*) being included in the chapter on immigrants of South and East Asian origins, the reason being that the Roma originally migrated from parts of the Indian subcontinent.[13] Gnisci is also particular about classifying first-generation immigrants as distinct from second generations, chiding editors that have masqueraded authors as second-generation immigrants when they are not.[14]

This attention to detail might be important for a comparative literary analysis, but is not very fecund as a cultural (or even linguistic) appraisal of both the Italian nation's unstable identity and Italy's remarkably heterogeneous immigrant population, which is made up of an astonishing variety of relatively ill-formed, small, ethnic, national, and generational groupings that inflict, to use a phrase by Homi Bhabha, a "classificatory confusion" (130) between identities and identifications. The diversity and fragmentary nature of the immigrant communities in Italy mirrors the fragmentation of the host nation's own identity (the instability of its *oikos*), thus creating a doubling/mirroring of already present confusions. It is important to note the bewildering diversity of the national origins of the immigrant community in Italy, which owes its pull-factors not to colonial ties (such as the dominant British immigrant community from the Indian subcontinent or the Algerian and Senegalese communities in France), but to contemporary global circumstances. As of 2013, some of the principal nationalities of immigrants in Italy are: Romania (21.27%), Albania (10.6%), Morocco (9.7%), and China (5%). Other major immigrant communities, comprised of numbers between 2 and 5 percent are: Ukraine, Moldovia, Poland, Tunisia, The Philippines, India, Bangladesh, and Peru.[15] It is for these two reasons that Italy's migration culture is in an extremely magmatic state, leading to solidarity, interaction, and identity creation between and across communities that can often seem unexpected. It is therefore imperative for scholars of Italian immigration culture to avoid making a categorical mistake while discussing hybridity in the analysis of migrant literature, film, and culture: stating or reinstating notions of multiculturalism that purport to explain it in terms of a contact or an interaction of two or more different cultures, thus assuming that these cultural differences exist "outside the realm of cultural discourse creation" (Smith 251). Abdul JanMohammed and David Lloyd put it excellently when they describe the counter-productive effects of such a world-view:

> [t]he semblance of pluralism disguises the perpetuation of exclusion insofar as it is enjoyed only by those who have already assimilated the values of the dominant culture. For this pluralism, ethnic or cultural difference is merely an exoticism, an indulgence that can be relished without significantly modifying the individual who is securely embedded in the protective body of dominant ideology. Such pluralism tolerates the existence of salsa, it even enjoys Mexican restaurants, but it bans Spanish as a medium of instruction in American schools. (Smith 251)

Put in this way, it is easier to see how the contemporary concept of multiculturalism can be interpreted as simply a more liberal heir to the Victorian notion of hybridity, which, as Robert Young illustrates, was a biological term used to classify and therefore create a scientific language that would obsessively and carefully separate the races (*Colonial Desires*). The mania of classifying hybrid multi-racial progeny of unions between colonizers and colonized only served to emphasize the notion that, in an ideal world, the various races were distinct and separate.

The ground reality in contemporary Italy most certainly does not resemble that of a multicultural Disneyland. Instead, it is a society where classificatory confusion abounds, which mirrors the contemporary Europe-wide classificatory confusion of different types of immigrants that I have discussed in the previous section. A distinct yet dramatic example of this instability is the public recrimination for the rape and murder of 47-year-old Giovanna Reggiani in Rome's Tor di Quinto suburb in November 2007. The suspect, Nicolae Romulus Mailat, resided in a temporary Roma camp, but hatred toward this group led to backlash against all Romanians (Roma and non), Eastern Europeans, and other immigrants in general. The then Prime Minister Romano Prodi hastily convened an emergency cabinet session in which a decree was passed "that will allow prefects—the local representatives of

Introduction

the interior ministry—to expel summarily the citizens of other EU states if they are judged a threat to public security" (Hooper). The Romanians in turn hastily tried to make the Italian public understand that the Roma are not the same as the Romanians, in vain. The fact that a major percentage of the Roma in Italy are Italian citizens was lost upon groups of angry middle-class people of Rome's periphery, as they organized *ronde della libertà* (freedom patrols) to police their neighborhoods against foreign criminals ("Ronde anti-rom dopo le sevizie").

Countless incidents such as those of the aftermath of Giovanna Reggiani's murder illustrate a situation of great identity confusion between shifting groups and sub-groups of Italians and immigrants in contemporary Italy. These cultural ambivalences are reflected within Italian new migrant cinema. Acts of canonization and classification of cultural sub-groups at this point of time are therefore, I believe, premature and often beside the point. Assessing Italy's magmatic migration culture is an extensive project that will require a collective effort by scholars to be fully accomplished, but in this book, I would like to suggest one viable theoretical definition of hybridity that will respect Italy's encounter with the South of the world and give justice to the state of classificatory confusion due to its status as an in-between culture vis-à-vis the categories of colonizer/colonized, center/periphery, the West/Orient.

As a result of this insistence on moving the discourse of immigration cultures away from multiculturalism toward hybridity, the films in this book are thematically divided rather than categorized according to the national or ethnic identities of its migrant subjects. This willed dissolution of the national labels given to both Italian and immigrant bodies shall hopefully demonstrate the underlying hybridity present in both the variety of stylistic approaches by filmmakers and the hybridity of the characters themselves within the diegetic worlds that have been created. To do so will not sidestep questions of cinematic voice as they are connected to hegemonic and subaltern identities on screen, nor questions about race and visible difference, but will actually allow us to tackle headlong subtle questions of power and representation within these cinematic products.

Indeed, as will be demonstrated time and again, despite an unusually fluid and confusionary cultural situation, representations of the immigrant encounter as a meeting between "us" and "them" abound, as they are ultimately a mechanism to safely constrain the boundaries of what constitutes the national Self. An example of such well-meaning but ultimately reductive understanding of cultural hybridity-as-multiculturalism is Agostino Ferrente's *L'orchestra di piazza Vittorio* (*The Piazza Vittorio Orchestra*, 2006). While I will not be exploring documentary film in this book, I believe the commercial success of this film (domestically, but especially internationally) and its implications to the analysis of new migrant cinema are compelling reasons to briefly discuss it here. Also, as Abigail Keating correctly indicates in her essay on this film, it is problematic to classify this film as a documentary. She states that: "it places a number of scenes of mimed musical performances within a film of chiefly original content; it has therefore been marketed as a 'documusical'" (Keating 197–209), thus revealing the slippery and problematic divisions present in this film between documentaristic and fictive representations.

L'orchestra narrates the creation of a multi-national orchestra representing the dazzling diversity of immigrants living in the Piazza Vittorio area of Rome between 2001 and 2006. With the help of the Apollo 11 association, composed of a group of writers, intellectuals and leftist community leaders, musician Mario Tronco decides to encourage the city of Rome to save the local Apollo theater which is in danger of being converted into a privatized bingo hall. Keating hints at the generic hybridity of the film but stops short of fully documenting the problematic representations of the international motley crew of musicians, all under the lead of a white male Italian orchestra director, and represented on the screen by another white male Italian. Paolo Favero is better at showing concrete examples of how the Self/Other dichotomy is (inadvertently?) maintained throughout the film, with the metaphor of musical harmony representing the meeting of diverse cultures having the effect of merely exoticizing them by promoting notions of difference. Writing about one of the protagonists in the film, an Indian man Mohammad Bilal, Favero says: "[the representation of] a Peter Sellers' stereotype of an Indian man [...] undermines the attempt to create a common platform on which to build equal dialogue between Italians and their contemporary 'Others'" (Favero 345). The fact that the story of the orchestra is narrated with a single "voice of God" by filmmaker Ferrente does

Introduction

not help ameliorate the problematic question of authorial voice and the resulting skewed power dynamic between hegemonic and subaltern subjects. Indeed, the non-Italian nature of the migrants is constantly emphasized, leading to it having an Orientalizing and commodifying effect—eclectic cultural difference to be sold in the Italian and international market. An example of film producers' descriptions for the publicity for screening events demonstrates this kind of marketing of reductive multiculturalism rather than a nuanced understanding of cultural hybridity:

> [...] if you want to see a Cuban practice yoga, an Indian on a white Vespa at the Coliseum without a helmet so as not to muss his hair, an Ecuadorian with pangs of love, a macho Arab wearing light pink, a man from Caserta sing in Hindi, an Argentinean who gets evicted from his garage, an Indian sitar player convinced he's Uto Ughi, a New Yorker playing tables, a Senegalese girot who marries one of his students.[16]

In their book *Bianco e nero: storia dell'identità razziale degli italiani*, Gaia Giuliani and Christina Lombardi-Diop persuasively analyze a long trajectory of images of black bodies in modern Italian commercial/media culture, from *Calimero,* a black, anthropomorphized chick, the only black one in a family of yellow chickens; to *Carosello*, an Italian comedy television show featuring sketches and light entertainment; right up to the United Colors of Benetton advertising campaign and other commercials such as that of a laundry detergent, Colorieria italiana, produced in 2006 (Giuliani and Lombardi-Diop). The authors conclude that these popular representations serve to domesticate and contain blackness by commercializing their bodies, and at the same time function as stabilizers of Italian whiteness by assigning the Italian audience the role of consumers of these black bodies that function as stand-ins for the products that these commercials advertise. The representation of the multicultural bodies of *L'orchestra* has a similar domesticating-through-commodification effect, in that it "fixes" them into readily consumed cultural stereotypes that, through detourism, stabilize the Italian *oikos* during a moment of cultural change rather than allow for the presence of uncomfortable liminal identities.

I believe that any approach to the study of Italy's encounter with its many Souths must give due vigilance for such simplistic contextualizations where Italians represent the hegemonic group and the immigrants the "multicultural Other" or categorization of immigrant groups into geographical and racial groupings without any questioning of the Self/Other dichotomy. Italy's immigrant crisis should be fully contextualized within the vibrant historical, geographical, and hence cultural tradition of a chronically hybrid nation. The classificatory confusion caused by Italy's own fraught identity between global dichotomies and the bewildering diversity of its immigrant population combine to make a very productive study of how cultural hybridity actually works. Outdated yet all-too-prevalent notions of multiculturalism, while comforting to many across a broad scholarly, cultural, and political spectrum, serve only to gloss over the essential constructedness of cultural identity and the complex relationships between national identity and its imagined representations. This situation therefore makes it crucial to distinguish and separate notions of multiculturalism and hybridity in any scholarly approach to Italian immigration cultures.

Framing Hybridity

The detourist nature of new migrant cinema in Italy is one of the factors that push the creation of cinematic spaces and bodies that are momentarily or permanently *hybrid* rather than simply multicultural. Therefore, my aim is not to describe the immigration question in terms of an encounter between cultures, but to contextualize this situation as a hybrid moment, where often repressed liminal identities present with the supposedly monolithic national Self as well as the Other come to the forefront, even if it is a fleeting moment. Hybridity, like "multicultural," is a term that is very often used colloquially but has a very specific meaning and mechanism in postcolonial theory. The next chapter establishes exactly what is meant by this word in the context of this book. However, let me give the reader a quick preview here. In his introduction to a key text of postcolonial theory, Robert Young uses the example of the Greenwich Prime Meridian to illustrate the understanding of hybridity as it is currently used in the field, and that is utilized in this book:

> The smooth gold band in the ground marks the Prime Meridian, or Longitude Zero. At the top of this small hill, you

Introduction

> have found yourself at the zero point of the world, at the centre of time itself. Paradoxically, for Greenwich to be the centre of the world in time it must be inscribed in the alterity of space. Stand to the left-hand side of the brass strip and you are in the Western Hemisphere. But move a yard to your right, and you enter the East: whoever you are, you have been translated from a European to an Oriental. Put one foot back to the left of the brass strip and you become undecidably mixed with otherness: an Occidental and an Oriental at once. (Young 1)

All identities are hybrid in Young's description of the word, as they are cultural constructions that provide baselines for measuring identities, geographies, and cultures. Just like a person straddling both sides of the Greenwich Prime Meridian, hybridity in new migrant cinema is sometimes placed right where you least expect it to be present—at the center of the Italian nation, rather than simply at the periphery of the immigrant Other. It should be emphasized here that this understanding of cultural hybridity is diametrically opposite to how the term was understood in colonial times in order to understand racial/biological hybridity:

> [...] hybridity works simultaneously in two ways: "organically," hegemonizing, creating new spaces, structures, scenes, and "intentionally," diasporizing, intervening as a form of subversion, translation, transformation. This doubleness is important both politically and theoretically: without the emphasis on the active, disjunctive moments or movements of homogenization and diasporization, it can easily be objected that hybridization assumes, as was often the case with the nineteenth century theories of race, the prior existence of pure, fixed and separate antecedents. (Young 25)

I therefore use the term "hybrid" to distinguish it from the mechanism that is commonly understood by the term "multicultural" which indirectly assumes separate precursors. This distinction will hopefully help separate the current use of the word by most postcolonial theorists and its historical and/or its colloquial usage. Further chapters in this book seek to demonstrate how Italian filmmakers consciously or unconsciously undertake detourism—move away from their declared intention of exploring the immigrant Other and seek, avoid, or unwittingly fall into innovative ways of representing the hybridity that lies at the core of the Italian nation through various stylistic and thematic devices. These films are therefore wonderful illustrations of cultural hybridity at work in cinematic texts.

Ferzan Özpetek is the one director that comes foremost to mind in any discussion of Italy's new migrant cinema. One of the most prolific and commercially successful directors in contemporary Italy, Özpetek's foreign-ness is often hard to locate and stabilize. Most of his films do not feature immigrants as their main protagonists, and barely explicitly tackle the subject of immigration. This is why it would be productive to discuss his profile as well as one of his most interesting and commercially successful films, *Le fate ignoranti* (*Ignorant Fairies*, 2001, released in America with a very different title: *His Secret Life*). Özpetek's Turkish-Italian identity is often used to categorize him as a migrant filmmaker, yet both his own personal identity and the "Turkish-ness" of his films are notoriously difficult to define. I would like to contend that this occurs because his works (like his own personal identity) are truly hybrid rather than multicultural, while his lush, operatic, and relatively big-budget productions make it even more difficult to designate his works as "accented." Not unlike the other films explored in this book, the classificatory confusion Özpetek's hybrid presence and his work incite therefore presents an interesting challenge for scholars of new migrant cinema in Italy. In contrast to the approach by Ferrente in *L'orchestra*, Özpetek's own personal cultural hybridity (which has allowed him to simultaneously be both Turkish as well as one of the most Italian of all contemporary directors) mirrors the perplexing hybridity of the characters in his films. The bodies in *Le fate ignoranti*, like in other films by Özpetek, elude facile categorizations at almost all attempts, and hybridity lies everywhere in the film—in the center as well in the periphery.

The film explores Antonia's (Margherita Buy) gradual discovery of her husband Massimo's secret parallel life, home, and family. After Massimo dies in a car accident in the first few minutes of the film, a painting with a hidden dedication of love launches Antonia on a hunt to discover its origin. She discovers that not only has Massimo had a lover for seven years, but that, far more shockingly for her, his lover is a man, Michele (Stefano Accorsi). Antonia's gradual entrance into Michele's life and home, which is visually and thematically configured as an alternate world, a hybrid space,

Introduction

causes her to unwillingly initiate a new journey where her personal cultural *oikos* will be radically reconfigured. Antonia's evaluations of her gender, class, racial, national roles are slowly changed and hybridized as she comes into contact with a motley crew that make up Michele's "family," which includes immigrants (principally Serra, a Turkish refugee) and other liminal social elements.

In her essay on the film, Silvia Marchetti describes how "through the character of Antonia, who encounters the foreignness of immigration while facing the Otherness of her husband's homosexual relationship with a man named Michele, the film shows that even within 'us' and not just in 'them,' lies a destabilizing element of otherness" (Marchetti 240). To restate this with the terms I have introduced, hybridity is shown to lie not just in the exoticized Oriental other, but also within the very center of the Italian *oikos*. Marchetti claims that "foreign immigration becomes a meaningful aperture through which Ozpetek brings to the fore other forms of otherness that reveal Italy as a fragmented country …" (240). While I agree with many points in this essay, I would like to argue that Özpetek's ideological move is even more original and radical than that described by Marchetti. Instead of using immigrants as a conduit to an understanding of otherness, the filmmaker utilizes a plethora of hybrid identities—or "marvelous bodies" on-screen that question social roles related to sexual orientation, race, gender, nationality, and family—in order to neutralize multicultural discourses of foreign immigration by internalizing, domesticating, and diffusing otherness. By placing hybrid identities in the center of the new *oikos* created in Michele's home, foreign immigration becomes just one of the many other factors that allow persons to partake in transformational experiences, or to use Young's phrasing: "hegemonizing, creating new spaces, structures, scenes, and […] diasporizing, intervening as a form of subversion, translation, transformation." *Le fate ignoranti* can therefore be characterized as the ultimate detourist film—it undertakes a journey into Italianness by placing hybridity in the center of Rome's urban Italian life rather than presenting otherness as multicultural difference that is meant to be appreciated or understood by the Self, as is the case with *L'orchestra*. The film negotiates a new *oikos* that does not stereotype the immigrant other or the Italian selves but repeatedly challenges viewers to explore in-between and fluid identities where established and pre-conceived patterns fall apart. I will not include a detailed analysis of this film as there are several essays written on the subject.[17] However, it is important to note that the director's difficult categorization as an "immigrant" director, and the fluid identities that populate the diegetic worlds in his films all serve to impress the importance of finding an appropriate framework that will not reduce the study of Italy's complex responses to immigration to an encounter between fixed multi-national antecedents.

The rapidly growing number of *extracomunitari* (the common euphemistic term used to describe immigrants, literally meaning "non-European Community" citizens, but actually used only for all visibly non-white immigrants) has become a leading issue in Italian political and cultural life that will not easily wane in the coming decades. I have described how this immigration crisis has brought about the re-kindling of Italy's own unstable *oikos* vis-à-vis the colonized Orient—the Other it would often rather not be identified with. This introduction on detourist films was accordingly framed by two contrasting responses to the crisis (*L'orchestra di piazza Vittorio* and *Le fate ignoranti*), as it is my aim to attempt to answer some of the range of questions they pose to scholars of new migrant cinema in Italy and beyond. While the productions studied in this book are indeed intentionally or accidentally detourist just like these two films, they are all primarily designed as cultural paths to understanding the dramatic changes Italian society has witnessed in the past few decades. The following chapter will therefore examine current understandings of cultural hybridity in the field of postcolonial studies and define some old and new terms that will then be used in following sections to analyze the rich and complicated cinematic wanderings into the world of migrants in Italy today.

Chapter One

Cultural Hybridity in Italy

Italy's detourist new migrant cinema presents scholars with a unique opportunity to test theories of cultural hybridity. As I have briefly described in the Introduction, postcolonial theory can be useful in carefully distinguishing the commonly used terms of multiculturalism from true hybridity, which is a far better term and mechanism to describe increasingly complex interactions between a variety of cultural groups in a globalized transnational world. In this chapter, I will primarily focus on defining some terms and elucidating aspects of Homi Bhabha's understanding of cultural hybridity that will be useful for the analysis of the films in the following chapters.

Postcolonial Studies: A Search for Discrepant Experiences

The field of postcolonial studies has evolved from its original intentions of analyzing primarily British Commonwealth literature. In order to establish a valid critical framework that will respect Italy's unusual cultural position on the crossroads of the Mediterranean and present a case for the pertinence of postcolonial theory to this study, let me begin with one of the first explicit definitions of "postcolonial," given to us by one of the early scholars in the field, Bill Ashcroft. In *The Empire Writes Back*, he argues that:

> We use the word post-colonial […] to cover all the culture affected by the imperial process from the moment of colonization to the present day. This is because there is a continuity of preoccupations throughout the historical process initiated by the European imperial aggression. We also suggest that it is

Chapter One

> most appropriate as the term for the new cross-cultural criticism which has emerged in recent years and for the discourse through which this is constituted. In this sense this book is concerned with the world as it exists during and after the period of European imperial domination and the effects of this on contemporary literatures.
>
> So the literatures of African countries, Australia, Bangladesh, Canada, Caribbean countries, India, Malaysia, Malta, New Zealand, Pakistan, Singapore, South Pacific Island countries, and Sri Lanka are all post-colonial literatures. (Ashcroft, Griffiths, and Tiffin 2)

Ashcroft, writing at a time when postcolonial theory was yet in its infancy, was trying to create a feasible container for the range and focus of the theory. The initial formulations of postcoloniality demonstrated the difficulty of creating a balance between establishing contained definitions of postcolonial times and spaces and yet maintaining an openness to other related phenomena. Ashcroft hints at this openness in his use of the term "continuity of preoccupations." The early container of the postcolonial theories was that of the literatures of the British Commonwealth nations. Ashcroft's definition, although allowing for a "continuity of preoccupations," still revolves around the interpretation of a precise historical moment—that of nineteenth- and twentieth-century European, and especially British imperialism—and its aftermath. The second point that I would like to draw our attention to is the vast range of the resulting list of nations and literatures that come to be included under the umbrella of postcolonial literatures. Ashcroft addresses a problem of legitimacy posed by an umbrella theory by pointing to the unifying experience of imperialism on cultures:

> What each of these literatures has in common beyond their special and distinctive regional characteristics is that they emerged in their present form out of their experience of colonization and asserted themselves by foregrounding the tension with the imperial power, and by emphasizing their differences from the assumptions of the imperial centre. It is this which makes them distinctly post-colonial. (2)

The problem, I purport, with such a definition of postcolonial culture, is *not* that it is too broad in its scope and ambition, but actually, it is not broad enough. In the process of trying to make sense of a complex set of theories and list its practical applicability to cultural studies, definitions such as these opened up a multitude of issues. Indeed, such definitions have at times had the unintended effect of restricting the potential reach of postcolonial theories, and limited the discussion to a critical squabble as to which cultures and nations get to be part of the postcolonial club and which do not. Postcolonial studies began in the context of a Commonwealth literature, but it has since then matured to take into account contemporary transnational societies. The recent growth of globalization and transnational studies, fields that have been derived from this effort by postcolonial theorists, are promising signs of a path forward. It is my hope that this book will provide yet another voice to the rapidly emerging field of postcolonial studies in Italy, which is still in its infancy.[1]

Edward Said is considered the founding father of a branch of postcoloniality called "Colonial discourse analysis," chiefly due to the success of his seminal work, *Orientalism*. He meditates on the importance of generating a realistic vision of the possibilities of postcolonial theories in *Culture and Imperialism*. Indeed, Said's definition of imperialism itself allows the field of enquiry to open up to a subtler and grander vision and analysis of a host of cultural phenomena, local, national, and transnational, without posting a list of historical or material prerequisites to the applicability of postcolonial criticism. Imperialism for Said, is "the practice, the theory, and the attitudes of a dominating metropolitan center ruling a distant territory" (Said, *Culture and Imperialism* 9). National and ethnic identities, for Said, are "historically created and a result of interpretation" (31) and it would be incoherent and counter-productive for postcolonial theories to try and posit these as essential in any way, since the very goals of the theories are to examine the relationship between identity creation and discourse and between power and knowledge. Said highlights his notion of "discrepant experiences" as a better way of understanding power relationships in culture at all levels, thus allowing for dialogue and interaction beyond the limits of Manichean oppositions of "colonizer" and "colonized" nation states. For Said, such discrepant experiences highlight the limitations of abstract ideas such as "East" and "West," and he proposes that theory must acknowledge the existence of these differences and understand how they are constructed, rather than utilize them to build artificial conceptual boundaries of all kinds. Said posits that all cultures assert identity. Thus, postcolonial studies, in such a situation, should work toward exposing and dismantling scholarship that "rather than affirming the interdependence of various histories on one another, and the necessary interaction of contemporary societies with one another, [perpetuates] the rhetorical separation of cultures" (38). The central question for Said in *Culture and Imperialism* is also the broader central question that I would like to propose to scholars of immigration cultures in Italy:

> What is the inventory of the various strategies that might be employed to widen, expand, deepen our awareness of the way the past and present of the imperial encounter interact with each other? (39)

Italy presents postcolonial scholars a concrete way to enable such a furthering of our knowledge of the mechanisms of imperialism and culture. This is because it plays an ambivalent role as both colonizer and colonized. It represents *both* the center and the periphery of the imagined Western Civilization and is as such, a discrepant nation. A study of immigration in Italy can be furthered only by a refinement of what we mean by terms such as imperialism, colonialism, and hybridity, and the Italian case provides us with the material and historical conditions to do just that. Postcolonial theories have grown to go beyond the "reified polarities of East versus West, and in an intelligent and concrete way attempt to understand the heterogeneous and often odd developments that used to elude the so-called world historians as well as the colonial Orientalists, who have tended to herd immense amounts of material under simple and all-encompassing rubrics" (*Culture and Imperialism* 26). With these words, Said encourages a more evolved and dynamic critical apparatus that will go beyond the "rubrics" that they initially set out to dismantle.

Bhabha's Hybridity

Homi Bhabha's theory of hybridity takes Edward Said's project of dismantling lingering postcolonial dualities to its logical conclusion, and is therefore, I believe, a useful tool in fully excavating the possibilities provided by the Italian case.[2] I would like to present a view of the Italian case through the lens of his enunciation of hybridity as outlined in the volume of his collected writings, *The Location of Culture* (1994). Bhabha's theory of hybridity is important in understanding this magmatic state, as it gives new relevance to the "post" in "postcolonial": no longer does the *post* simply denote the linear temporal framework of colonial and after-colonial time, and the specific spatial territory of the land occupied under European imperialist forces. The *post* now signifies *beyond*— beyond a critical vision that employs cultural comparativism to create notions of "homologous national cultures, the consensual or contiguous transmission of historical traditions, or 'organic' ethnic communities" (7). Indeed, for Bhabha, the understanding of identity creation through such a discourse "can only be achieved through the death, literal and figurative, of the complex inter-weavings of history, and the culturally contingent borderlines of modern nationhood" (7). Bhabha, in effect, strikes at the heart of underlying notions that form the basis of the idealized neoliberal ideas of both nationhood and multiculturalism, which, as I have noted in my introductory chapter, "[rely] on the assumption that there were primeval, separate, and distinct global cultural orders which are only now beginning to meet in the context of global migration."

To fully answer the question of why it is so essential to conceptually re-negotiate identities that go beyond the duality of Colonizer/Colonized, especially in the Italian case, it would first be important to summarize the various historical and material conditions that make Italy and Italian immigration culture a particularly apt model for the understanding of hybridity as Bhabha envisions it. Since the word "hybrid" has had a long and convoluted usage, and is currently used to convey a broad range of cultural situations, it would also be prescient to underline the distinctness of Bhabhian hybridity, and especially demonstrate the importance of the role of "mimicry" and "menace" as hybrid strategies of representation. There are various ways in which these concepts can be useful in the study of literary or cinematic texts, also in the way they suggest caution upon an excessive use of the literary and textual approach to the study of cultural upheavals, opening up the study to a more interdisciplinary approach. Another important characteristic of Bhabha's hybridity is its neutral connotation. Bhabha goes beyond an optimistic or naïve

Chapter One

celebration of hybrid states and articulates a more nuanced and complex understanding as a difficult, yet all-pervasive presence in cultures.

Italy's Chronic Ambivalence— The Ghosts of Crises Past

I would like to expand upon my suggestion in the Introduction that the Italian nation has a relatively unstable *oikos*. Indeed, Italy's contemporary crisis of immigration can be situated within a thematic continuation of a very ancient and vibrant national cultural *leitmotif* of fragmentation. This narrative of fragmentation is inscribed within the Italian literary and cinematic canon, its history, and also its geography. As Parati rightly mentions, Italy is a nation at the "cultural crossroads of the Mediterranean." It is also a geographical bridge, a long and narrow peninsula that not only spans North and South, but also East and West. Francesco Cossiga, the Christian Democrat leader who served as the President of Italy from 1985 to 1992, describes this geographical four-way split in an appropriately striking manner:

> Anche se gli storici la prendono sempre a male quando devono citare la calzante intuizione del principe di Metternich che riduceva l'Italia a una semplice "espressione geografica," secondo me non aveva torto! O, per dirla con più pertinenza, sbagliava a negare all'Italia risorgimentale il diritto di farsi Stato, ma aveva molte ragioni nel rappresentare l'Italia così come la vedeva campita sulla mappa d'Europa. L'Italia deve tutta la sua storia alla sua geografia: ancorata alle Alpi, "insuperabile confine" già per Tito Livio, ma distesa sul Mediterraneo, punto d'approdo di popoli e culture. Oltre che ponte fra Nord e Sud, crocevia obbligato fra Est e Ovest: all'estremità adriatica del Puglia il sole sorge quaranta minuti prima che in Ventimiglia, perchè Otranto è più a oriente di Trieste. Perciò siamo nati meticci ... (Cossiga and Chessa 8)

> Although the historians are always reluctant to cite the fitting intuition of the Prince of Metternich, who reduced Italy to a simple "geographical expression," I do not think that he was wrong! Or, to be more precise, he was wrong to negate Risorgimento Italy the right to declare itself a State, but he had many reasons to represent Italy just as he could see it situated

> on Europe's map. Italy owes all of its history to its geography: anchored to the Alps, "the insurmountable barrier" for Livy, but spread upon the Mediterranean, the point of meeting for peoples and cultures. Other than bridge between North and South, an obligatory crossroad between East and West; at the Adriatic end of Puglia the sun rises forty minutes before it does in Ventimiglia, because Otranto is to the east of Trieste. This is why we are born mestizo …

Indeed, as Cossiga implies, any discussion of Italian immigration cannot exclude Italy's own history as Europe's internal, hybrid Other, and I would like to accentuate the importance of this otherness within by very briefly mentioning the chief ways in which Italy connotes or embodies otherness:

1. The "Belated" Nation: Italy had witnessed a relatively late and complicated formation of the Nation-State in the late nineteenth century. The complexity of the relationship between political unification and cultural formation of the nation is well described by Derek Beales and Eugenio Biagini: "While it is in a sense possible to treat Italian unification as an affair of war and diplomacy, more or less completed within two years, and then to explain it just in these terms, no historian of unification would limit himself or herself to this period and these aspects. [Unification] was a result or a stage of national revival, known as the Risorgimento, which originated in the eighteenth century, and has lasted, according to many writers, into the twentieth. [...] it seems to us that the precise relationship between Risorgimento and unification is exceedingly hard to determine." (Beales and Biagini 2)

2. The "Fragmented" Nation: Italy has had a relatively fragmented and diverse population speaking a myriad of languages and dialects (Massimo D'Azeglio's aphorism comes to mind here, "Abbiamo fatto l'Italia; si tratta adesso di fare gli italiani" ("We have made Italy, now we must make the Italians"). Beales and Biagini again make a persuasive claim that the *questione della lingua* was a national problem that has often been blown out of proportion and context. They problematize Tullio de Mauro's claim that official standard Italian was alien to a majority of the new citizens, conclusively claiming that the language problems accentuate class differences rather than problems of cultural unity (75–80). This further highlights my point about the subjective

Chapter One

nature of Italy's material situation of ambivalence with respect to European identity.

3. The "Southern Question": Italy's relatively heterogeneous economic development, leading to a sharp divide in wealth between the North and the South, is a consequence of historical political inequalities. This combination of inequities resulted in a wave of internal emigration from the mostly agrarian South toward the industrial North. The South, in effect, is historically Italy's internal Other, just as Italy is Europe's internal Other, a situation illustrated by the term *La questione meridionale* (The Southern Question).³ The Southern Question has continued to be a political and cultural concept that has been used to great effect in Italian public life. We only have to listen to any of the Northern League's ex-leader Umberto Bossi's denunciations of Italy's South (whose metonymic image is *Roma ladrona/padrona*, "Robber/ Master Rome") to observe that the Southern Question has remained relevant, and is intimately connected to Italy's identity relationships with Europe, Africa/Orient, and the immigrants:

> Finalmente con la Lega Nord per la prima volta il Nord ebbe un suo partito e quindi la possibilità di passare dal borbottio dell'insoddisfazione contro Roma alla denuncia chiara e forte dell'oppressione centralista. Era nata cioè ufficialmente la questione settentrionale; esplose il risentimento che si era accumulato contro Roma nella nostra società fin dal dopoguerra. Dapprima sul Nord si erano riversate forti immigrazioni per sostenere lo sviluppo industriale che avevano distrutto l'identità delle nostre grandi città [...] la cassa del mezzogiorno, opere faraoniche sempre pagate da noi ma spesso neppure realizzate [...] alibi per incassare oltre un milione di miliardi. Il Nord trasformato in un pozzo di San Patrizio senza un limite e senza fine. (Bossi)

> Finally, with the Northern League, the North was able to have its own party and therefore the possibility of passing from dissatisfied mutterings against Rome to a clear and strong denouncement of centralized oppression. Thus was born, that is, the Northern Question, and the sentiments accumulated against Rome by our society since post-war years exploded. From the beginning, strong waves of immigration had destroyed the identity of our great cities [...] the Fund for the Mezzogiorno, pharaonic works always paid for by us but often

never constructed [...] alibis made in order to take in more than a million billion [lire]. The North transformed into St. Patrick's well, without a limit and without an end.

That political parties should naturally find a complement to xenophobic rhetoric toward the nation's *extracomunitari* (the external Others) in vitriol toward its historical *terroni* (internal Others) serves to highlight the importance in linking these seemingly discrete phenomena.

4. The Italian Global Diaspora: Economic woes, especially in the South, led to internal migration but this was coupled with and complemented by external migration in the twentieth century, creating a massive Italian diaspora around the globe. Indeed, economic woes led Italy to be the epicenter of mass emigration in the fin-de-siècle and in the early half of the twentieth century, with impoverished Italians leaving for Northern Europe, the Americas, and Australia. The remarkable switch from being a nation of emigrants to a nation of immigrants most certainly places Italy in a complex situation in terms of understanding how national memories are repressed, forgotten, or harnessed in the creation and negotiation of a new national *oikos*.[4]

5. The Failed Colonial Legacy: Italy's colonial policy was relatively belated and cruel but ultimately unsuccessful in controlling large swaths of vital foreign territory. Mussolini's invasion of Ethiopia, for example, marked, according to Ruth Ben-Ghiat, "the apex of the fascist myth of national regeneration. Celebrated as a triumph of collective action that would free Italy from the 'prison' of the Versailles treaty, the colonial enterprise provided putative proof that Mussolini had transformed Italians from spectators to agents of historical change" (Ben-Ghiat 123). Italian colonization was, amongst other things, a cultural maneuvering toward elusive European respectability, an attempt at salvaging its unstable national *oikos*. The complex interactions between Northern Italians, Southern Italians (Italy's internal Others), and African colonial subjects in its colonial territories present some of the most revealing examples of the nation's fraught and complicated racial positioning.[5] The historical amnesia with regard to Italian colonial culture, especially in the Italian academe, is representative of the culture's disavowal of this uncomfortable past.

6. The "Sick Man" of Europe: In contemporary times, Italy continues to be called the "sick man of Europe," a metaphor connoting a systemic political, economic, and cultural malaise. While the title of "sick man" has been historically applied to various countries, its latest iteration referring to Italy can be traced back to articles such as "Addio, Dolce Vita" in *The Economist* in May 2005 and one in *The Telegraph* from 2008, "Italy: The Sick Man of Europe," to name just two. Post-war Italy is seen, from within and without, as a nation that continues to be dominated by a politics of *trasformismo*, where governments were formed under awkward coalitions only to fall and be replaced by the same leaders in different positions of power. The perception of Italy's position in the European Union is yet again that of all-encompassing corruption and opaqueness in financial, legal, political, and administrative matters.

These conditions, many of which are related to each other, all capture the *relative* otherness of Italy in relation to Western Europe, consistently *perceived* from within and without as a nation resigned to only partially assume all the requirements of a "Western-European-style democratic" nation. I would like to collectively term the discourse that is inscribed upon these various factors of fragmentation as Italy's "chronic ambivalence." The word *chronic* is a deliberate choice, as it both trans-historicizes Italy's hybridity through its literal meaning (as a habitual or recurring phenomenon) as well as through its allusions to the medical terminology of illness.

As Fabrizio De Donno and Neelam Srivastava correctly point out, the inspirational nature of the *Risorgimento* "can perhaps be linked to the peculiarities of Italy's historical evolution as a nation and its *ambiguous* position as regards Europe and modern European colonialism. A primary ambivalence is given by the fact that the pre-unification Italian states had been colonies of various European empires before united Italy became a colonial power itself" (De Donno and Srivastava 375). The authors point out, in other words, that it is due to its chronic ambivalence that Italy's radical and nationalist traditions, ranging from Gramscian and Marxist thought to that of nationalist leaders such as Giuseppe Mazzini, have been inspirational to independence movements worldwide, despite being itself a colonial power: "Gramsci's works in general, his work *The Southern Question* in particular, have been relevant to Liberation Theology movements from Central and South America to the Indian sub-continent, to the Zapatista movement in Chiapas, and to the continuing debate between Italian North and South. For Italy, the terms of this debate are now, in part, defining its role within the European Union" (Verdicchio 191–212).

Chronic ambivalence, I believe, does not simply indicate a *controstoria*, an alternative or subaltern narrative line in relation to the national story of Italy encapsulated in the *Risorgimento*. It is the central parallel narrative of the nation, although it is often disavowed. It is important to realize that this narrative of fragmentation and alterity stands in parallel rather than above or below Italy's narrative of unity and European-ness (one must not forget that Italy was one of the founding nations of the current European Union, while other peripheral European nations such as Spain and Greece were not). This split—the contradiction of being quintessentially European, but not quite—is represented by one of Italy's chief *topoi*—the *questione*, a "question mark." The *questione* is a central image, a ghost that constantly accompanies, or may I say haunts, the essentialist discourses of the Italian nation as a complete whole, just like the liminal bodies in Özpetek's *Le fate ignoranti*, described in the Introduction, cause a sudden irruption between past and present crises. The linguistic hybridity of regional dialects versus the need for a standard national language (*questione della lingua*) and the economic disparity between the colonial North of the country and Southern Italy (*questione meridionale*) are some of the more famous question marks. These *questioni* clear a space that is a *tabula rasa* that invites and sets up a constant debate as to the terms that should define it and constantly eludes definition. Terms and opinions jostle in this metaphorical space, factions fight, question, argue, make peace, co-operate, and then die off only to be replaced by another generation of ideas. The space of the *questione* remains a difficult but nevertheless vibrant and defining aspect of Italy's collective psyche. Indeed, the *questione postcoloniale* that we have been discussing here presents all the hallmarks of these other previous *questioni* that have marked Italy's cultural history. In recent decades, the new and hotly debated *questione* to emerge has been, of course, *la questione dell'immigrazione*.

Chapter One

The Centrality of Ambivalence

Bhabha's understanding of culture does justice to the complex reality of the working of power relations and cultural identities both on an individual and a community level. Indeed, his development of the concept of hybridity is key to a better understanding of complex colonial and postcolonial interactions. I therefore believe that Bhabha's hybridity can do justice to the implications of Italy's chronic ambivalence upon its immigration culture. He provides an exceptional theoretical core for the Italian case for two principal reasons: first, due to the centrality of ambivalence in his understanding of the condition of hybridity; and second, due to his fusing of the identities of "colonizer" and "colonized" into a common entity—that of the "colonial subject."

The hybrid location of Bhabha's notion of culture is, according to Stephen Slemon, "temporally discontinuous and spatially disunified, [and] provides a space for the theorist or historian to begin to formulate a critical understanding of the disparate and differential social processes" by which agency is created within marginalized peoples (Slemon 114). In this way, Bhabha describes culture at the location of the interstices, shifting "theoretical concern away from the monolithic building blocks of culture—nation, race, class, colonizer, colonized—toward a reading of the 'in-between' spaces, the spaces in excess of the sum of the parts of social and cultural differences" (114). Italy, a nation comprised of extensive interstitial cultural spaces, is thus a prime example of such hybridity. Bhabha's hybridity is this "in-between" space, the space where culture forms and "works." This mechanism also allows us to clearly distinguish the term from other terms that discuss syncreticism, such as creolization. As Robert Young emphasizes: "Hybridization as creolization involves fusion, the creation of new form, which can then be set against the old form of which it is partly made up of" (Young 25). Bhabha's description of hybridity, on the other hand, with its emphasis on ambivalence and interstitiality, underscores a sometimes menacing, restless, and fluid cultural situation where identity subverts, fuses, mingles, and also sets up new spaces for the formation of completely new and unexpected identities and hegemonies. It is for these reasons that contemporary Italy's classificatory confusion is such an apt subject to illustrate the workings of Bhabhian hybridity.

Mimicry and stereotype-as-fetish are the two terms that expose the disquiet caused by the ambivalence of hybridity. Together, these two strategies of representation expose Bhabha's hybrid or "third" space. While the stereotype is useful in understanding ways in which antithetical identities are fixed in colonial discourse by the colonial subject, mimicry is particularly relevant to my exploration of the chronic ambivalence that haunts identities, in particular Italian and non-Italian identities in new migrant cinema. In other words, Bhabha explains how the colonial subject, (1) seeks (in vain) to "fix" distinctive identities through the stereotype-as-fetish, while (2) mimicry exposes the ways in which such identities constantly "slip," revealing their essential hybrid nature.

The Stereotype-as-Fetish

By his deliberate dissolution of Manichean divisions between colonizer and colonized (both are subsumed under the term "colonial subject"), Bhabha's vision of colonial power becomes far removed from that of the all-authoritative subject: colonial power, for Bhabha, is charged with disquiet and menace from within. He insists that in order to locate this disquiet, the study of the structures of colonial discourse must be complemented by an analysis of subjectivity and consciousness. For Bhabha, the colonizer and the colonized meet at the realm of the stereotype—it is in the stereotype that both find a means of subjectification and an "articulation of forms of difference" (96). Here too, the key Bhabhian term that characterizes the stereotype is ambivalence. Bhabha says that colonial identity lies in-between the identities of colonizer and colonized. A duality of derision and desire marks colonial discourse: there is a splitting (a wanting to be the same but also be like the other) and a doubling (a desire to be at two places at the same time) in the colonial subject. This presence of constant ambivalence, created by a splitting, a doubling, is expressed in the compromise that the colonial subject arrives at—the stereotype.

The structure of the stereotype acts as Freud's fetish in that they are both substitutes that provoke the split feelings of fear and pleasure. The fetish is "a non-repressive form of knowledge that allows for the possibility of simultaneously embracing two contradictory beliefs, one official and one secret, one archaic and one progressive, one that allows for myths of origins, the other that articulates difference and division. Its knowledge 'value' lies in its orientation as a defense toward external reality" (115). The stereotype and the fetish are structurally similar, in that they both link what is unfamiliar or fearful (sexual or racial difference) to that which is familiar and accepted (the fetish object or the stereotype). For Bhabha, the colonial stereotype, like the fetish, provokes the subject to vacillate between delight of the well known, the comforting, the exotic, and fear/contempt of the unknown. The stereotype and the fetish are also functionally similar, since both do two things—first, they figure difference between race/culture/gender as an anxiety about lack/difference; second, the stereotype and the fetish both affirm completeness or similarity. This is the compromise of the fetish and the stereotype, brought about by the substitution of the fetish object for the real thing that is lacking. Thus, the stereotype normalizes racial and cultural difference and masks its otherness through a fixed representation. It fixes the essential fluidity of identity and makes it easy for the subject to categorize and in general ascribe meaning to cultural entities.

Stereotype-as-Fetish: The Importance of the Visible and of Repetition

In this discussion of stereotype as fetish in the context of film, it is important to note the principal place that Bhabha assigns to the visual aspect of the difference. Visible difference authorizes the stereotype, says Bhabha, quoting Paul Abbot, as the visible is often conflated with the natural (113–14). This description by Bhabha of the manipulation of the visual as "natural" as an important aspect of stereotyping is the exact same mechanism which we can locate within the classificatory zeal of biological map-making by natural historians in colonial times. But just as the visible "authorizes" discrimination, Bhabha explains that it also sets up the representation to be inadequate:

> It is through this notion of splitting and multiple belief that, I believe, it becomes easier to see the bind of knowledge and fantasy, power and pleasure, that informs the particular regime of visibility deployed in colonial discourse. The visibility of the

> racial/colonial Other is at once the *point* of identity ("Look, a Negro") and at the same time a *problem* for the attempted closure within discourse. (115–16)

Just as the visual recognition of the point of identity ("Look, a Negro") fixes identity, so does it also set up the seeds for its own failure, as the visual basis upon which this fixing is based is also the problem for its attempted closure. Thus, the stereotype works as Freud's fetish, in that it requires the simultaneous existence of contradictory beliefs. The colonial stereotype of the "native" or the "negro" sets up a repeated cycle of readily accessible characteristics, and yet it is those very features that provide the gateway to dismantling these images.

This importance of the visible is central to the question of how immigrant bodies are imagined on the screen and presented to Italian audiences. Indeed, as Derek Duncan has argued in his pioneering essay on Italy's new migrant cinema, contemporary Italian films that represent immigrants must be critically analyzed in terms of how they racialize (or to use the Bhabhian terms I am using here, stereotype through fetishization) the non-Italian subject (Duncan 195–211). In Chapters 4, "Ambivalent Desires," and 5, "Ambivalent Moralities," where I discuss explorations of desire and fear respectively in relation to immigrants, I draw connections between the description I have given here of Bhabha's colonial/racial stereotype and Laura Mulvey's understanding of the regulation of desire vis-à-vis gendered bodies on screen. Both Bhabha and Mulvey use the idea of the fetish to understand how imbalances in societies are replicated in cinema. I therefore believe that they can together provide a very fruitful framework to our understanding of the various films studied in this book.

The "regime of visibility" that Bhabha describes in the quote above also leads him to connect the working of the stereotype to another important psychoanalytic mechanism that is useful to the study of power dynamics in film: Lacan's Imaginary. The Imaginary is a phase of childhood described by Lacan in which questions of identity arise for the first time. Lacan calls the point of entry into this phase the "mirror stage." When the child looks at his own complete image, he experiences a split feeling toward this image: there is a feeling of great pleasure in his identification with his own complete image, and there is also a feeling of displeasure, arising from the awareness that he is not his image, that he is like his image, but somehow different. This split feeling gives rise to, respectively, the feelings of narcissism and of aggressivity.

For Bhabha, the construction of colonial representation relies on the two tropes discussed above: the stereotype-as-fetish and the Imaginary. Fetishism masks difference by providing a compromised substitute—it works, in other words, as a metaphor. In the representation as stereotype-as-fetish, the object that substitutes is adjacent to, or associated with, the actual subject that is being constituted—in other words, it is a *metonym*. For Lacan too, the unconscious is structured like language, as it works through metaphor and metonymy, which are linked to the twin dream processes described by Freud—condensation and displacement, respectively.

Therefore, to summarize, Bhabha describes the colonial stereotype through its four-way strategy that is split between metaphor, metonymy, the narcissistic image, and the alienating/fearful image. The colonial stereotype functions in the manner of a metaphor since it masks/substitutes that which it is supposedly similar to. It functions also as a metonym as the subject is represented only by some of its putative elements. The stereotype is also a split image, narcissistic, as it is complete and unified, fearful and alienating, as it is different and less complete than the actual experience.

This central ambivalence that Bhabha describes within colonial representation of the colonial subject is also, he argues, the fundamental way in which it gains its currency. Bhabha describes that these colonial representations *must be anxiously repeated*, as though they cannot be proved. Stereotypes, which cover fears and negotiate authority, therefore, need to be compulsively repeated.

As noted above, the fetish "allows for the possibility of simultaneously embracing two contradictory beliefs [...]. Its knowledge 'value' lies in its orientation as a defense toward external reality" (115). Such a knowledge value is especially important to Italy's encounter with its internal and external others, considering the state of chronic ambivalence within which it is taking place.

Mimicry

Mimicry is Bhabha's term to represent the principal menace that pervades colonial discourse. It is therefore his description of the essential destabilizing process already inherent within authoritative discourse. In other words, it is an opposite yet complementary process to the fetishization of the stereotype. Italy's unique position in the ambivalent zone between the "colonizers" and the "colonized" thus provides a prime example of a mimic-nation, a culture that exposes the unstable nature of both authority and subalternity. The mimic-body is a constant reminder of the constructed nature of the stereotype-as-fetish, and shows that despite its potency, the stereotype-as-fetish is inherently set up for failure. The anxious repetition of the stereotype (such as that of the eroticized black woman in colonial Italy, to give one example) only exposes its fallibility.

Bhabha describes mimicry as another ambivalent mode, since it contains both a similarity and a dissimilarity. It is a difference that is "almost the same but not quite" (122). I have briefly mentioned the ways in which Italy is the "almost, but not quite" European nation. Mimicry is thus, I believe, a central figure of Italian-immigration culture, as it brings the "not quite" cultural entities to the forefront of cultural discourse. Mimicry, for Bhabha, relies on resemblance between colonizer and colonized, and it should not be seen as an example of colonial dependency or sycophancy, but as a mode of disruption of colonial authority. It is a parody, a mockery, an unmasking of fixed absolutes constituted by colonial stereotypes. Mimicry, however, is not resistance, but a part of the colonial process of representation. It is an ambivalent assertion of similarity and difference: on one hand, the mode is an *appropriation* of the other as part of the colonial system, and at the same time, it is an "*inappropriate*" (122) form of the original. Just as in the way that "to be Anglicized is *emphatically* not to be English" (125), in Italy's migration cultures, to be Italianized is to decisively not be Italian.

In the detourist new migrant cinema studied here, mimic—that is to say marvelous—bodies are often used to expose the structural instability of the racialized/stereotyped body. To illustrate the concept of Bhabhian mimicry, let me provide here a brief cinematic example of the cultural work carried out by the mimic-body from an intriguing film that I will analyze in more detail in Chapter 3: *Lamerica* (1994) by Gianni Amelio. The film describes the journey of Gino, an Italian assistant to an Italian entrepreneur through a chaos-strewn Albania as he tries to relocate Spiro, an

Chapter One

old Albanian prisoner (Figure 2). Spiro has been made president of a fake Italian-Albanian shoe company that Gino works for in order to illegally procure European development funds. The entire first quarter of the film establishes Spiro's Albanian identity for the audience, although he does seem to have grave mental disabilities to the point that he believes he is twenty years old and is unable to speak. In an important scene in this film that presents a turning point, Gino (and the audience whose point of view has until now been firmly aligned with his) is suddenly faced with the possibility that Spiro might actually not be Albanian. Not only is he possibly not Albanian, but he also seems—of all things—to be Italian. This dramatic revelation sets in motion a realignment of personal and national identities, geographies, and histories, leading to a final *suspension* of Italian- and Albanian-ness in the final scene of the film. Spiro's striking turn from belonging to the category of the

Figure 2: Spiro/Michele boards a bus in Amelio's *Lamerica*

colonized to that of the colonizer, from turning from the Other to the Self can be considered as an archetype of a mimic trait I have been describing here, where characters and people are successfully capable of negotiating outside the realms of national, cultural, and ethnic identification, thus dissolving essentialist dichotomies of "us" and "them," of "same" and "other." There is a cultural reality in Italy where identities and identifications are given moments of fluidity even though authoritative processes try to "fix" them, instances where Italians mimic the *extracomunitari* and vice-versa. The racial and cultural zone of ambivalence in Italy is thus extremely prone to the slipping away of essentialist discourse. In a zone of chronic ambivalence, identities and identifications fall apart.

The Menace of Mimicry and the Reinscription of the Stereotype (or, Of Ministers and Orangutans)

It is important to note that the unstable and fluid condition provoked by a mimic-nation or mimic-man such as Spiro/Michele does not simply offer a celebratory escape from fixed identities. It is also a source of distress. Indeed, Italy's in-betweenness has been an important factor in the violent backlash that many immigrants have faced in contemporary Italy. I believe that Bhabha articulates the distress caused by hybridity through his description of the "menace" that accompanies mimicry. Like the figure of the Italianized native, or the nativized Italian, mimicry, as a "metonymy of presence" (129), creates a menace, which results in what I would like to call a momentary *suspension* of fixed identities.

A recent memorable yet depressingly familiar example of the forceful reinstatement of the stereotype-as-fetish provoked as a reaction to the distressing suspension by the mimic-body can be found in Lega Nord leader Roberto Calderoli's speech discussing Cécile Kyenge, Italy's first black minister. Calderoli, the most sensationalist of the leaders of the anti-South, anti-immigrant Northern League party and Vice-President of the Italian Senate in the Gianni Letta government, compared Kyenge to an orangutan while at a political rally. I choose to mention this example because analyzing the transcript of relevant part of Calderoli's speech, made on 13 July 2013, can illuminate Bhabhian stereotyping and mimicry at work in cultural texts:

> E rispetto al ministro Kyenge, veramente voglio dirgli, sarebbe un ottimo ministro, forse lo è. Ma dovrebbe esserlo in Congo, non in Italia. Perché se in Congo c'è bisogno di un ministro per le Pari Opportunità per l'Integrazione, c'è bisogno là, perché se vedono passare un bianco là gli sparano. E allora, perché non va là? Che mi rallegro un pochino l'anima, perché rispetto a quello che io vivo ogni volta, ogni tanto smanettando con Internet, apro "il governo italiano," e cazzo cosa mi viene fuori? La Kyenge. Io resto secco. Io sono anche un amante degli animali

> eh, per l'amor del cielo. Ho avuto le tigri, gli orsi, le scimmie, e tutto il resto. I lupi anche c'ho avuto. Però quando vedo uscire delle—non dico che è—delle sembianze di oranghi io resto ancora sconvolto. (Calderoli, "La questione")
>
> With regard to Minister Kyenge, I would really like to tell her that she would be an excellent minister, maybe she is. But she should be one in the Congo, not in Italy. Because in the Congo they do have a need for a Minister for Equal Opportunities and Integration, there is need there because if they see a white man, there they would shoot him. So, why doesn't she go there? It would ease my mind a bit, because compared to what I have to experience every time, once in a while, when I am surfing on the Internet, I look up "Italian Government," and what the hell shows up? Kyenge. I remain dazed. I am also an animal lover eh, for goodness sakes. I have had tigers, bears, monkeys, and everything else. I've also had wolves. But when I see—I am not saying that she is—a resemblance of an orangutan, I once again remain shocked.

In a masterful act of national and racial stereotyping, Calderoli first sets up the discourse by mentioning that Kyenge should have stayed in her native country, yet at the same time magnanimously allows for the possibility that she could someone be with the requisite professional skills to hold a high official government post. She is therefore represented as a good example of a mimic-woman, an "almost-minister" due to her professional skills, yet, as we see in the second section of the quote, "not quite," due to her race. Thus, she is a mimic-minister and mimic-Italian, establishing for the narrator what Bhabha terms as a "metonymy of presence." We have already mentioned that this mimic-status provokes a menace. Forced upon the colonized, mimicry forces the colonizer to see traces of himself in the colonized, as sameness begins to slide into otherness. The colonized subject's sudden realization of inauthenticity, of being ideologically constructed and fixed in representation, is the menace of mimicry:

> The ambivalence of colonial authority repeatedly turns from mimicry—a difference that is almost nothing but not quite—to menace—a difference that is almost total but not quite. (Bhabha 131)

Mimicry, and the menace it constitutes, forces the problematic question of what it is to be the "original" in the first place, just like Kyenge's image as a minister of the Italian government forces the question of what the proper criteria of being an elected representative of the Italian nation should be in the first place (citizenship, or race?). According to Bhabha's description of colonial discourse, the only resolution to this menacing and destabilizing image of mimicry can be through the reinscription of the stereotype-as-fetish. Calderoli's speech accomplishes its reinscription in two ways. In addition to describing Kyenge's mimic-body, Calderoli first contextualizes the stereotyping of Kyenge that follows in the second half of the quote by first stereotyping her country of origin (the Democratic Republic of Congo): through the typical mechanism of Orientalist citation, it is fixed as a barbaric "anti-*oikos*" where civilizational niceties toward whites do not exist. He mentions the word "there" several times while referring to the Congo in order to emphatically separate it spatially and therefore culturally from "here," Italy's own stabilized *oikos*. The image-fetish of the gun-brandishing, white-killing Congolese native "fixes" the nebulous Italian audience of the speech as conclusively and irredeemably white, and in the position of imagining the scene of being potential victims of violence by the brutal black Other. The description of the shock ("resto secco") of seeing Kyenge's face appear as *the* face of the Italian government on the Internet suspends her identity. The sight of this mimic-body is the final provocation—a menacing image where the definitively pre-established black Other of the Congolese anti-*oikos* has become integral to the very center of the national *oikos* (its government). The menace, the threat, posed by the mimic-man such as Kyenge comes from a partial resemblance, from a revulsion and fascination that such a kinship suggests. The differences constructed by colonial discourse are thus threatened by resemblance, creating, in effect, a double vision: "The menace of mimicry is its double vision which in disclosing the ambivalence of colonial discourse also disrupts its authority. And it is a double vision that is a result of what I've described as the partial representation/recognition of the colonial object" (Bhabha 126). Mimicry is a repetition that is "almost but not quite the same" and thus questions not only the definition of the original, but also its self-identity. Yet at the same time, mimicry also sows the seeds for the reinscription of the stereotype—as I have already mentioned, visible difference authorizes the stereotype. Therefore, this situation of mimicry (the image of the mimic-minister representing the Italian government on the Internet) causes the viewer of the image/narrator of the speech to react by forcefully reinstating the stereotype-as-fetish through a somewhat long-winded and disingenuous discourse about wild animals. By comparing the threatening, visible mimic-body of Kyenge to an orangutan, Calderoli's anxious repetition of the much-repeated visual stereotype-as-fetish of blacks is complete. The fantastical image-fetish of the minister-as-orangutan successfully usurps her legitimacy as a genuine minister and serious representative of Italians in government. While the words I have analyzed from the speech end here, the oscillating cycle of stereotype/mimicry/stereotype, etc., does not stop at these words, but begins anew, since Bhabha mentions that the stereotypical fetish-image, by its very nature, also sets up the seeds of its failure and consequent slip (once again) into mimicry.

As my examples of Spiro/Michele in *Lamerica* and Calderoli's description of Cécile Kyenge demonstrate, Italy, located at the crossroads of the Mediterranean, is a prime mimic-nation due to its capacity to generate and repeat multiple such "double visions" of identities. The Kyenge example mentioned above particularly indicates how the racial stereotype needs to be anxiously repeated in order for it to maintain currency and hold the menace of mimicry (unsuccessfully) at bay. Calderoli's racist populist tactic had weighty political value for his constituents for this very reason, and is indicative of the backlash a person's mimic-status (in this case, Kyenge, as an almost-minister—but not quite, due to her blackness) can provoke in society.

The Marvelous: Locating Hybridity on Screen

Now that I have established that Italy's *chronic ambivalence* is a defining concept in the cultural analysis of the encounter between Italians and immigrants, I would like to re-read the examples of hybridity in the film *Lamerica* and Calderoli's description of Minister Kyenge to introduce my concept of "the Marvelous" to represent cinematic moments of the suspension of identities. By using the word "marvelous," I am deliberately recalling the title of Stephen Greenblatt's book, *Marvelous Possessions: The*

Wonder of the New World. Indeed, this word connects my new and very different formulation of the concept of the Marvelous in the context of the migrant experience to a long tradition of its use by travelers, as described by Greenblatt.[6] I chose the word "marvelous" for several other reasons. The word comes from the old Latin *mirabilis* or "wonderful" ("Marvelous," *Online Etymology Dictionary*). *Mirabilis* emphasizes the visual connotation of the feeling of wonderment, which has a particular resonance while studying a primarily visual medium such as film. The Italian word *mirare* is "to look, scan, or scope out visually," and *ammirare*, "to admire." But the *marvelous* also has a contradictory and ambivalent meaning when we understand it as a "fascination." "To fascinate," as Elisabeth Grosz points out, quoting the *Oxford English Dictionary*, is "to attract, irresistibly enchant, charm" but also "to deprive the victim of the powers of escape or resistance by look or by presence." (Grosz 6) The experience of the Marvelous, caused by mimicry as Bhabha defines it, "trips" the cyclical repetition of the stereotype-as-fetish, causing a *momentary suspension* of a scale of norms and comparisons that ordinarily function to create rigid stereotypes such as the smelly or criminal immigrant. It will be my task throughout this book to isolate situations that I define as "marvelous"—a representation within the cinematic text of a usually temporary "marvelous subject or experience" in which characters deploy the feeling of their identity going beyond the values by which it is defined, and are thus effectively suspended and unmasked to expose its mimic status and thus, its hybrid nature. These are, in other words, the cinematic "discrepant experiences" that Said talks about while explaining the need to go beyond dualities.

I will use the Marvelous as a central trope while interpreting the films in this book. I use the word "trope" to indicate both its meanings: first it is a figure of speech, a "word or expression used in a figurative sense." In the visual media, it is also used to mean "a common or overused theme or device" ("Trope," *Merriam Webster Online Dictionary*). For example, when we say that a film "contains all the hallmark horror-film tropes," we mean that it exhibits all the visual editing, or sound, or mise-en-scène qualities we commonly identify with the genre of horror films. For the purposes of this book, I mean to use the word as a collection of stylistic devices that seek to suspend rather than fix identity, thus providing a common theme in the new migrant cinema studied here.

In her essay "Deanimations: Maps and Portraits of Life Itself," Donna Haraway, while discussing the notion of map-fetishism, describes the fetish as a trope, in that it is a kind of "substitute" for the real:

> In Greek, *trópos* is a turn or swerve; tropes mark the non-literal quality of being and language. Fetishes—themselves "substitutes," that is, tropes of a special kind—produce a characteristic "mistake"; fetishes obscure the constitutive tropic nature of themselves and of worlds. Fetishes literalize and so induce an elementary material and cognitive error. Fetishes make things *seem* clear and under control. (In Jones, Galison, and Slaton 181)

Employing Haraway's use of the Greek root of the trope, *tropos*, the marvelous represents a turn, or a swerve. However, it is a visual representation that provides a feeling that is antithetical to that which is represented by the trope of fetishism as described above. Instead of recognition of the stereotype, it indicates the moment in which the trope of fetishism is "swerved back," or unmasked, however temporarily, by mimicry, to expose the constructedness of the initial act of fetishism, to unmask the "constitutive tropic nature of themselves and of worlds." The moment of the marvelous is in this way a visual or thematic moment of the *suspension of a cyclical repetition of identification*. In *Lamerica*, the moment when Gino (and the audience) understand that the main premise of the film's main plot, Spiro's Albanian identity, might be untrue is the very moment when Spiro becomes a marvelous body, whose identity is suspended between these national categories. Similarly, the moment when Cécile Kyenge's image appears on the results of an Internet search for the "Italian Government" is the exact moment in Calderoli's speech when her body is suspended between that of the stereotypical poor/dirty/violent black immigrant and of the authoritative Italian politician. The Marvelous, that unsaid eruption of an ambivalent feeling provoked by the marvelous body, coincides with a moment of *stupor*—a feeling of being dazed but also astonished, where the viewed spectacle becomes not one of pleasure in access to the stereotype but an experience of disorientation, of going *beyond*.

My use of the Marvelous in analyzing *Lamerica* and Calderoli's description of Cécile Kyenge is a deliberate attempt to undertake not only a close reading, but also a "symptomatic reading" of cultural imagery. This term, coined by Louis Althusser, describes a widely accepted method of undertaking cultural analysis of literary and critical texts. In his re-reading of Marx and his formulation of "ideology," Althusser introduces the concept of the "problematic." A problematic is the underlying series of questions that command the answers given in the text; it is the ideological or theoretical structure that frames the text. The aim of the critical reader or theorist then, is to deconstruct the underlying problematic of the text by focusing on both what is said, *and what is not said within the text*. This kind of reading is symptomatic reading. Althusser describes Marx's reading of Adam Smith as symptomatic, because:

> It divulges the undivulged event in the text it reads, and in the same movement relates it to a different text, present as a necessary absence in the first. Like his first reading, Marx's second reading presupposes the existence of two texts, and the measurement of the first against the second. But what distinguishes this new reading from the old is the fact that in the new one the second text is articulated with the lapses in the first text. (Althusser and Balibar 28)

My description of the Marvelous is an attempt to expose the unsaid structures of identity formation present in the new migrant cinema analyzed in this book. Sometimes a symptomatic reading is required to unearth the hidden tensions of identity negotiations (their hidden detourist nature), while at other times, it is brought to the fore by the various members of a film's vast production team's conscious intentions, thus diminishing my need to employ symptomatic reading. My reading of the cultural work carried out by Spiro's ambivalent presence at the heart of the film *Lamerica* and Kyenge's ambivalent presence in the Italian government shows them to be examples of the function of such interpretations to analyze representations of identities in cinema, literature, or any other relevant cultural text.

Chapter One

Postcolonial Studies and Italy—A Few Paths Forward

Italy's national identity, formed by a complex history charged with multiplicity and simultaneity, fragmentation and unity, is Europe's historical internal Other, and therefore is and has been chronically ambivalent and permanently hybrid. The nation's narrative of chronic ambivalence with regard to the imagined civilizational "blocs" of Europe and Africa/Orient runs parallel to its strong narrative as a successfully unchanging monocultural and European nation, making any stabilization always partial. When migrants begin to hybridize an already hybrid nation, they provoke a "classificatory confusion" (Bhabha 130) and a "double vision" (126); resulting in a menace that can point to a possibility of either change and liberation or fear and closure within society. The common presence of xenophobia in Italy is, I believe, another glaring symptom of Italy's underlying chronic cultural ambivalence toward its constitutive Others. Much can be gained by avoiding a simplistic interpretation of the current situation as yet another instance of the stable national Self negotiating a relationship with an essential migrant Other.

Bhabha's hybridity opens up the question of methodology in the study of Italian immigrant cultures. Teresa de Lauretis, in her essay "Difference Embodied: Reflections on *Black Skin, White Masks*," points at the radical shift implied in Frantz Fanon's text from a purely literary understanding of otherness to an embodied conception of culture:

> Indeed, what spurred my critical interest in *Black Skin* was its psychoanalytic cast and the centrality it thus confers to sexuality in racial—or rather, raced—identity. Fanon's unique apprehension of the body as the material ground of subject formation, which led him to add the notion of "sociogeny" to Freud's ontogeny and phylogeny, extends the theoretical reach of psychoanalysis to a conceptual space located between them, a place beyond the individual's psychic history (ontogenic development) but closer to home than species history (phylogenetic inheritance), that is to say, the place of culture. (De Lauretis 54)

Bhabha's envisioning of the various strategies of hybrid representation underlines Fanon's insistence on the importance of the body and of desire, thus co-joining the private/personal with the collective/communal. Indeed, "in both Fanon and Bhabha [...] the space of difference and otherness is a historically and culturally constituted borderland between the perceptual/conscious and the unconscious" (De Lauretis 56). It is this promise of embodiment rather than the challenging abstraction of the language that drew me to Bhabha's work in the first place. I agree with Robert Young's reading of *The Location of Culture*; he argues that Bhabha's work is not incompatible with action, and it includes a politically and practically engaged view of culture (163). Understanding Bhabhian hybridity through the Italian case must therefore allow for an openness toward an exploration of both textual and non-textual forms of cultural knowledge and praxis.

The inconsistent understanding of the word "postcolonial" in the Italian scholarly context belies the discomfort posed in locating Italy's own ambivalent historical identity as colonizer or colonized or the difficulty in placing Italian culture into one of these rubrics. A conscious decision needs to be made in order to address Italy in a postcolonial framework. One could continue to use the term sometimes understood in Italy: *postcoloniale* referring to cultural manifestations that have strictly to do with Italy's relationship with its former colonies (including only immigrants residing in Italy from these former colonies). But to do so, I believe, is to repress Italy's own ambivalent positioning in the colonial/postcolonial spaces. I would suggest that in a global context, but especially for scholars of Italian culture, "Postcolonial Italian Studies" must be understood as signifying a general assemblage of theoretical work that can help us understand a *postcolonial condition*: where separate yet interconnected studies of colonial history, colonial cultural legacy, nationalism, contemporary immigrant literature and culture, Orientalism, diaspora, and transnationalism interact, dialogue, and dissolve into each other.

Chapter Two

Beyond Neorealism
The Cinematic Body-as-Nation

Chronic ambivalence has been a ubiquitous feature of Italy's cultural life, and immigration has forced yet another reconsideration of a national *oikos* that is dramatically split between West and East. In the previous chapter, I have explained how Bhabha's descriptions of the stereotype-as-fetish and mimicry can be useful conceptual tools to understand this ambivalent cultural situation and the cinematic products created therein. The mimic-body's capability to be "almost, but not quite" unmasks the constructedness of Italian-ness in the first place, carrying out a cultural operation that has subversive connotations as it maintains and adds to a national narrative of chronic ambivalence. I have also hypothesized that the cinematic representations of immigrants are fundamentally detourist, in that they inadvertently undertake voyages to survey the Italian Self while they explicitly aim to voyeuristically explore Europe's external Others. These contemporary films are therefore cultural operations in the creation of a new Italian *oikos* in a moment of great identity flux. The Italian directors' inward-looking gaze at its external Others is influenced by the nation's rich cinematic past, its contemporary reality of televised consumerism, identity politics in the age of Berlusconism (roughly, the *ventennio* from 1994, when Silvio Berlusconi first became Prime Minister, to 2013 when he was convicted of tax fraud by the Court of Cassation), continued globalization, instability in the Middle-East and Mediterranean regions, and the increased assertion of a supranational European institutional structure.

My task in the following chapters will be to demonstrate how this new generation of film directors undertakes a repopulation of cinematic spaces with ambivalent mimics—the "marvelous bodies" of the title of this book. This operation of

Chapter Two

imaginative repopulation of Italy's cultural spaces, as surely as it asserts hybridity through the creation of marvelous bodies, also simultaneously (re)asserts Italy's chronic ambivalence. Yet before I undertake that analysis, I would like to establish a historical context for contemporary films of immigration, because if Italy is indeed chronically ambivalent, then Italy's national cinema, a privileged national art form that has historically earned global recognition, should reflect the inherent tensions generated by this ambivalence.

In his essay on the origins of Italian neorealism, Vito Zagarrio poses a question that is also central to this chapter:

> Continuity or rupture? This is the central dilemma of much of twentieth-century Italian history. Is there continuity between Fascism and the Christian Democratic regime that followed it? [...] The question of continuity/discontinuity also arises in the political and cultural fields, especially on a terrain as delicate as the analysis of film." (Zagarrio 19)

Indeed, if Italy's new migrant cinema is detourist, only the contextual lens provided by Italy's postwar cinematic history can properly unveil the complex cultural dialogue being carried out by these films. I will therefore place the key works of the Italian cinema of migration in its correct cultural context, vis-à-vis two broad historical categories of Italian cinema—neorealism and post-neorealism. The categories are useful not only because of the historical relevance in Italy of these terms per se, but also because the question of realism is intimately connected to how nation-building has been understood and carried out in Italy through cinematic representation of individuals and communities. This theoretical chapter will therefore serve to highlight the presence of or departure from direct or indirect influence of these two conceptions of postwar Italian cinema on contemporary filmmakers that explore immigration. This "detour" into postwar Italy's cinematic history is relevant and necessary, as it will serve to defend my contention that most films on immigration *cannot* be defined as being neo-neorealistic despite the fact that they do indeed borrow the *impegno sociale* and a few stylistic parameters of neorealism. It will also allow me to suggest that in Italy's new migrant cinema, faith in the cinematic medium that characterized neorealism is mostly lost, and is replaced by irony, or at least some form of self-consciousness or unease. I will explore Bazin and other scholars' considerations of neorealism, as well as include thoughts about post-neorealism, the *commedia all'italiana,* and Luigi Pirandello's concept of humor in order to prove that contemporary filmmakers who are exploring immigration are caught between the urge to represent the reality of the humanitarian crisis in an indexical way and their partial or complete realization that the contradictions in society that they need to represent in order to characterize this reality are in many ways unfilmable with a purely neorealistic aesthetic. Due to this dilemma, I contend that new migrant cinema tends to be hybrid in genre—split between what I will call a "realist" and a "humoristic" mode.

The Body-as-Nation

The body on the screen has explicitly represented the Italian nation at least since the founding of the Cinecittà film studios in Rome under Fascism. It has been a principal tool for the imagination of the Italian national community. This strong element of self-reflexivity in the Italian cinematic tradition encourages filmmakers, critics, and/or the audience to represent and recognize the body on the screen as a metonym of the nation. Much of this self-reflexivity can be attributed to a Gramscian vision of the role of the intellectual in society. I would like to categorize postwar Italy's national filmmaking into two principal strains—neorealism and post-neorealism. Post-neorealism principally includes the *commedia all'italiana* and the various auteur films of the Sixties by directors such as Fellini, Antonioni, Pasolini, and many others. These two main strains of cinema contain the two principal divergent stylistic and, more importantly, ideological views of representing the condition of the nation in postwar Italy. Both traditions, despite their fundamentally different kinds of self-reflexivity, are persuasive manifestations of the nation's chronic ambivalence and its need to explore and/or seek its resolution through cinema. Conversely, the legacy of and the tension between these two divergent traditions demonstrate the cultural potency of this chronic ambivalence.

As Angela Dalle Vacche has very astutely pointed out, postwar Italian cinema, more than any other art form, was profoundly invested in the creation of a collective social narrative for the new

Italy that had emerged out of the ruins and shame of Fascism. This body of film, setting the styles, themes, and tones with its auspicious and spectacular initiation through neorealism, has aimed to provide its spectators with "terms of identification, an image of how they need to see themselves in order to have access to a national identity and imagine their roles in a historical process" (Dalle Vacche 277). If this is indeed so, new Italian cinema's recent turn to set its gaze upon the migrant body is indeed a sign of the recognition, and absorption, of the immigrant condition within the postwar discourse of a national self.

The question of the body is highly pertinent to Italian immigration film. The migrant body exists, according to Graziella Parati, "in a cultural and legal context that restricts his/her right to integrate outside the workplace. Consequently, his/her right to produce is accompanied by a duty not to reproduce, have a family, and occupy a cultural space" (Parati, "Migration Italy" 144). Since the productive and reproductive values of bodies are central to the question of the migrants (the permission for them to stay in the host country depends on how these values are measured or perceived), the bodies of both immigrants and Italians become chief objects of the exploration in new migrant cinema. Of course, the body has also been key in Italian cinema in the past due to both the nature of the cinematic medium, and Italy's special relationship to cinema as a national art form *par excellence*. In order to highlight this "special relationship," Millicent Marcus, taking the cue from Dalle Vacche, draws a trajectory in her book *After Fellini*, of a national narrative within the history of neorealism and its legacies, right up to contemporary times, where the "body in the screen serves as a reflection of a fictional, national self" (Dalle Vacche 254).

> Fascism, for example, inscribed its will to power in the genres of epic and of "muscular cinema" and Renzo Renzi has seen in the series of Maciste films, starring the strongman in an astonishing variety of settings (Maciste in the Lion's Den, Maciste the Alpinist, Maciste in Hell, Maciste vs. the Sheik) the model of the polyhedric hero that the Duce himself would become (Mussolini the Aviator, Mussolini the Equestrian, Mussolini the Diplomat, Mussolini the Drainer of Marshes, Mussolini the Farmer, etc.) in the extensive newsreel footage and press coverage devoted to him. The collective identity of neorealist cinema, instead, would be figured in the suffering, martyred body of

Beyond Neorealism

> Open City's Giorgio Manfredi, whose death, together with that of Don Pietro, heralded the resurrection of a nation in a Utopia that was never to be. Since then, the body as social signifier has adapted itself to the expressive needs of various categories which compromise postneorealist practice, from auteur cinema, to *commedia all'italiana*, to *cinema politico*. Thus, Pasolini's filmography revolves around the subproleteriat's body as the privileged object of desire, practitioners of political cinema such as Rosi and Petri make the body the site of institutional violence which literally guns it down, while Italian comic filmmakers personify social stereotypes in the *maschere* of Alberto Sordi, Ugo Tognazzi, Nino Manfredi, Vittorio Gassman, et al. (Marcus 233–34)

The examination of the migrant-subject or migrant-object's body in new Italian cinema becomes highly relevant to understanding Italy's projection of its national self, given the centrality of the cinematic body in the history of Italian culture due to the treatment of the body as a social signifier. While I am in complete agreement with Marcus's analysis of postwar Italian cinema in *After Fellini* and *Italian Cinema in the Light of Neorealism*, I would like to redirect her narrative by placing post-neorealist film as a principal player in Italian cinema's creation of a national collective self, equal to, if not more important than neorealism. In doing so, I would also like to problematize the primacy of neorealism in the scholarship of Italian cinema.

The central reason for my stress on the various forms of new cinematic languages that gained prominence after the main phase of neorealism, such as the *commedia all'italiana* and the auteur films of the Sixties, is the importance of the relationship, until now unexplored, between films from this period and today's corpus of new migrant cinema. Many films that will be analyzed in the next chapters have been praised for their contribution to the birth of a neo-neorealism. I would like to demonstrate that such a conceptualization of these films is not helpful, since neorealism itself is a slippery term that represents a broad category of cinematic strategies. In addition, Italian post-neorealist films have a more prominent mark on these contemporary films than has been previously acknowledged. Another important reason for my interest in the post-neorealist period is the unparalleled popularity of these films with Italian audiences at the height of another socially and culturally contradictory period, the "economic miracle" of the Sixties. I do not think that it is a mere coincidence that the post-neorealist aesthetics developed in a moment of a mass movement of people from the rural periphery to the urban centers, from the poor South to the industrial North as internal migrants, or simply as upward mobility threatened to shake the well-established class structures of Italian society.

Neorealist works, although highly praised in the international scene and by the critics, especially the French *Cahiers du Cinema* led by the prime exponent of neorealism, André Bazin, were, with a few exceptions, not very successful with the Italian audiences.[1] The films that are collectively classified as *commedie all'italiana* (simply called *commedia* from now on), on the other hand, were often commercial successes, or in other words, the audience favorites, a true popular cinema in the golden age of Italian cinema.[2] Critics and intellectuals have historically ignored or derided the genre (the "*all'italiana*" term was initially used disdainfully) and only recently has there been a restoration of critical and academic value to this body of film.[3] *Commedia*'s powerful grip on the nation's collective imagination cannot be, in my mind, underestimated, as it has often been in the scholarship on Italian cinema. The auteur films by the cinematic heavyweights such as Fellini, Pasolini, Antonioni, and Bertolucci, have received better scholarly treatment, of course, but their works are often treated as separate from the contemporaneous *commedia* films. For the purposes of this book, I would like to frame these seemingly disparate strategies of "art" and "popular" cinema into a single body of films that can be collectively defined as "post-neorealism."

Neorealism Is Dead, Long Live Neorealism!

How can one accurately define neorealism and contrast it to the variety of post-neorealistic films that succeeded it? By engaging with scholars that have tried to answer this fraught question, I would like to suggest that neorealism is based on a rigorous intellectual self-reflexivity of the filmmakers/intellectuals with regard to the relationship between cinema and the social and cultural reality of Italian society. By a "self-reflexive film," I mean a film that makes reference to its own contrivance or artificiality. This constant auto-referentiality is paralleled by a freedom from the burden of self-reflexivity for the viewer of these films through stylistic naturalism. Essentially, neorealism is a historically contained tradition in which the quantity of analysis, opinion, debate, and reaction about what it *is* superseded the actual number of films that were created in the tradition.

In contrast to neorealism, post-neorealistic films shift this burden of self-reflexivity from the filmmaker and/or the intellectual/critic to the audience through the stylistic use of artifice. This does not imply that filmmakers are not self-reflexive when they depart from neorealism, only that they at least feel the need to share the demands of such reflection with their audiences. Indeed, I would suggest that these evidently non-realistic representations of bodies and landscapes call upon the audience to directly reflect upon the relationship between the cinematic reality and the world outside that artificial representation. Both these traditions, neorealistic and post-neorealistic, are strategies that have been historically used to represent the contemporary state of the Italian body on screen, and are reference points for filmmakers in the new migrant cinema. Understanding these historical traditions therefore provides us with the model upon which today's marvelous bodies are built.

My analysis of the importance of post-neorealist genres such as the *commedia* is of course by no means a task of substitution of the cultural and cinematic authority of neorealism in Italy, but it is a way to recuperate the important cultural work undertaken by these genres in the (re)creation of an alternative discourse to that of the optimistic (and largely theoretical) one heralded by neorealism. Also, my comparison between these two major "streams" of Italian cinematic tradition is meant to supply general benchmarks in understanding complex gradations of realism actually employed by the directors today, and is not intended to create two mutually exclusive categories of Italian film. Indeed, neorealism shares its roots in the *commedia dell'arte* as much as the *commedia* does. As Dalle Vacche insists, this common tradition has often been repressed in favor of a more idealized critical explanation of neorealism *à la* Bazin:

> Critics have downplayed the link between the commedia dell'arte and neorealist cinema in favor of a horizon of international literary and cinematic influences. I would attribute this to an oversight in the history of the representation of the body in Italian culture. More specifically, it points to a lack of

> awareness that the body on screen serves as a reflection of a fictional, national self. Were we to connect neorealist casting and the masks of the commedia, we would more easily contrast Fellini's carnivalesque construction of character with Pasolini's unsettling depiction of marginality. [...] Most film historians associate the spectacular-allegorical style of Italian cinema with opera, without acknowledging that spectacle and allegory also belong to the stage of the commedia. (Dalle Vacche 254–55)

Such a revised perspective of neorealism goes further to place stylized, post-neorealist filmmaking traditions such as the *commedia all'italiana* as the dominant stream of Italian national cinema, rather than neorealist film.

While neorealism derives much of its recuperation of the "living body" from the *commedia dell'arte*, I believe that post-neorealist film, through its emphasis on the representation of ambivalence, is more successful at making the discourse of Italy's chronic ambivalence explicit.[4] It achieves this through innovative thematic and stylistic means that depart from the false holy grail of stylistic realism. The idealized notions of representing the "truth" in neorealism must repress these ambivalences in order to create a coherent national image, something that post-neorealism deliberately refutes. Indeed neorealism has often needed to suppress the ambivalent social and political roles of the nation's institutions in order to construct a coherent image of a morally unified nation. Post-neorealist films on the other hand exemplify the key relevance of mimicry in the projection of a discourse of a national chronic ambivalence, while still maintaining certain aspects of the uniquely Italian humanistic discourse present in neorealism (especially the concern for the proletariat). Each of the films examined in the following chapters is a unique and innovative Italian cinematic response to the social crisis of immigration, and as I shall try and demonstrate, continue the debate on Italy's chronic ambivalence by either recalling or departing from the two illustrious national cinematic periods of the past. Indeed, the thematic detours into Italy's past history are paralleled by stylistic and ideological detours into the postwar history of Italian cinema.

Containing Neorealism

Neorealism is the single most revered institution in Italian cinematic history; it occupies a privileged status as harbinger of both cinematic and cultural revolution in the immediate postwar Italy, and yet, defining it has been a notoriously difficult and polemical concept. Without wishing to open up a Pandora's box of questions on the nature of neorealism, I would like to present some of the more consistent ways in which this important moment in Italian cinema has been understood and is currently understood. Alessia Ricciardi summarizes the two major meanings attributed to neorealism:

> Neorealism in Italy may be said to rather encompass two somewhat different meanings. The term comes to be associated, on the one hand, with the project of reformulating the nation's identity in the period immediately after World War II and, on the other, with the notion of a privileged instrument for the recuperation of reality either in its immediacy (Zavattini) or in a critically mediated form (Aristarco). (483)

While it is undeniable that forms of neorealism did exist within a coherent set of filmic examples, I would like to sidestep an attempt at stylistic definition of these films and use a historically contained, cultural, and social definition.[5] Neorealism is a progressive humanism of the *immediate* postwar period that stressed the common man in an ideologically chaotic Italy. The generation of directors that made the important and canonical neorealist films were seeking a new language of realism to create a national story of rejuvenation, a new *oikos* that would become a point of reference for the reconstruction of the country. Ideological ambiguity and chaos dominated Italy's violent and problematic relationship with the Nazi-fascist, Resistance, and Allied armies in the last bitter years of the war; after the final armistice, therefore, there was a great need to undertake structural changes in society through a new cinematic language (a collective language *par excellence*), in order to purge the nation from fascism on all levels. The stylistic approaches of Rossellini, De Sica, and the other major neorealist masters were all ways of fulfilling this cultural need for collective salvation. This salvation would be based on the ideals of the resistance and inspired by the Gramscian ideal of a "national-popular" art. Roberto Rossellini, director of the seminal neorealist film *Roma città aperta* (1945), declares that neorealism is "the greatest possible curiosity about individuals: a need, appropriate to modern man, to speak of things as they are,

Chapter Two

to be aware of reality" and for him, it is "nothing other than the artistic form of truth" ("A Few Words" 89). The director's affirmations might strike the contemporary reader as naïve, believing as we sometimes do that nothing, even the "real," is what it is, but the need to affirm the "truth" and reality "as is" was a very urgent and palpable cultural need in an Italy that had just gone through the black years of fascist rule. Fascism, driven by empty rhetoric that deceived the people, would be purged by neorealism, which was to be a cinematic method of overturning the moral, and therefore aesthetic, decadence of this shameful period. It would also turn the camera to the individual common man rather than focusing on the heroics of an undifferentiated mass of fascists or the heroic, melodramatic leaders. Thus, realism for Rossellini and his colleagues was a Gramscian restoration of a national-popular culture by a purge of the ideological decadence of Fascism and its associated artistic styles. What do I mean by ideological decadence? Rossellini, describing his motivations for making *Germania Anno Zero* says:

> The Germans were human beings like all the rest. What is it that could have carried them to this disaster? A false philosophy, the essence of Nazism; the abandoning of humility for a cult of heroics; the exaltation of strength over weakness, vaingloriousness over simplicity? That is why I chose to tell the story of a child, an innocent, who through the *distortion* of a utopian education was brought to the point of committing a crime while believing he was accomplishing something heroic. But a small ethical flame still burned within him; he killed himself to escape his sense of moral disquiet. (100; my italics)

Through a tale of personal tragedy on an individual level of the child, Rossellini thus constructs a national allegory of the sickness of Nazi-fascist propaganda that distorted rather than showed reality "as is." This distortion of reality is the decadence that the neorealists abhor. The stylistic choices, made with heterogeneous results and conclusions by the varied group of directors that are classified as neorealists, all to varying degrees were going against a style that would distort the banal reality of everyday life to artificial, melodramatic, extraordinary, or heroic levels. As Caesare Zavattini declared, "I believe that the world continues to evolve towards evil because we do not know the truth: we remain unaware of reality" (72). It is perhaps now in 2017 that one may perhaps better empathize with Zavattini's deep concern for questions about truth and reality in dominant cultural representations, as global culture becomes increasingly dominated by "fake news" and "alternative facts."

Neorealism, therefore, would go against the escapism allowed by the cinematic style of spectacle, which masked "reality" and shows the banality of everyday living. The "style" of neorealism can be summarized through three major criteria:

1. SPACE/LANDSCAPES: the opening up to the external world and cultural landscapes through lesser reliance on "sets" and studio productions.

2. BODIES: the reliance on real bodies and faces of the proletariat through decreased use of studio-system divas, and

3. TIME: the recalibration of dramatic narrative structures.

These criteria can all be attributed to methods with which the integrity of the pro-filmic reality could be respected: the "documentary-style" of the on-location filming that is frequently understood as eponymous with the term neorealism, the hiring of non-professional actors, and the insistence on the filming of non-dramatic events are some of the ways in which neorealist films tried to be faithful to the pro-filmic social and cultural reality of the times. Lack of interior monologues becomes another stylistic consequence: for example, in the final sequence in *Germania Anno Zero*, which lasts an entire seven minutes and culminates in Edmund's unpredictable suicide. The orientation of the camera in this whole sequence is toward the outside of the building in which Edmund meanders. There is no foreshadowing of a tortured psychological state of the child, and the audience is given no recourse to internal thoughts. There is only an abrupt jump into thin air. In terms of the disappearance of dramatic narrative structure, Zavattini mentions the need to not conform to Hollywood-style cinema of spectacle:

> For example: let us take two people who are looking for an apartment. In the past, the filmmaker would have made that the starting point, using it as a simple and external pretext to base something else on. Today, one can use that simple situation of hunting for an apartment as the entire subject of the film. It must be understood, of course, that this is true only if the situation is always emphasized with all the echoes, reflections, and reverberations which are present in it. (71)

Thus, capturing the spontaneity of everyday life becomes a chief theoretical concern in neorealist works. The word "theoretical" is important, because while the cultural and intellectual dialogue around neorealism seemed to observe a stylistically compact endeavor, the reality was a far more heterogeneous body of work. The undeniable aspect of neorealism is therefore its ideological commitment to understanding society, its *impegno sociale*. The common man on screen strived hard to function as testimonial to the trials and victories of the populace in the face of grave adversity. Cinema was to become a tool of pedagogy and documentation on a collective, national level. The stylistic means of achieving this spontaneous cinema of testimony, however, would be varied and heterogeneous. The pedagogic function of cinema that neorealism eulogizes continues to be a preoccupation with new Italian directors seeking to represent immigrants.

André Bazin, the editor of the French *Cahiers du Cinéma* who almost single-handedly brought neorealism to the forefront of global critical attention, believed that the neorealist style is radical in the importance it places on the realism of the body. He describes the way in which neorealist directors foreground the property of the cinematic medium, thus enhancing ontological realism (Bazin 195–211). While reality in the plastic arts is often mediated through the artist, photography, by its very nature, is a mechanical transposition of vegetal reality: the light reflected by the bodies in front of the camera is the light that imprints itself upon the filmstrip. Bazin argues that neorealist directors utilize this close relationship between objects and their representation in film (or to put it in technical terms, of the indexicality of the photographic image) to create an acute psychological bond between characters on screen and audiences. He describes the neo-realists, therefore, as the proponents of "true realism" as opposed to the "pseudorealism" of the perspectival arts that strove to give viewers an "illusion of reality":

> The quarrel over realism in art stems from a misunderstanding, from a confusion between the aesthetic and the psychological; between true realism, the need that is to give significant expression to the world both concretely and its essence, and the pseudorealism of a deception aimed at fooling the eye (or for that matter the mind); a pseudorealism content in other words

Beyond Neorealism

> with illusory appearances. [...] Perspective was the original sin of Western painting.
> It was redeemed from sin by Niepce and Lumière. (197)

Photography, therefore, is the truly realist medium, because it gives both the artist and the viewer the psychological experience of mummification, thus fulfilling a primal need that Bazin calls the "mummy complex:"

> If the plastic arts were put under psychoanalysis, the practice of embalming the dead might turn out to be a fundamental factor in their creation. The process might reveal that at the origin of painting and sculpture there lies a mummy complex. The religion of ancient Egypt, aimed against death, saw survival as depending on the continued existence of the corporeal body. Thus, by providing a defense against the passage of time it satisfied a basic psychological need in man, for death is but the victory of time. To preserve, artificially, his bodily appearance is to snatch it from the flow of time, to stow it away neatly, so to speak, in the hold of life. It was natural, therefore, to keep up appearances in the face of reality of death by preserving flesh and bone. The first Egyptian statue, then, was a mummy, tanned and preserved in sodium. (195)

Mummies, as well as photographs and the cinematic images are preserved indices of life. Indices are, by their nature, time-bound and change mummified. They hint at a totality that forever seems to escape us. Therefore, cinema, and in particular Bazin argues, neorealist cinema, affects us profoundly in the ways we experience both time and physical reality. The objective nature of the photographic image of the actual body, he argues, produced by a mechanical process, is highlighted by the neorealists, who allow for a greater respect for this ontological integrity of the pro-filmic reality by the sundry methods variously employed.

The classic sequence in Vittorio De Sica's *Umberto D.* (1952), hailed as the final great neorealist masterpiece, is a good illustration of Bazin's theoretical framework. Particularly relevant is the famous sequence in which the maid, Maria, wakes up and goes about her morning chores. The seven-minute-long sequence seems to be shot in "real time," unhindered, as it may seem, by narrative constraints, melodramatic acting that externalizes psychological truths to the audience, or dialogue. Maria is presented in a realistic middle-class setting, her body is not reference-deprived, and the entire mise-en-scène contributes to heightening the ontological realism of the character and her pro-filmic reality. The stress on temporal realism can also be understood by Rossellini's concept of "waiting":

> In the narrative cinema, "waiting" is essential. Every solution is born from waiting. It is waiting which makes people live, which unchains reality; it is waiting which, after the preparation, gives liberation. (Rossellini, "A Few Words" 91)

Or in "Ten Years of Cinema":

> Neo-realism consists of following someone with love and watching all his discoveries and impressions; an ordinary man dominated by something which suddenly strikes him a terrible blow at the precise moment when he finds himself free in the world. [...] What is important for me is the waiting. (Rossellini 98)

The stylistic result of this yearning for "waiting" translates into two stylistic choices: the frequent long takes, with the resulting opening up to uncertainties being "imprinted" on the film; and a de-dramatization of the narrative structure, as exemplified by the sequence I have described from De Sica's *Umberto D*.

To summarize, neorealism is a humanism that tried to locate ideological and stylistic principles that would create an ethically and artistically "distortion-free" cinema in which the proletarian body could be witnessed in a "direct" way that heightened ontological realism by foregrounding the indexicality of the photographic image. If this body was indeed a national social signifier, then it can be said that neorealism strove to provide a truthful indexical "mirror" of the new national collective-self. Neorealism was neither an organized movement, nor a consolidated style, and was generated in the context of the need to be a testimonial to the anti-fascist social ideals of the resistance. Alessia Ricciardi is correct in asserting the need for a historical interpretation of neorealism more commonly attributed to Italian criticism, rather than the French idealization of a theoretical neorealism, through its proponents such as André Bazin, Gilles Deleuze, and right up to Jean-Luc Godard:

> The somewhat regressive overtones of Bazin's and Deleuze's interpretations of neorealism as an intuitive, artistic impulse awaiting its fulfillment in the philosophical theorizing of French critics or the cinematic innovations of the *Nouvelle Vague* give way in Godard's *Histoire(s)* to an overt recitation of the most shallow stereotypes of Italian society. Let us observe in conclusion that, from Bazin to Godard, French criticism has tended to neglect the idea of neorealism as a well-defined period in Italian film history stretching from 1945 to 1952 and instead has taken neorealism as the ideal face of modern cinema, an aesthetic on which the redemption of modernity as such may be predicated. (Ricciardi 499–500)

My focus on neorealism in this chapter has concentrated, accordingly, on the very curious socio-cultural context within which neorealism grew, in order to view it from within the very peculiar historical moment in which it was generated. It therefore is a helpful category only when it is restricted to this special period in Italy's cultural history. I have been suggesting that there are many conflicting ideas on the precise definitions of the traditions of neorealism and the post-neorealistic traditions such as the *commedia*. There is a pragmatic need to depart from an unspecific understanding of neorealism in order to retain it as a useful category of film that was produced in the immediate postwar decade in Italy. Categories are only useful to a point, and bringing up the many dead bodies of neorealism in a book on contemporary Italian film is a particularly impractical and counter-productive move. Yet this is exactly what scholars, including myself, will be tempted to do; a majority of the films discussed in this book, including those that I have already mentioned, such as Amelio's *Lamerica* and Garrone's *Terra di mezzo* have been declared important examples of the renewal of neorealism in contemporary Italy, while in reality, few of these products are visually or even culturally connected to this tradition. This is the reason I have had to tackle this matter here. Neorealism, in the sense of a generalized *impegno sociale* has indeed been resuscitated in contemporary films of immigration due to the complex humanitarian and cultural crises and the need for filmmakers to present an alternative to the television versions of this reality. This is the prime reason for which the term has been overused to the point of becoming synonymous with any film that deals with contemporary issues, however tenuous or complex its relationship with that reality.

It is my belief that most of the films on immigration *cannot* be defined as being neo-neorealist despite the fact that they do indeed borrow the *impegno sociale* and a few stylistic parameters of neorealism. The directors' consciousness of the subjective nature of "truth" and "identity" denies most of them that optimism of neorealism of the Forties and Fifties. They therefore, I believe, develop highly innovative personal strategies of accessing some form of cinematic "truth" without succumbing completely to neorealistic aspirations. I would like to suggest that the faith in the cinematic medium that characterized neorealism is mostly lost, and is replaced by irony, or at least some form of self-consciousness or unease. The reality of contemporary Italy's mediatic and therefore civil and political life has created a moral fatigue and depression that cannot be compatible or comparable to the decade of restored hope in the cinematic medium immediately following World War II. All Italian films of immigration are therefore cinematic paths that go *beyond* neorealism, precisely because they are forms that try to resist the "tele-reality" that is, in many ways, a perverse version of the neorealist ideal. The precise and very conservative definition of neorealism proposed here allows us to highlight the various contaminated forms that follow it in the post-neorealist decades of the Fifties and especially the Sixties and to identify forms that are borrowed in the contemporary films of immigration.

Despite the many stipulations that I have established around the use of the term "neorealism," it is nevertheless important for our understanding of contemporary Italian films of immigration, because it gives us some of the basic aesthetic and ideological vocabulary to understand Italy's continued tradition of cinema as a national signifier. Essentially, I believe that the baby must not be thrown out with the bathwater. In addition to the continued presence of echoes and ghosts of neorealism in today's films of immigration, the discussion of this period of Italian film is also helpful in the contrast it offers to what came after—the various collection of genres and styles I categorize as "post-neorealism." Despite it never really being a monolithic movement and having a variety of techniques and versions and moments of ambiguity, neorealism can be said to have exerted a "gravitational pull" on the collection of body and cultural-images that it produced, retroactively producing an image of a modern democratic nation. Post-neorealism, in contrast, began to embrace the more ambivalent aspects of the national body, and therefore represents a chaotic force, where the coherence of collections of national images is pulled apart, causing the indexical neorealist body to split and distort. Just as the *post-* in postcolonial signifies "beyond" for Bhabha, the *post-* here once again signifies a stylistical, conceptual, and therefore cultural leap away from neorealism, and encompasses both what was to become the popular medium portraying the national body in the end of the 1950s (the *commedia*), as well as the art-house favorites such as *8½* by Fellini. As Italy passed from the initial decade of optimism of the reconstruction period (roughly the decade of 1945–55) into a period of paradoxical social and political upheaval in the late-Fifties, so did centripetal forces overtake the centrifugal, and the national body would break apart, turning into a multiplicity of ironic, self-reflexive mimic-bodies of the *commedia* and the auteur films of the Sixties.

The Centrality of Chronic Ambivalence in Post-Neorealist Film

Italy began to move past the initial physical and moral ruin of Fascism and war, and by the mid-Fifties, had begun to rapidly industrialize, leading to the years of the economic miracle, or simply, the "boom." Frenzied development continued steadily under the governance of the now already entrenched Christian-Democrats but it was mostly in the North, leading to mass migrations of dispossessed people from Southern Italy to the major industrial centers in the North. Initial optimism for a moral rejuvenation under the ideals of the Resistance quickly faded to a realization that the project of identifying ex-Fascists and bringing them to justice had failed, and even any clear ideological boundaries between ex-fascists and communists began to erode. Instead of a new path, politics had stagnated, and had turned into something more ambiguous and paradoxical rather than optimistic. One of the most important directors of the *commedia all'italiana*, Mario Monicelli describes his concerns about the ambivalent political situation, which seems surprisingly relevant to the contemporary situation in Italy:

> Noi siamo in un periodo di transizione fra una società e un'altra […] Il contesto politico è cambiato. Prima era chiaro e preciso:

> il potere della Chiesa, la destra. Ma oggi è tutto ambiguo, le carte sono mischiate, il Partito Comunista fa parte, o quasi, della coalizione e noi ci chiediamo quale debba essere la nostra posizione [...]. (Gili 191)

This specific socio-political scenario, encapsulated in the term *trasformismo*, resulted in the need for a new cinematic language that could better portray the new ambivalent national *oikos* that inflicted a moral and political classificatory confusion. This was the condition in which the *commedia* was born and flourished. These social concerns were also of prime interest to a new generation of directors such as Fellini. That *trasformismo* has been and continues to be perceived as a prominent feature of Italian political life can be witnessed by its resurgence in today's Italy. The first reactions in the press to the news that, after two months of wrangling, Enrico Letta has finally been able to form a government through a grand coalition between his Democratic Party (PD) and their arch-nemesis, Berlusconi's People of Liberty Party (PDL) was to insinuate that we still may be well within the age of political *trasformismo* in Italy:

> It is the most famous quote in modern Italian literature, because it captures so well the cynicism and conservatism of modern Italian politics. "If we want everything to remain as it is," says Tancredi in Giuseppe di Lampedusa's "The Leopard," "everything needs to change." For once, Italy's politicians have turned the saying on its head. On April 20th they arranged for things to stay as they were in order to make them change. ("Letta in Post")

The origins of the *commedia*, as Tullio Masoni and Paolo Vecchi explain, are as varied as are its many forms and facets: the *commedia dell'arte*, with its masked characters and rampant improvisation, the *teatro dialettale*, the circus and the figure of the clown, the *caffè concerto* of the late nineteenth century, and especially the *teatro di varietà* (in Napolitano 75–86). While having many facets, one common feature to all the forms of the *commedia* and the major post-neorealist films lies in the ambiguous moral and physical attributes of its characters, which deliberately generate an ambivalent feeling in the audience, rather than feelings of easy identification. This is a great departure from the (ideally) ethical or corrupt characters of neorealism. Writing about Mario Monicelli's *La grande guerra* (1959), considered as one of the first classic *commedie*, Pietro Pintus explains some of the main characteristics of the *commedia*:

> Ma *La grande guerra*, insieme con gli indubbi meriti intrinseci, avrebbe messo in evidenza anche talune caratteristiche—che sarebbero poi divenute costanti—di un certo cinema che proprio in quelli anni cresceva, destino a diffondersi, e che si sarebbe a posteriori chiamato *commedia* all'italiana: la commistione di comicità e di dramma, la predilezione per il tratteggio di eroi tutto sommato negativi, una viva attenzione al presente se non addirittura l'attualità, e l'intreccio spesso ambiguo di satira, denuncia morale e irridente caricatura priva di un autentico spessore etico. (In Napolitano 18)

I believe that a better understanding of these unique "in-between" ethical qualities of the un-heroes of the *commedia* and the "serious" art films of the Sixties can be better understood through a study of what Luigi Pirandello called "humor," in contrast to the "comic," in his ground-breaking essay *On Humor* (1908). I believe that the various loose definitions of *commedia* as "a mix of comedy and tragedy" and the unsettling qualities of the auteur films of the post-neorealist period do not fully explain the unified cultural work they carried out in the context of their time. The collection of qualities that Pirandello describes as humor can give us more insight into the primary characteristic of this genre, i.e., *the centrality of ambivalence* rather than resolution in the representation of the body-as-nation. Humor, as opposed to the comic, allows us to connect the genre of the *commedia* to Bhabha's understanding of the destabilizing quality of mimicry in hybridity.

I have described how André Bazin considered the indexicality of the photographic image as a primary source of "true realism." He defines the works of the neorealists as a variety of styles that highlight this indexicality. Realism, for Bazin, therefore, is not about an aesthetic that gives the viewer an "illusion of the real" but an objective, mechanical one that fulfills the viewer's psychological need for "embalming" space and time: "Thus, neorealism is more an ontological position than an aesthetic one" (Bazin 204). Photography, and cinema are, consequently, the privileged media that satisfy the human urge to "mummify" bodies and their environments, and neorealism is the culmination of the understanding of this psychological need. I have described how this faithfulness to realism is manifested in neorealist films' formal aspects, i.e., in their representation of spaces, bodies, and time. In contrast to the neorealist stylistic ideal then, stands post-neorealism, which prescribes a set of very subjective aesthetic positions that serve to complicate the understanding of the body on screen not merely as a physical "imprint" of reality, but the organic base upon which cultural discourse "imprints" itself—leading to the split between the face and the social "masks" that are worn upon it, a split creating ambivalence and mimicry. It is no wonder that the *commedia* is also called the *commedia di costume*—in other words, a study of what happens to the body when it becomes a conduit between individual values and societal norms. *Costume*, in Italian does not mean "costume" but "customs or traditions," reflecting the common Latin root *consuetudinem* for both words. The contradictions or discrepancies that emerge between the desire of individuals and cultural rules and traditions become the primary sources of humor, and the body visually distorts itself on screen to perform its various roles as a mimic. The main stylistic characteristics of all post-neorealist films, including the *commedia* are:

1. SPACE/LANDSCAPE: Spaces are re-arranged into a stylized mise-en-scène. City peripheries and other liminal areas are often the setting of choice. Instead of masses and crowds of people filmed in medium or long shots, interior landscapes of the mind come to the forefront, resulting in a primacy of individual bodies and faces.

2. BODIES: Instead of non-professional actors, highly accomplished and recognizable actors are used. Their gestures and movements are highly stylized at times, up to the point of being grotesque in the *commedia*. Psychological intricacies are externalized onto the body and face.

3. TIME: The extended shots of "waiting" in neorealism transform into elaborate montages with dramatic consequences, where time is now experienced in either very long or very short durations. There is often extreme disruption of pro-filmic time through extensive manipulation of narrative arcs (uses of flashbacks, flash-forwards, ellipses, etc.).

When compared to neorealism, then, the visual distortions of the bodies in the *commedia all'italiana* are somewhat analogous to the distortions present in Mannerist bodies that contrasted with the symmetry and naturalism of the bodies in Renaissance paintings. Pirandello's description of humor points to the existential disjunction, the contradiction that is created due to the split between the desires of the individual and the rules of the society in which he/she lives, and I believe that this is exactly what resides at the heart of all the *un*-heroes of post-neorealist film, from Risi's grotesque social monsters to Antonioni's neurotic women to Fellini's permanently dissatisfied men. The stylization and departure from neorealism described above are the formal methods of representing the contradictory content of these new films.

Humor, for Pirandello, is distinct from the comic. The most frequent comment I hear from students taking my Italian Comedy course is that none of it is very funny at all. This is because these films tend to be humoristic rather than comic. Humor in these films is the kind of humor described by Pirandello. It can be deeply unsettling, even tragic or sad. The contradiction that we are shown in a character leads us to perceive the split between appearances and the real, between *what is* and *what should be*. This causes an initial comic effect and therefore induces laughter. After an inner psychological process of *reflection* upon this contradiction (coaxed by the humorist), the viewer who perceives this contradiction or discrepancy experiences the "feeling of the opposite"—which is humor:

> I see an old lady whose hair is dyed and completely smeared with some kind of horrible ointment; she is all made-up in a clumsy and awkward fashion and is all dolled-up like a young girl. I begin to laugh. I *perceive* that she is *the opposite* of what a respectable old lady should be. Now I stop here at this initial and superficial comic reaction: the comic consists precisely of this *perception of the opposite*. But if, at this point, reflection interferes in me to suggest that perhaps this old lady finds no pleasure in dressing up like an exotic parrot, and that perhaps she is distressed by it and does it only because she pitifully deceives herself into believing that, by making herself up like that and by concealing her wrinkles and gray hair, she may be able to hold the love of her much younger husband—if reflection comes to suggest all this, then I can no longer laugh at her as I did at first, exactly because the inner working of reflection has made me go beyond or rather enter deeper into, the initial stage of awareness: from the beginning *perception of the opposite*,

> reflection has made me shift to a *feeling of the opposite*. And herein lies the precise difference between the comic and humor. (Pirandello, Illiano, and Testa 113)

Therefore, in short, humor is a complex process in which the viewer/reader of the character in the work of art may first experience the comic, and then, through an evaluative process, which is an emotionally highly cathartic one, arrives at a feeling of humor:

> We said that, as a rule, in the conception of a work of art, reflection is almost a mirror in which feeling looks at itself. In pursuing this image, one could say that, in the conception of a work of humor, reflection is indeed like a mirror, but a mirror of icy water, in which the flame of feeling not only looks at itself but also plunges in it and extinguishes itself: the sizzling of the water is the laughter that the humorist evokes, the vapor which it emits is the fantasy, often somewhat murky, of the work of humor. (118)

In our discussion of the cinematic body then, the "fantasy" described by Pirandello is that stylistic distortion of the body in the "mirror," the bending of the realist aesthetic that would like to portray reality "as is" and which strives to heighten indexicality of the photographic image. The viewer, due to this distortion, becomes aware of the artificiality of the representation and is therefore tugged simultaneously by the opposite feelings of laughing and weeping, as he mirrors the humorist's curiosity of ambivalence and contradiction:

> Every feeling, every thought, or every impulse that arises in the humorist immediately splits into the contrary: every affirmative into a negative, which finally ends up assuming the same *value* as the affirmative. At times, perhaps, the humorist can pretend to have only one feeling; meanwhile, inside him, the other feeling speaks to him, a feeling that at first seems to lack the courage to expose itself; it speaks to him and it begins to advance now a timid excuse, now an attenuation, which reduce the warmth of the original feeling, now an acute reflection which deflates its seriousness and induces laughter. (125; my italics)

We have been discussing bodies and spaces in terms of representations of the individual and collective "values" attributed to bodies. Pirandello's description of humor allows us to fully flesh out this conception of the crucial cultural "work" that humor potentially undertakes through its subversive re-evaluation of individual and societal values and identities—in other words, of its *oikos*. Indeed, post-neorealist directors strive to do precisely that. By inciting a "classificatory confusion" within established embodied values by highlighting its contradictions rather than its integrity, these films masterfully produce characters caught in between the roles of society's heroes and villains. Rather than easy categorization by the audience, these films sought to provoke disorientation or stupor. It is not a coincidence that its critics will harshly, and usually wrongly, dub most films as "cynical."[6] The stylistic and cultural departure from the delimited period of neorealism as I have described it ascribes a definite political value to Pirandello's humor, in addition to its existential importance. When viewed through the lens of postcolonial theory, Pirandello's understanding of humor in the visual arts can be understood as an artistic trope that represents Bhabhian hybridity, the uneasy, often menacing interstitial space where contradiction, discrepant experiences/images, and new identities are formed.

In their discussion of one of the films that will be explored in detail in Chapter 4, *Bianco e nero* (*White and Black*, 2006), Bernadette Luciano and Susanna Scarparo correctly distinguish between bodies in comedies that reinforce stereotypes (for example, the blackface tradition in the United States) and those that question and transgress them. Quoting Mick Eaton's article "Laughter in the Dark," Luciano and Scarparo say that laughter can "have either a consensual or a transgressive effect" (Luciano and Scarparo 136). Since the ideological function of comedy is so important to a study of new migrant cinema, I have utilized Pirandello's distinction between the "comic"—an evocation of consensual laughter, and the "humorous"—a cinematic image and a mechanism that promotes reflection through a marvelous body—an inherently transgressive type of laughter. Creating this distinction here will help the analysis of comedy films of new migrant cinema in further chapters immensely.

If neorealism highlighted the indexicality of the photographic image through the use of non-professional actors and radically de-dramatized screenplays that involved lots of "waiting," post-neorealist films do just the opposite. In the *commedia*, for example, we have a deft alternation between the comic and the dramatic, and the use of highly professional actors who soon became iconic as masters of *commedia*: Vittorio Gassman, Marcello Mastroianni, Ugo Tognazzi, Nino Manfredi, and Alberto Sordi, to name a few important ones. Each of these actors embodied various regional or class stereotypes, fetishizing their stereotypical characteristics to such an extreme that they provoke transgressive (rather than consensual) laughter. The act of reflection, prompted by the swift alternation between dramatic elements, typical in the *commedia*, prevent stabilization of the stereotypical "masks." Instead, these fetishized identities now seem to the viewer to be grotesque "mimic-men" that expose their very constructedness and point to the underlying contradictions upon which their entrenched identities were built. Thus we have the unmistakable mix of *both* utter shamelessness/lack of remorse and extreme fragility/sensitivity of the iconic un-heroes of the *commedia*, who strive with utmost determination to "perform" the roles of someone they can never really be: Gassman's macho boxer who has a speech disorder in *I soliti ignoti*; Mastroianni's neurotic and sexually frustrated Sicilian aristocrat in *Divorzio all'italiana*; Sordi's attempt at performing American-ness in *Un Americano a Roma*, memorably foiled by an innocuous plate of spaghetti, are only a few examples of the rich cast of Italian un-heroes. The personal failures of these characters occur to great humoristic, rather than comic, effect. The psychological neutrality of the neorealistic faces turns to melodrama, caricature, grotesque exaggeration of facial expressions, and regional gestures, movements, accents, and typologies embodying ideological stereotypes.

While neorealism focused on trying to gain an objective view of the body situated within the external world, with its external pan shots, uninterrupted tracking, and long shots, the *commedia* explores the contradictions of the hybrid mimic-body split and doubled in all its horrific and fascinating detail: gone are the long shots and takes, replaced by close-ups of faces wracked by psychosomatic illnesses, nervous tics, lisps, snickers, winks, wet lips, twitches; grotesque faces with missing teeth, crossed eyes, hooked noses that become caricatures through exaggeration of expressions. The extreme theatricality of these "masked" performances undoes the stereotype, exposing the underlying ambivalence. Thematically too, ambivalence pervades the so-called societal values. They are often upended as cultural roles are exposed in all their hypocritical detail; for example, in *I soliti ignoti*, there is a mass confusion of personal and professional "roles:" prisoners turn out to be better than the lawyers at the understanding of the justice system, non-criminals take the rap for real ones for economic advantages, honest persons try to become professional thieves, Southerners try to pass themselves off as Northerners, healthy people fake illness or injury, while the sick pretend to be healthy, etc.

In short, post-neorealist films are a collection of strategies to better place the body-on-screen as an updated accurate contemporary social signifier of a new Italy, a hybrid *oikos* that characterized ambivalence rather than certainty. In an age of contradiction and ethical decadence, these films peruse the variety of mimic-bodies rather than taking the cultural roles of various bodies "as is" for granted.

The Realist and Humoristic Modes of Representation

I would like to suggest that contemporary filmmakers are caught between the urge to represent the reality of the humanitarian crisis presented by immigration in an indexical way and their partial or complete realization that the contradictions in society they need in order to represent this reality are in many ways unfilmable with a purely neorealistic aesthetic. They are split, as were the other post-neorealist filmmakers I have described above, between the need to entertain and the need to document historically significant moments. The result is therefore a collection of films that are essentially hybrid forms, containing some elements of neorealism in their content and aspiration (the ever-present conscience of the *impegno sociale*), yet very often post-neorealistic in form. In order to better illustrate these hybrid forms in today's films that focus on immigration, forms that contain elements of both the intellectual self-reflexivity of the filmmakers of neorealism and the self-reflexivity imposed upon the audience by the stylized traditions of post-neorealism, I would like to introduce the terms "realist mode" and "humoristic mode." These modes reflect general stylistic and thematic tendencies in a film toward the very different self-reflexive approaches of neorealism I have described above, and the later post-neorealistic traditions that depart from it. In other words, the collection of disparate stylistic strategies I have listed in the neorealist and post-neorealist periods correspond to choices belonging to the realist and the humoristic modes respectively. The realist mode tends to be problematic in its representation of truly hybrid identities while humoristic films tend to present a far better representation of the contradictions that underscore cultural hybridity in Italy today.

As Italy moved rapidly from Europe's under-developed Other into a mainstream European economy, the collection of visual strategies that define post-neorealism accurately portrayed the in-between-ness of the Italians through the depiction of the Italian body wearing masks. These faces, bodies, and masks "perform" modern society but fail miserably in the resulting humoristic performance, thus exposing the chronic ambivalence and hybridity of the nation in relation to fixed social identity. Post-neorealist films thus exposed the constructedness of Italy's ambition to become a modern consumerist society, a society that was to be achieved by the ruthless expulsion of its internal Others—the *meridionali*, the poor, the old, the disabled, etc. Post-neorealist films effectively use various methods that depart from neorealism to tackle its failed promises: Pasolini develops a "cinema of poetry" in order to culturally recuperate the disavowed abject qualities of society; Antonioni represents the psychological impact of the new Italy on the relationship between the sexes in the new upper middle classes; Bertolucci finds stylistic means to embody and analyze the perceived moral decadence of the Left; Risi, Germi, the *commedia* in general fetishize unto grotesqueness the battles between old and new generations; Fellini wholly indulges in (yet also feels guilty about) personalized access into the promised surplus of an upwardly mobile modern Italy.

Pirandello's wonderful description of humor (as the "shadow" following the "body") gives us a useful description of how these films make an incisive cultural critique of the society of the *boom economico* by paying attention not only to the Italian "body" (the mainstream narrative of a successful industrialization) but also hybrid identities, its "shadows" (the *panni sporchi*, disavowed problems, mentioned famously by then Prime Minister Giulio Andreotti):

> The ordinary artist pays attention to only the body; the humorist pays attention to both, and sometimes more to the shadow than to the body: he notices all the tricks of the shadow, the way it sometimes grows longer, sometimes short and squat, *almost as if to mimic the body*, which meanwhile is indifferent to it and does not pay any attention to it. (145: my italics)

Post-neorealist cinema's unique uses of humor (in Pirandello's strict understanding of that word) made audiences reflect on their social roles in a rapidly changing Italy. It is an evocation of laughter that is transgressive rather than consensual, as it calls to attention the body's mimic-status, a situation that evokes menace rather than comforting familiarity, as we have discussed in the previous chapter. I will demonstrate in the following chapters that this self-reflexivity is one of the principal characteristics of many of the most interesting examples of new migrant cinema. The generation of those who turn their cameras upon the migrant body are often conscious of Italy's ambivalent historical position and aware of Italian cinema's unparalleled legacy of chronicling these contradictions in its moments of crisis. The stereotypical images in the media that have created an alternate "tele-reality" weigh heavily on their minds as they seek solutions that balance the need to document reality and the need to interpret and entertain. They therefore seek innovative means of depicting characters that are fraught by a radical destabilization of the self by harking back to their own strong traditions of social cinema that have successfully represented marvelous bodies in the past.

It is important to restate here that there is no defining line that hermeneutically separates films in the realist mode from the humoristic. The contemporary films of immigration in Italy can, and often do, switch from one mode to another. Contamination, variations, and hybrid genres become common. This was also the case historically: the humoristic aspects that reside in the interstices of films such as *Roma città aperta* and the realist aspects of *Divorizio all'italiana* or *Deserto rosso* are important to a better understanding of those films. Indeed, hybridity between the two traditions of neorealism and post-neorealism often lies at the root of some of the most critically successful films in the history of Italian cinema: Fellini's episodic *La dolce vita*, Antonioni's existential hyper-realism in *L'avventura*, Bertolucci's expressionism in *Il conformista*, even Pasolini's cinema of poetry possess elements of both the realist and the humoristic modes. These two modes are strategies that are once again employed by the "detourist" films on immigration explored in the next three chapters. One of the characteristic features of the films analyzed in *Marvelous Bodies* are their generic hybridity in relation to more exclusive categories of neorealism and post-neorealism. The historical tension between "reality" and "artifice" as represented by the two modes that I have defined, is now being consciously or unconsciously harnessed by a young generation of directors, producing an astonishing variety of marvelous bodies in the Italian cinema of immigration.

All the films studied in the following chapters treat the migrant-subject's body on the screen either more in the "humoristic" vein or more with a "realist" sensibility. The humoristic films focus on the essential ambivalence demonstrated by the characters and utilize that ambivalence to drive the plot. Mystery, rather than pedagogy, becomes central to the humoristic plot, as identities are split, doubled, or hidden, creating embarrassment, unease, and "menace." These films will be especially explored in Chapter 5, "Ambivalent Moralities." The claustrophobic weight of stereotypical popular images of the immigrant body that project a continuous, soothing, and uninterrupted narration of a monolithic national *oikos* pushes filmmakers to use stylistic strategies that highlight the cinematic medium rather than mesmerizing the audience with yet more commercial/television-like worlds. The visual marvels of the sight of marvelous bodies are precisely these disruptions in the continuous flow of migrant stereotypes that soothe the audience into critical torpor. The *torpor* is shaken by *stupor*, that precise moment of dazed yet uneasy amazement caused by the suspension of identity rather than the repetition of expected stereotypes. The more successful films on immigration are, through these moments of stupor, attempts at the creation of cinematic ruptures that move away from popular images, in that they seek to override default stereotypes and discourses of the nation that bodies in visual media represent. They therefore often result in humoristic tropes to be used, such as grotesque or absurd situations, disruptions in narrative structures, thematic ambivalence or disorientation through misunderstandings between characters, or provoked misidentification of characters for the audience.

Beyond Neorealism

Even films created in a realist mode, such as Marco Tullio Giordana's *Quando sei nato non puoi più nasconderti* or Vittorio de Seta's *Lettere dal Sahara* cannot fully reclaim the ideals of neorealism of the Forties and Fifties. Neorealism, if one defines it strictly as a critical yet optimistic humanism of the immediate postwar period, is effectively dead, but as I have mentioned before, it is still important to recognize the neorealistic *intentions* of some of these filmmakers. Despite mirroring some of the aesthetics and the progressive social ethos of the original neorealists, the new directors cannot deny the historical consciousness of Italy's chronic ambivalence (i.e., its contradictory relationship vis-à-vis the Other) and their contemporary preoccupation with visual media's corruption to create alternate realities for political purposes. The films that approach the immigrant-subject in the realist mode are often problematic, as they tend not to undertake a critical approach to the question of Italian-ness, often subscribing to the outdated notions of multiculturalism that Bhabhian hybridity questions.

Regardless of their bent toward the realist or the humoristic mode, the films studied in this book are attempts at using various strategies of representation that can be said to form hybrid genres that work between these modes, with a much more self-reflexive and troubled depiction of identity roles of the Italians and migrants. They often exemplify strategies that try to create "classificatory confusions" of the screened bodies, rather than stereotypical "fixing" of immigrant identities, fetishized for the sake of easy identification by the audience. The result of all these different explorations, whether tendentially more humoristic or more realist, is a fascinating variety of marvelous bodies on screen.

Chapter Three

Ambivalent Geographies

Mount Vesuvius dominates the screen. The establishing shot is that of an instantly recognizable object of great power that immediately grounds the film geographically and culturally for all Italian audiences to the metropolis of Naples, capital of the Campania region, cultural capital of the entire South. The aerial tracking shot then angles slightly downward, showing us a bird's eye view of the urban sprawl at the foot of the massive volcano, further confirming the specificity of the location. But then we perceive something slightly unsettling, unfamiliar. There is nothing uncommon visually, at least not yet. Yet the sound does not match the images of the cityscape. We do not hear the urban bustle of the metropolis of the Italian South, but the sound of the wind. We feel disoriented in space and time. The superb extended shot continues to track over the city, and suddenly amongst the typical urban imagery of endless buildings, roads, and traffic, we are presented with a marvelous body, just as the musical soundtrack cues in over the sound of the wind. This body now completes the director's evasive operation that destabilizes rather than establishes spatial and temporal location for his viewers. We see, from far above, the marvelous body of an animal rather than of a human. It is a horse, its pure white color catching the eye as a reverse-negative stain in an otherwise dark and traffic-packed streetscape. The horse is drawing a carriage, but this too is not any ordinary carriage. It is heavily gilded in gold with a seventeenth-century rococo design. The horse and the carriage seem suspended in another dimension. Are we in Naples today or Versailles during the reign of the Sun King? The camera slowly nears the marvelous image from above as it weaves its way through heavy traffic.

This hallucinatory and manifestly discrepant image, so much in contradiction with its surrounding landscape and time, makes up the first brilliant sequence of Matteo Garrone's *Reality* (2012). This one tracking shot is an example of the director's humoristic and ironic preoccupation with the relationship between cinema and the individual and collective realities of Italy today. An acute concern with this relationship makes Garrone an ideal first candidate for the study of Italy's ambivalent geographies in the context of immigration.

The question of locations, landscape-images, and imagined geographies is central to the question of immigration in Italian national cinema, because, as Noa Steimatsky claims, in Italian cinema "The act of filmmaking [...] constitutes an imaginary re-inhabiting of the landscape. Such assertive use of locations is posited as a historical project and as cultural and aesthetic self-realization" (Steimatsky 3). It is no surprise, that the identity crisis provoked by immigration has inspired several Italian filmmakers to direct their gaze to seek culturally ambivalent, marvelous landscapes of the nation. Neorealism, focused on rebuilding a vital nation from the ruins of Fascism and World War II, cinematically imbued both urban and rural landscapes with a strong sense of "Italian-ness" (3). The directionally opposite humoristic post-neorealistic traditions of either emptying the bodies and landscapes of this national signification or overemphasizing their regional specificities at the cost of its national connotations (which occurs in the *commedia all'italiana*), began in the Fifties and matured in the auteur films of the Sixties. Antonioni's eerily deserted urban landscapes and precise yet unusual architectural framing of bodies and Pasolini's vital, chaotic peripheral landscapes where urban gentrification has yet to establish repressive order are some of the best examples of directors who were preoccupied with representing the absurd/fantastical/disorienting or liminal instead of the nationally recognizable. The new Italian films of immigration continue to engage with these ideological tensions by visually exploring the nation's new cultural landscapes.

Oneiric Spaces in Matteo Garrone's
Terra di mezzo

Garrone's first films focus on immigrants and other peripheral humans dwelling in Rome's urban periphery. He is a young director who has truly excelled in creating an aesthetic of suspended identities and locations. I shall now examine his first full-length feature, *Terra di mezzo* (*In-Between Land,* 1996) and define his unique strategy of representing liminal embodied landscapes in the context of immigration. Garrone catapulted to worldwide fame after his film *Gomorra* won the Grand Prix at the 2008 Cannes Film Festival. He has created a distinct style that can be seen to be growing in maturity in an arc that stretches from *Terra di mezzo* to *Gomorra* to the recent *Reality*. He is often referred to as a neorealist, but I would like to demonstrate that he is actually a keen exponent of a humoristic style of cinema. Garrone can be called an heir of neorealism only if we specifically focus on his interest in basing the pro-filmic environment upon actual contemporary social landscapes and spaces. Many non-Italian critics have done exactly that, and by focusing on his Italian identity, have praised him for his gritty, neorealistic aesthetic in *Gomorra*,[1] revealing a superficial understanding and use of that term and partial familiarity with the director's filmography. *Gomorra* is a consciously post-neorealistic film, a visual pastiche of the *noir*, science fiction, and stylized expressionism, despite it being an adaptation of a smash-hit book by Roberto Saviano that reveals factual details of Naples's organized crime system, the Camorra. The director's interest in representing the complex reality of the Camorra organization is undeniable as is his consistent commitment to social issues that began right from his first film, *Terra di mezzo*. As he himself states, his style is founded primarily upon a great visual interest in human bodies and faces, and their relationship to the landscapes and objects that they inhabit:

> In realtà si può dire che da quando ho girato il mio primo film *Terra di mezzo*, fino a oggi, il mio metodo di lavoro non è cambiato molto. Già da allora ero mosso da desiderio di perlustrare dei territori alla ricerca di un'idea figurativa del film, attraverso i luoghi e attraverso i volti. (De Sanctis et al. 67)[2]
>
> In reality, one could say that since I shot my first film *Terra di mezzo*, until today, my working method has not changed much. Already then, I was moved by the desire to chart territories in the search of a figurative idea of film, through places and through faces.

Indeed, like in *Reality*, the bodies and landscapes that populate the screen in *Gomorra* are culturally imbibed with the specificity of the Campania region. Not only are most of the actors non-professional locals or professional actors from the region, but their regional identity is also further grounded for Italian audiences by the strict use of a variety of Campanian dialects rather than standard Italian. The linguistic specificity is such that local audiences from the Campania region can not only recognize it, but can also perceive clear differences between various regional dialects used, such as Mondragonese or Neapolitan. Despite this very specific and groundbreaking use of dialect for a film with a national audience, Garrone, as he did in *Reality*, contradicts this realist specificity by the utilization of a profoundly stylized mise-en-scène. There is a distilling of the images of real territory and bodies by careful composition, framing, and editing so as to make this reality simultaneously disorienting, distorted, and therefore *oneiric*. In other words, he departs from the realistic mode precisely because he is not as interested in sociological analysis as he is curious about expressing the consequences of social rules upon landscapes and bodies ("the search for a figurative idea of film"). The contradiction between the languages we hear (the realist specificity they represent) and the mise-en-scène and framed bodies we see creates the central moral tension and stylistic suspension in *Gomorra*. The end result is more humoristic than realistic.

Italian audiences are conditioned to expect extremely strictly defined linguistic parameters as a result of being gifted with the largest and most sophisticated dubbing industry in the world. They normally only hear the best Italian language-speaking artists using standardized Italian, bereft of regional accents and even slight traces of cadences on all dialogue soundtracks, both Italian and foreign. This complacency is brought to an abrupt end as they are forced, in *Gomorra*, to read Italian subtitles for 137 minutes in order to comprehend the Campanian dialogue. It is easy to see why critics would praise a film that deals with contemporary social issues with such a rebellious attitude toward the national language as a masterpiece of neorealism. Yet one can imagine how such a forceful insistence on regional identity, reinforced by the use of local, non-professional actors, could inadvertently be fetishized into caricature or stereotyping of the Southern typology. This is a possible outcome to which Garrone is most sensitive and would most like to avoid. I believe that he is successful in his difficult attempt to both specify yet universalize the economic, political, and socio-cultural situation in Campania. The jarring recall to a Campanian rather than an Italian reality that I have described above has an effect that is the opposite of stereotyping. Garrone does this by contrasting the regional identity with ethereal or absurd juxtapositions of landscapes and bodies, creating a split-identification by viewers that results in suspension rather than easy identification, and therefore, stereotyping of the Neapolitan type, or the sensational mob/gangster type. The Campanian faces and bodies, in other words, become marvelous. An operation of suspension of such an order in *Gomorra* demonstrates the work of a master who has reached stylistic maturity. Yet, this film is not a single brilliant work that emerges out of nowhere. Garrone's training in creating exquisite representations of suspended identities began with his interest not in Italy's internal others, the Southerners (*meridionali*), but its external others, its immigrants.

When Garrone interferes with conventional verisimilitude, he is making a cultural commentary rather than simply trying to document reality "as is." His background as a painter gives him a sensibility that allows him to make minute observations of landscapes, buildings, objects, and people, and then re-present them to the film viewer. He is not interested in "documentary truth" or providing an "illusion of reality" in as much as he is interested in how cinema can make full use of its capabilities as a medium to show a stylized *hyper*-reality—a reality that has passed through the subjective eyes of the painter/director, is interpreted by him, and is then *re*-presented on film. Indeed, Garrone's absolute comfort with his status as an interpreter of reality rather than simply an observer has helped him create a unique style in which the line between documentary and fiction is completely blurred. It therefore seems that the most important of the many in-between lands explored by Garrone in his first film is that "in-between" generic zone where documentary slides into fiction and vice-versa. Speaking again about his method, Garrone says:

> È un metodo, questo, che certamente ha origine dal documentario—anche se queste categorie, fiction e documentario, sono sempre un po' approssimative—che diventa un'ideazione di personaggi che vengono verificati continuamente, a volte anche con dei cambiamenti dolorosi in corso d'opera. (De Sanctis et al. 68)

Chapter Three

> This is a method that certainly has origins in the documentary—although these categories, fiction and documentary, are always a little vague—that becomes a creation of characters that are continuously revisited, even sometimes with painful changes during filming.

Indeed, Garrone's style is characterized by a complete open-ended relationship to the screenplay. Often, big changes are made in the editing stage, and Garrone frequently returns to film more scenes after editing, having reconsidered thematic or aesthetic elements within the plot because of the experience of montage. This is not improvisation for Garrone, rather, it forms the heart of a "painterly" strategy of interpreting and representing actors, bodies, faces, and spaces:

> Un paragone lo si potrebbe fare con la tecnica delle velature utilizzata in pittura. Nella pittura all'olio, per arrivare a una partocolare tonalità, si usano tanti strati di colore sovvraposti, le velature appunto, che poi danno vita all'effetto finale. (De Sanctis et al. 68)

> A comparison could be made with the technique of layering used in painting. In oil paintings, one uses many layers of superimposed colors, what we call *velature*, to arrive at a particular tonality, which end up giving life to the final effect.

The drive to such meticulous interpretation of embodied landscapes comes from the director's curiosity about society, but without any interest in analysis, and a strong will to cinematically *express* rather than *comment*:

> Non so bene perché, ma da [*Terra di mezzo*] si è creato un equivoco sull'importanza per me della denuncia o dell'impegno [sociale]. Sono sempre stato dell'idea che sia più importante l'espressione che l'informazione, tutto questo discorso anche vale per *Gomorra* che richia di essere frainteso, perché ha una componente di denuncia sociale ma questa rappresenta solo un aspetto delle sue varie motivazioni. (De Sanctis et al. 69)

> I don't know exactly why, but from [*Terra di mezzo*], an ambivalence was created in me with regard to the importance of social cinema (*denuncia* and *impegno*). I have always been of the idea that expression is more important than information. All this discourse is also valid for *Gomorra*, which risks being

> misunderstood because it does contain an element of social cinema, but that represents only one of its various motivations.

Garrone's *equivoco* is important, as it points to his deliberate ambivalent positioning with regard to his capacity as a film-maker to take ethical standpoints by claiming a moral high ground. Even when speaking about *Gomorra*, Garrone downplays his role of social commentator: "Non aspettatevi un film di denuncia, ne' una inchiesta. Non voglio fare il moralista. Mi sono soffermato sui personaggi. Studiare questa umanità è stato l'aspetto che mi ha interessato maggiormente." ("Primissima: *Gomorra*") ("Do not expect a social commentary or investigative film. I do not want to be a moralist. I stopped at the characters. Observing this humanity is what interested me the most"). While not abdicating social responsibility, Garrone's films thus consciously try to strike a balance that prevents the director's gaze upon reality from becoming didactic. Instead, he allows his aesthetic interpretation of the bodies and landscapes to make a social commentary through their visual impact. Speaking of his work, and that of Paolo Sorrentino, Garrone says:

> Per noi conta più l'idea visiva legata al racconto che l'informazione. Il mio augurio è che i nostri film possano emozionare e colpire allo stomaco il pubblico. Mi piace pensare che la razionalità resti in secondo piano rispetto ad una risposta emotive da parte degli spettatori. Emozionare è per me la cosa più importante. (De Sanctis et al. 9)

> For us the visual idea connected to narration is more important than information. My hope is that our films will be able to move and provide gut-emotions to the public. I like to think that rationality remains secondary to an emotional response from our spectators. To make people feel [strong] emotions is the most important thing.

Perhaps the most important consequence of this stress on the visual rather than the textual component of the film can already be seen in Garrone's first film: a radical de-dramatization of the plot. In *Terra di mezzo*, narrative dissolves into atmosphere. The film is composed of three distinct episodes, although they are not hermeneutically separated. Indeed in a few instances, minor characters from one episode "slip" into another episode on different occasions. The three episodes are: *Silhouette*, which portrays a day in the life of three Nigerian prostitutes; *Euglen e Gertian*, which follows two Albanian youths in their quest for a day's worth of manual labor; and *Self Service*, which depicts the story of an Egyptian gas-attendant. All three episodes are characterized by an almost non-existence of a plot, and yet, through a certain visual realism, unique to Garrone, the viewer is left with a palpable sense of melancholy and ambivalence toward the migrants and Italians in the film. The seemingly un-scripted dialogue, the casual appearance of highly dramatic moments and their quick disappearance, the mixture of actors and of non-professional actors who masquerade as "actors" playing themselves, and most importantly, the peculiar rarified yet realistic visual style, all contribute to creating an affect of ambivalence in the viewers toward the characters. The viewer becomes one of the "ghosts" inhabiting the marvelous and ethereal "in-between" land within which the principal characters seem to be stuck in a *dormiveglia*—a permanent waking sleep. The de-dramatization of the plot, in which nothing really seems to happen, shifts the focus of the viewer from the content to the form, and radically dilates the temporal reality for the viewer, furthering this marvelous feeling of participating in the unending in-between economic, social, temporal, and spatial limbo in which the migrants and Italians in the film find themselves. Indeed, *Terra di mezzo* is, I believe, one of the best and most extreme contemporary cinematic examples of what Rossellini extols as the art of "waiting":

> In the narrative cinema, "waiting" is essential. Every solution is born from waiting. It is waiting which makes people live, which unchains reality; it is waiting which, after the preparation, gives liberation. (Rossellini, "A Few Words" 91)

Crucially, in deference to Rossellini's "waiting," as we "wait" along with the filmmakers and the characters, in *Terra di mezzo*, truly nothing dramatic happens. Even the extremely transgressive content of the audience being able to gaze at the forbidden bodies of the Nigerian prostitutes is made banal and awkward rather than desirable by the subtle visual irony of Garrone's compositions, script, and editing. This irony of radical de-dramatization causes the film to slip from the realistic to the humoristic mode. The "drama," or the emotional punch, that Garrone prizes happens

Ambivalent Geographies

precisely because we realize how difficult are the daily lives of the characters in the film, both Italian and migrant, because they are condemned to be restricted to social liminality. The seemingly unscripted violences, both great and small, that erupt into and upon the landscapes and bodies in the film are thus all the more painful to the viewer, because they seem regular, eternal, and cyclic rather than exceptional traumas.

Silhouette, the first episode (Figure 3), was made as a short film and won the top prize, the *Sacher d'Oro*, in Nanni Moretti's Sacher Film Festival in 1995. The prize money was then used to fund, in part, the other two episodes of the film. *Silhouette* is indeed a remarkable short. Filmed in the periphery of Rome, in that "in-between" area where urbanity melts onto the surround-

Figure 3: Title Credits, *Silhouette*, in *Terra di mezzo*

ing countryside, this episode gains much of its power through its manipulation of the camera's point of view to either align the audience with the gaze of the prostitutes or with that of its clients. There is a continuous spatial dialectic between the dark and claustrophobic *insides* of the various cars that pass by and stop by the Nigerian women, and the *hyper*-real wide-open *outside* landscapes that show a dystopic scenario where urbanity plunders and rapes nature. The viewers are implicated in this play of spaces. They are allowed to transgress by gazing upon the migrant woman's sexualized body, but are then deftly stripped of that power and made to become victims of that gaze themselves, as they are placed in the position of being leered at by the clients.

In most of the episode, the Nigerian women, played by real prostitutes, are placed upon a makeshift living space made up of

Chapter Three

pieces of lost-and-found furniture. This stylized mise-en-scène, with the couch and a few other pieces of furniture perched upon a jutting rock on the edge of the road, could be seemingly "real" in the documentary sense, but is also highly aestheticized because it works as an elevated "stage" from which the women can perform or can themselves view their surroundings. The central emotion of ambivalence toward these *sur*-real bodies on an elevated stage is generated by the consistent use of the low-angle shot when using the shot-reverse-shot method of filming the conversations between the prostitutes and their clients (Figures 4 and 5). As the clients themselves are gazed upon from above, they seem to lose their privileged point of view, as does the viewer who associates his gaze with that of the clients. Viewers also find themselves, in the instances of the scenes that are shot from within the confined space of the client's cars, in the uncomfortable position of being the objects of leering gazes by characters, such as cyclists in their space-age-looking suits, who pass the cars and look "inside" the camera from "outside" the cars.

Garrone's use of an aestheticized humoristic style rather than a didactic social realist style can be seen frequently in the disturbing juxtaposition of visual images: at one point, for example, a client asks one of the prostitutes to urinate in an open field while he

Figure 4: Clients viewed by the prostitutes. *Silhouette*

watches. The viewer is placed in the very uncomfortable position of gazing with the point of view of the client, but what makes the shot extremely striking is the remarkable framing of the prostitute, shown as she hunches down, by a medium shot with a large depth of field that juxtaposes her body with an eerie landscape of massive

Ambivalent Geographies

Figure 5: Clients (and us) viewing the prostitutes in the reverse-shot. *Silhouette*

new building constructions that loom menacingly in the distance behind her (Figure 6). The visual analogy is to great emotive effect: cement visually plundering the countryside while the viewer/client visually fetishizes the woman's productive and reproductive body. Garrone's dictum of "qualsiasi imagine, qualsiasi inquadratura deve essere rigorosa" ("every image, every frame must be rigorously

Figure 6: Uncomfortable juxtapositions. *Silhouette*

studied") is thus successful in creating a strong emotional discomfort in the viewer through the careful framing of bodies within a hyper-real mise-en-scène. The improbable location in which we see the prostitutes practice their trade is visually represented by a curious mix of reality and the subjective re-arrangement of the elements of this reality: thus the shepherds grazing their sheep are juxtaposed to the group of prostitutes as both human and animal bodies stumble in the muddy fields, the sheep searching for grass

95

and the prostitutes seeking some abandoned shack where they can host their clients. This visual re-arrangement is the motor of drama in *Terra di mezzo*; it gives the viewer a humoristic "feeling of the Other" through the visual contradictions that abound in the film, creating an "in-between" marvelous and oneiric landscape that defies rational descriptions of objective "truth" that can categorize and create meaning. The rarefaction of the living body is brought to its climax in the final scene of *Silhouette*. As African music plays on the soundtrack, the sun sets on the horizon, and the ladies are shot between the setting sun and the camera. Their cultural specificity as racialized, gendered subjects, which has already been suspended through stylization in earlier moments, is finally erased. Despite the soundtrack, which could be interpreted as a feature that grounds the bodies as African, visually, all that remain of these women are their contours, the two-dimensional outline of bodies, symbolizing radical liminality in an already in-between land.

The second episode, *Euglen e Gertian,* has an example of the "social realism" that seeks to make a much more direct social statement on the marginality of the immigrants, but again, Garrone keeps his distance from such commentary (and such cinematic treatment) by inserting it within the dialogue, which borrows heavily from the *commedia all'italiana* tradition that I have described in detail in Chapter 2. When Euglen is taken to the house of an upper-middle-class lady to fix some broken tiles, the conversation, led by the Signora, flows into the commonalities between Italy and Albania. The Signora identifies with Euglen's marginality rather than with her fellow-Italians through the common experience of poverty, which she says she suffered through during the war, while Mario, the man who has hired Euglen, becomes increasingly uncomfortable and slightly offended by the comparison:

> SIGNORA: (*A Euglen*) In Italia, cinquant'anni fa, era come l'Albania, distrutta, solo che tu, non te lo puoi ricordare.
> EUGLEN: No ...
> SIGNORA: Mario sì che lo ricorda ...
> (*Mario accenna con incertezza ...*)
> MARIO: Eh, mica tanto ...
> SIGNORA: Dai, come "mica tanto"? C'avevi dodici anni. E vabbe' che lei viveva in campagna ... mangiavate ... avevate del vino buono ... l'olio. Noi a Roma ci siamo mangiati tutti i topi e i gatti.

Ambivalent Geographies

> MARIO: (*Bisbigliando*) E … purtroppo …
> Tutti quelli del Colosseo abbiamo mangiati noi …
> […]
> SIGNORA: E addesso bevono solo l'acqua minerale, figurati!
> (Garrone)
>
> LADY: (*To Euglen*) In Italy, fifty years ago, it was like Albania, destroyed, only that you cannot remember any of it.
> EUGLEN: No …
> LADY: Mario surely remembers …
> (*Mario nods uncertainly* …)
> MARIO: Eh, not that much …
> LADY: Come on, what do you mean "not that much"? You were twelve. Oh well … you who lived in the countryside … you all ate … you drank good wine … *oil*. We in Rome, we had ourselves all the rats and cats …
> MARIO: (*Mumbling*) Eh … unfortunately …
> All those from the Colosseum … we ate them …
> […]
> LADY: And now we only drink bottled mineral water … imagine!

Mario, who would like to repress the memory of the abject, is forced to confront it by the old Signora, causing him discomfort and embarrassment. He does not like to place Italy and Albania on the same level as it affects the fragile power relationship he has created with his two Albanian workers.

Instances of even such indirect social commentary are rare in the film and are treated with extreme caution by Garrone. In a sequence that precedes the one mentioned above, the director inserts a meta-cinematic discourse about the futility of words that undermines even the sympathetic identification by the old lady with the plight of the Albanians, because for Garrone, it seems sentimental pity is in itself problematic. In a scene where Gertian is helping a plumber fix a sink at a woman's house, the woman, sporting a wild hair style and obviously a little socially awkward, gives an unexpected monologue:

> DONNA: (*All'idraulico*) Scusa …
> L'IDRAULICO: Dimmi …
> DONNA: Ti posso dare del tu, no?
> L'IDRAULICO: Certo.
> DONNA: Siccome … tu sei molto proiettato sulla realtà, mi sei molto utile. Perchè io … avrei sempre bisogno di diventare

> amica di queste persone che fanno questi lavori ... l'idraulico ... macchinista ... che ne so ... salumiere. Però non lo so ... se fossi amica di un salumiere ... perchè vedi ... la parola ... serve a comunicare. Cioè ... io mi sto sforzando a comunicare con te. Non è che ti voglio far perdere del tempo, però mi piacerebbe così ... svelarti.
> L'IDRAULICO: (*Guarda in silenzio, un po' imbarazzato.*)
> (Garrone)
>
> WOMAN: (*To the plumber*) Excuse me ...
> PLUMBER: Tell me ...
> WOMAN: I can address you informally?
> PLUMBER: Sure.
> WOMAN: Since ... you are oriented toward reality, you are quite useful to me. Because I ... would always need to become friends with those who do these kinds of jobs ... plumber ... machinery operator ... who knows ... a delicatessen owner. But I don't know ... if I was friends with a delicatessen owner ... because ... you see ... the word ... is used to communicate. That is ... I am trying very hard to communicate with you. It's not that I want you to waste your time, but I would like to in this way, reveal you.
> PLUMBER: (*Looks at the girl in silence, a little embarrassed.*)

This scene contains the most obvious meta-cinematic discourse on Garrone's position in understanding and communicating the reality of Italy's working class communities and migrants. Using tongue-in-cheek humor, Garrone distances his project from any claim of description/analysis of social malaise and fetishization of the "real people"/working class by making a deliberate comment on both his ethical and aesthetic statement of intent.

Indeed, instead of description and explanation of the "real," Garrone prefers ellipses and temporal dilation, which provide the viewer a very different, and more "direct" representation of the contradictions that result from the experience of liminality. Perhaps the most striking example of Garrone's use of these stylistic techniques of spatial and temporal disorientation is in the third and final episode of *Terra di mezzo*, entitled *Self Service*. This episode, in contrast to the other two, concentrates on one character, Ahmed Mahgoub, played by himself. The irony of the title is evident as it centers on Ahmed, who is a night-worker illegally manning a "self-service" gas station to provide a full service to customers. When asked what his name is, he replies with the Italianized "Amedeo" instead of Ahmed. The entire episode, which lasts approximately twenty-four minutes, consists of snippets of conversation between Ahmed/Amedeo and clients who stop to buy gas. In between clients, time seems to stand still, as does a sense of diurnal time, with the background being a gas station only illuminated by an electric blue from the in-scene lights (see Figure 1). The resulting images are cloaked in a bluish sheen that is echoed in the famous tanning salon establishing shot in *Gomorra*. The station itself seems to be shot as if it were an island, sealed from its contiguous urban landscape and thus made to resemble a stage rather than a real location in Rome, with Ahmed/Amedeo a contemporary Robinson Crusoe. The attendant seems to vanish in the many extreme close-up shots that characterize this episode, his very dark skin almost melting into the blue-black darkness of the night.

Any sense of time and space is further disoriented for the viewer by three ellipses, in which a black-and-white film appears on screen. The film presents an Egyptian man reminiscing about his successful life in Italy. He is surrounded by photos and mementos from Italy, and is clearly financially successful and happy. Importantly, we do not know if this person is Ahmed/Amedeo, or if these ellipses are indeed flashbacks, and although the man in the film is physically similar to Ahmed, Garrone leaves the question open. Another possibility suggested by the visual similarity-yet-dissimilarity between the two Ahmeds is that the one portrayed in the flashback sequences is the present Ahmed's father. Although the nature of the relationship between the two Ahmeds remains elusive, the emotional impact of the contrast between Ahmed's situation and the other Egyptian man's experience is undoubtedly definitive. It serves to make Ahmed's experience even more oneiric and un-grounded in reality, with his clients coming and going like phantoms in the night. The visual contradiction, where the film inside the film presents a completely different outcome to the protagonist's life represented in the broader film, is to a great humoristic effect. Two instances of extreme dramatic tension occur in this episode. The first one occurs in the beginning of the episode, when a man in his fifties stops to fill his tank and asks Ahmed about the whereabouts of the usual "women" that hang around in the area:

Chapter Three

UOMO: Senti ... ma conosci delle ... donne qui di questa zona?
AHMED: Sì, ma adesso vengono qui di sera ogni tanto ... non è come una volta.
UOMO: (*Indicando*) Si mettevano giù, lì in fondo ...
AHMED: Sì sì tanti anni venivano.
UOMO: E ... come mai stasera non ci sono?
AHMED: Boh ... perchè vengono tardi. Non è come prima. Ormai hanno fatto i soldi. All'inizio tutti vengono presto.
UOMO: E come sono, bianche, nere ...?
AHMED: Bianche, nere, tutto ... gialli, mulatto ...
UOMO: Io mi ricordo, ci sono stato con una nera. Ma non è che mi piacciono tanto. Oddio, non è niente di personale ...
AHMED: No no no, neanch'io manco io con le nere.
UOMO: Neanche a te piace? Ah, non si direbbe ...
AHMED: Io non vado bene con la donna nera, con la donna bianca subito ...
UOMO: Eh beh, io ogni tanto ... ci vado ... ma non come le bianche ...
AHMED: Sì ma io non vado per niente, capito, perchè non mi tira. Io con la donna bianco ci vado subito. E una bella soddisfazione. Con le donne nere no. Non sono mai riuscito a capire.
UOMO: Eh, strano, non mi sarei mai aspettato ...
AHMED: Eh, la gente pensa che sono scuro allora mi piace la scura ma no, è il contrario. (Garrone)

MAN: Listen ... do you know of any ... women in this area?
AHMED: Yes, but now they come here once in a while on evenings ... it's not like it was before.
MAN: (*Pointing*) They used to sit there ... down there ...
AHMED: Yes, yes, they came for many years.
MAN: And ... how come they are not here this evening?
AHMED: I don't know ... because they come late. It's not like before. Now they have made money. Initially everyone arrives early.
MAN: And how are they, white ... black ...?
AHMED: White, black, everything ... yellow, mulatto ...
MAN: I remember, I was with a black woman. But I don't like them too much. Well, I don't mean that personally ...
AHMED: No no no, I neither, me too, not with blacks.
MAN: You too don't like them? Ah, One wouldn't have guessed ...
AHMED: I don't go well with the black woman, with the white woman ... immediately ...

> MAN: Eh yes, I once in a while ... I go with them ... but not like with whites ...
> AHMED: Yes, but I don't go at all, you understand, because I can't get it up. I with white women go immediately. It is a very satisfying thing. With black women, no. I have never understood it.
> MAN: Eh, strange, I would never have expected that ...
> AHMED: Yea, people think that since I am dark, so I like a dark woman, but no, it's the opposite.

The man is obviously stupefied by the transgressive sexual choices of Ahmed, and he quickly finishes the conversation that seems to have gone awry. He has just been experiencing an extremely discrepant moment in his understanding of the Egyptian attendant, and must therefore quickly fetishize him in order to re-establish the stereotype. The man asks his name and Ahmed replies "Amedeo," thus presenting yet another element of menace to the fixed identities of Italian and non. When questioned pointedly by the man, Ahmed/Amedeo says that it is his Italianized name. Ahmed's declared object of desire threatens the Italian man's position, and he therefore picks a fight with Ahmed on the ruse (real or false) that he did not fill the tank with the right amount of gas and pocketed the money. He constantly calls the gas attendant by his Egyptian name, avoiding the Italianized "Amedeo" that Ahmed prefers, as if to further repress any possibility of marvelousness. This altercation ends up with the man racially fetishizing and verbally abusing Ahmed as a migrant criminal, and threatens to call the police so that he is expelled from Italy.

The only other situation that causes a disruption in Ahmed's oneiric and timeless suspension in space and time is another altercation between Ahmed and a few teenage Romans. Even here, the conversation seems to proceed in the usual repetitive and contractual way between customer and worker, and the dramatic high-point, where one of the young men calls Ahmed a "*tartufon*," occurs unexpectedly and passes without pause or elaboration. This scene is perhaps one of the most powerful examples of the denunciation of racism in Italian film, because of its unexpected and casual viciousness and its occurrence within a unique visual and narrative context that studiously avoids direct social commentary.

Chapter Three

Self Service ends with a lyrical and oneiric sequence that ties it to the ending of *Silhouette*. In the final sequence, Ahmed/Amedeo returns to his apartment and falls asleep. We do not get any glimpses of the urban scenery outside the specific location of Ahmed's claustrophobic apartment. There are no long or medium shots, only tracking shots that keep close to Ahmed/Amedeo. This further suspends this body from the landscape-images that would allow the audience to establish location and time. The scenes of his return are juxtaposed via jump cuts to show other barely unidentifiable bodies who are also asleep in the emerging dawn. The viewer can see that they are (probably) the prostitutes from the first episode. All the bodies are dark and seem to blend into the surrounding emerging light. In an in-between time between night and day, the oneiric phantom-bodies seem to fade away on screen and fall asleep, while the rest of the world awakes.

In *Terra di mezzo*, Matteo Garrone has masterfully invented a new language that swerves away from a strong realist premise into the humoristic mode, just as plot concerns dissolve into reflective mood and atmosphere. Rather than create a film that would understand "them" and "their life," Garrone problematizes the question of what it means to be Italian or not through his unusual visual treatment of landscapes and bodies. With this highly original treatment of internal/private and external/public spaces and landscapes, Garrone approaches the question of the nation's external others in a sophisticated way. By manipulating the Italian audience's expectations and desire of seeing, and thus gaining access to prohibited spaces reserved for the exotic immigrant Other, he inserts the migrant-subject's body right within the heart of the national cinematic discourse. The oneiric landscape and body-images in *Terra di mezzo* successfully represent the disavowed marvelous "in-between" that pervades the heart of Italy's social spaces. Garrone's humoristic aesthetic style and narrative structure, honed in his first feature films and matured in films such as *Gomorra* and *Reality*, brilliantly slide into the in-between realities of inside/outside, city/country, day/night, real/artifice, migrant/Italian, thus making several highly original contributions to Italy's historic discourse of chronic ambivalence.

Meditalamerica: *Lamerica* and the Recuperation of Embodied History

I began my analysis of Italy's equivocal cultural situation in my Introduction to the book with an example from the film *Lamerica*. I would now like to analyze this rich film in more detail, particularly its depiction of embodied landscapes. The director, Gianni Amelio, is undoubtedly one of the innovators in the newer generation of Italian filmmakers. He has been consistently concerned with countering his nation's tendency to allow itself a collective, yet selective, historical amnesia. It can be said that all of his films, from *Colpire al cuore* (1982), right up to *La stella che non c'è* (2006), explore Italy's multiple and contradictory roles in history, and the ramifications of these roles upon the films' characters. All his films, in some way, are journeys of temporal "psychosis" that recuperate forgotten or repressed national histories. In *Colpire al cuore*, Amelio examines the ambiguous positions of characters vis-à-vis the political polarization of the 1970s; *Porte aperte* (1990), an adaptation of Leonardo Sciascia's famous novella, juxtaposes repressive practices of the Fascist era with contemporary political repression; *Il ladro di bambini* (1992) is a story of Italy's continued social problems as they affect its children; *Così ridevano* (1996), which won the *Leone d'oro* at the Venice Film Festival, narrates the story of two Sicilian brothers who emigrate to Turin in the late Fifties. In an interview about the latter film, the interviewer reminds Amelio that the brothers' last name is *Scordia*, similar to *scordare*, "to forget." He replies:

> I'm very happy to be reminded that Scordia has its roots in the word *scordare*, because the ultimate meaning of the film is really the lack of historical memory. That is also the meaning of *Lamerica*, *Open Doors* and *Stolen Children*. In other contexts, the theme is very similar to losing your memory. (Crowdus, Young, and Brey 15)

No other film better encapsulates Amelio's obsession of re-presenting Italy's repressed identities than *Lamerica* (1994). He does this visually by defamiliarizing the bodies and the specific cultural landscapes of Albania and Italy. Indeed, while set in the post-communist chaos of Albania, the film is very much a detour into an exhumation of Italy's own history of colonization and emigration to the New World. The film's first images are archival footage of Mussolini's conquest of Albania. As the titles end, the black-and-white images cut jarringly to color, and for a brief moment the viewer is suspended between the color images that suggest contemporary times, and the historical images that continue to linger in the mind.

The title of the film already points to a post-neorealistic film that goes beyond a purely realist representation of Albania's chaotic reality. It is a misspelling of "l'America," the destination of the millions of Italian emigrants who set sail for the New World throughout the twentieth century. The title, on one hand connects the historical migrations of the Italians to the contemporary Albanian exodus, creating a transnational and transhistorical equivalence between them. But "Lamerica" is distinct from "l'America" both in the way it is written, but more importantly as it is conceived. The former is a metaphorical land, where the personal economies of desire can fantasize about a new *oikos* of unlimited surplus and success. Indeed, the phrase "hai trovato l'America" ("you have found America") is idiomatic, meaning that a person has found success, whether it is personal or material or both. The phonetic usage of the word as the title of the film with the exclusion of the important apostrophe marks the division between the metaphorical landscape of a magical personal topography of desire and the actual territory of the New World, the continents of North and South America. Visually and thematically, Amelio is concerned with this metaphorical land, as he strives to reconcile the historical destination of Italians with the contemporary *lamerica* for Albanians, Italy itself. The focus of action is nevertheless set in present-day Albania. It can be therefore pardoned that the film has been often reviewed as a neo-neorealistic drama about the state of the Balkan nation:

> Its powerful interweaving of fictional narrative and recent historical events, and its use of authentic locations and a supporting cast of non-professional actors prompted several reviewers to invoke the masters of neorealism. (O'Healy 246)

I, however, agree with O'Healy's assessment that the film, while having some superficial neorealistic elements, departs fundamentally from the genre in many of the most important aesthetic and thematic elements:

> Though *Lamerica* is generally discussed in terms of its realism, which demands the successful masking of the techniques of illusion, it should be noted that the film frequently draws attention to the constructedness of its own realistic effects through citation and other self-reflexive strategies, thus distancing itself from any claim of representing an unmediated reality. (O'Healy 247)

The film is actually both *epic* and *humoristic* rather than realistic—deliberately epic in order to first to trans-historicize and trans-nationalize the specific social situation in Albania in the early Nineties, and second to bring in the main meta-cinematic discourse of the mythical image of television in the creation of the migrant-subject's desire for Italy. It is a humoristic film due to its central plot of mistaken identities rather than stabilized ones. This *equivoco* (misunderstanding) of national bodies and landscapes is the key to the film, just as the misspelling of America is central to the peculiarity of the film's title.

The film recounts the story of Gino Cutrari (Enrico Lo Verso), a young Sicilian entrepreneur, and Fiore (Michele Placido), his older boss, who travel to Albania, which is in the throes of complete social and political turmoil, to set up a shoe factory "Alba Calzature." The name of the factory "Alba" or "Dawn" is satirical because the two Italians do not actually intend to help Albania enter a "new era" in an industrialized and globalized economy as they seem to paternalistically remind everyone, but only use the fake establishment as a façade in order to swindle grant money from the European Economic Council, which was to formally become the European Union with the signing of the Maastricht Treaty in 1993, a year before the film was shot. In order to make use of the grant, Fiore must have an Albanian "president" for their company. They finally find their puppet-president in the form of a senile and wizened old man who is called Spiro Tozaj (played skillfully by the non-professional actor Carmelo Di Mazarelli). Calling Spiro the "face of a New Albania" (Fiore promises the director of the horrific labor camp where Spiro is found that he will be interviewed on Italian television) adds further irony to the situation—for all appearances, Spiro is so debilitated mentally and physically, both with age and hardship, that he seems to be almost on the verge of death. Spiro, as if to mirror this age-confusion, seems to be unable to speak, his senility bordering on a return to the infantile (he wets himself in Gino's jeep a little later, much to Gino's rage). When asked what his age is, Spiro gesticulates that he is twenty years old. When Fiore decides that Spiro is the perfect stand-in, because "Non potevamo trovare un uomo più rincoglionito di questo!" ("We couldn't have found someone more idiotic!"), he assigns Gino to the task of finishing up the bureaucratic details and leaves Albania. Gino, again reflecting Amelio's deliberate confusion of Spiro's age, takes him to a local orphanage and pays the nuns in return for lodgings. The silent Spiro is seen wandering, as if in a daze, among the children of the orphanage, further heightening the audience's wonderment at this mentally and physically destabilized and *dis*-placed character. The displacement of Spiro is mirrored in the ruinous landscape that we witness in the early part of the film. Everything is in flux. The first sequence, filmed from the point of view of the passengers in a car, avoids any direct reference to geography, instead disorienting the viewers with masses of bodies that throw themselves in front of us (the passengers traveling in the car) and the chants we hear in unaccented Italian "Italia, Italia, tu sei il mondo!" ("Italy, Italy, you are the world!"). The contradiction between the linguistic specificity and geographical uncertainty of this scene will be amplified throughout the film, reaching its climax in the final scene of the film, which seems completely suspended from any geographical or temporal signs.

Amelio deliberately chose a non-professional unknown actor to play Spiro, because he wanted to keep the audiences unaware of his identity:

> I wanted to specifically work with a nonprofessional actor because he's a character who changes his identity during the course of the movie and I didn't want him to be portrayed by someone the audience could identify [...] Besides, in the beginning he doesn't speak. Other people talk to him in Albanian and he understands and responds in Albanian. For an Italian audience, it is a surprise the first time he speaks Italian, which isn't until about forty minutes into the film. (Crowdus, Young, and Brey 14–18)

Spiro is a marvelous body, suspending actual identity—in terms of not only his national identity but also in his apparent senility that causes him to be stuck in time. What follows the prologue, where Spiro is introduced into the film, is Gino and Spiro's epic journey through a sun-scoured, elemental countryside crisscrossed by large and chaotic masses of people wandering, stumbling, running aimlessly. One of the most non-realistic or non-documentary aspects of the visual quality of the film comes from Amelio's choice of filming in Panavision. This anamorphic format gives the scenes a spectacular quality that is unparalleled in any previous Amelio film, and is a deliberate choice by Amelio, who did not want to be accused of creating a spectacle while Albania reeled in utter chaos:

> Il Cinemascope che disegna interni e paesaggi mai a misura umana [...], il teleobiettivo che schiaccia gli emigranti sui mezzi di trasporto precari e sovraffollati, la musica, i toni lividi della luce, non spettacolarizzano una narrazione epica, ma riflettono lo sguardo spaventato di quell'uomo che scopre, là dove gli avevano promesso la cuccagna, un girone dantesco. (Preziosi and Bernardis 49)

> Cinemascope, that never portrays internal scenes or landscapes on a human scale [...], the wide-angle lens that squashes the emigrants on precarious and overcrowded means of transport, the music, the livid tones of the light, do not create a spectacular narrative epic, but reflect the frightened gaze of a man that has been promised a land of abundance but has only found himself in one of Dante's circles of Hell.

This elemental visual quality of Albania's chaotic landscape serves to further highlight Spiro's marvelousness. He escapes the orphanage because, as a furious Gino hears from an unconcerned nun, "Voleva andare a casa" ("He wanted to go home"). Spiro's escape to find his *oikos* will launch a journey for both characters that mimics the Albanians mass-migration across the countryside to the "escape point" of the port of Tirana—the synapse that leads to the mythical *Med-Ital-America*.

Spiro and Gino's journey mirrors the journey of the masses of Albanian migrants to Italy, but it mimics theirs, it is "almost but not quite" that journey, first because Gino himself is, technically, "Italian," and second because, as we find out, Spiro, too, is not the Albanian Other but an Italian citizen. His real name is Michele

Chapter Three

Talarico and he deserted the army during Italy's Fascist occupation of Albania and subsequently "performed" Albanian-ness for decades in order to escape prosecution. His performance, however, has destabilized his sense of time, and he is "stuck" in the time of Mussolini's war, not understanding that the chaos that surrounds him is a very different situation. The humor that characterizes most of the film comes from the fact that Spiro's historical mis-recognition is actually the only wise perspective, while Gino, with his callous behavior toward the Albanians, stemming from his complete lack of historical education, ends up being the one lacking a basic understanding of history. The representation of geography, in most instances, mirrors Spiro/Michele's viewpoint that he is indeed in Italy rather than Albania. We see images of bleached and parched land and mountains, unrelenting in their simultaneous anonymity yet recognizably Mediterranean specificity.

Spiro/Michele's marvelousness consists in both a spatial and temporal destabilization, remarkably akin to the "legendary psychasthenia." As Elizabeth Grosz explains, identification of the ego is acquired along with a simultaneous acquisition of spatiality and temporality. A marvelous body creates a temporary destablization of the self, so much so that it momentarily loses its imagined form, and also momentarily loses its capability to negotiate its own boundaries with the surrounding space. Grosz mentions a paper by Caillois that had a great impact on Lacan's thinking, "Mimicry and Legendary Psychasthenia." Caillois argues that mimesis in nature (such as when an insect mimes a leaf, or another species of insect) is not a consequence of adaptive evolutionary function, but rather "has to do with distinctions [the insect] establishes between itself and the environment, including other species" (Grosz 46). Caillois likens this mimicry to a kind of psychosis called "legendary psychasthenia," a state in which the patient cannot locate himself or herself in space: "It is with represented space that the drama becomes specific, since the living creature, the organism, is no longer the origin of the coordinates, but one point among others; it is dispossessed of its privilege and literally *no longer knows where to place itself*" (46). In other words, this kind of psychosis takes away a primary anchor that is a condition for a coherent sense of identity. The "coordinates" with which the individual "maps" himself or herself as well the world around him or her cannot be calculated because the point of reference is lost. Psychosis is thus, for Caillois, "the human analogue of mimicry in the insect world" (47). Migrancy, a state of being fraught with actual displacement of the self, as I believe, can therefore be represented as a kind of induced psychosis, which is exactly what Amelio does. It is no wonder that when the spectator comprehends, forty minutes into the film, that Spiro might actually be Michele, an Italian, they are stupefied. This *stupore* is that moment where two signs strongly contradict each other so much so that there is only a sense of marvel and suspension. This feeling of momentary confusion, akin to a deer being caught in the headlights, is key to the dramatic force of the film.

Spiro/Michele's destabilization in *Lamerica* is so great that, at one point in the epic journey, Spiro/Michele and Gino pass by a gigantic sign written along an entire mountainside that says "Enver Hoxha." There could not be a clearer cultural marker to finally ground the ambivalent geography of the film to not only a nation but also its recent history. Yet Spiro/Michele says, "Sò quello che c'è scritto lì—Mussolini" ("I know what is written there—Mussolini"). The reading of the sign by a marvelous body—that indeed suspends even the supposedly objective and agreed-upon meaning of language and political history—further removes any potential stereotyping of the Albanian situation and consolidates the position of the contemporary Albanian-abject within the core of Italian-ness. As Spiro/Michele's spatially and temporally destabilized journey makes him believe they are actually traveling down Italy's "boot" in order to arrive to his hometown in Sicily, Gino's journey occurs as a counterpoint to Spiro/Michele's journey, as a slow sliding from the Italian "Self" into the Albanian "Other." He is stripped of all the "things" that make him Italian—firstly his jeep, then his clothes, his sunglasses, his passport, his money, and then, finally, he also loses his capacity to speak—the ultimate journey out of identity and into suspension and marvelousness (Figure 7). The slide into suspension occurs through the realization of the historical links between Albania's present and Italy's abject histories of Fascism, colonization, emigration, and perhaps, most importantly, utter poverty of the masses. Indeed, for Amelio, *Lamerica* is a film that highlights repressed commonalities between Italy's history of economic deprivation and Albania's contemporary desperation:

Chapter Three

Figure 7: Gino's final transformation into a marvelous body. *Lamerica*

> Actually, I want Italians and everyone else who sees this film to remember something simpler but deeper and more important [than common political and historical links between Italy and Albania]. In fact, if I were to explain the meaning of the film, I would say it is the ability to understand the importance of a piece of bread, which is a theme repeated throughout the film. I think that the memory of history is important to all of us—not to remember the date of a battle, let's say, but to remember who we were, to understand who we are today and where we are going. A person who was hungry once will always be able to understand the feelings of someone who's hungry today. (Crowdus, Young, and Brey 17)

Gino's descent into understanding, then, occurs with the historical knowledge of a common *embodied* experience of suffering, something that is *beyond* the specificities of national and linguistic identities. Gino's journey is from that of stereotypical Italian exclusivity with respect to the Albanian-abject, into a marvelousness of embodied historicity. He finally "enters" the magmatic and pulsating masses that crowd the stark outdoor locations in *Lamerica*, not fighting them anymore but merging into them as one. Spiro/Michele's temporal psychosis makes him psychologically better suited to endure the bodily suffering of migration, unlike Gino, whose body has never felt this level of trauma and deprivation.

This embodied marvelousness finally occurs definitively in the elegiac yet awe-inspiring final sequence, which slowly fades-in to show a crane-shot of a monstrous and aging ship bursting at its seams with thousands of marvelous bodies, all suspended in a deep blue sea that seems to have no end. The Mediterranean in this way becomes a final "third space," that of complete suspension. Spiro/Michele believes he is aboard a ship going to New York, while Gino is completely speechless, as if he had reverted into the child-like state in which he found Spiro/Michele at the beginning of the film. Language, a stabilizer/fixer of national identity, is once again irrelevant in this metaphorical Mediterranean, and the film aptly closes with close-up shots of the migrant-subjects, repeated for minutes on screen. As the audience gazes and seeks specificity by asserting the gaze, they only beget a multiplicity of gazes from silent faces deflected back at them.

The Politics of Sentimentality:
Quando sei nato non puoi più nasconderti

I have demonstrated examples of two successful films, through which the directors allow the audience to explore various dimensions of embodied landscapes in the humoristic mode, thus disrupting a stable Italian identity. In the final sequence of *Lamerica*, the Mediterranean becomes a *locus amoenus* of suspension. These final images of suspension are deliberately radically different from the televised images of Albanians arriving at the coast of Puglia that entered every Italian living room during the Albanian exodus, fanning hysteria of a potential invasion. Amelio's visual treatment of a very dramatic contemporary event is a form of resistance to the televised message, and therefore, fundamentally self-conscious of the limits of journalistic and cinematic realism.

The Mediterranean has often been used as a trope in Italian cinema for the renegotiation, or rather, the temporary suspension of identities; Wertmüller allows a deserted, uncharted island in the Mediterranean to become a clean space for the renegotiation of gender roles and political/ideological affiliations in *Travolti da un insolito destino nell'azzurro mare d'agosto* (*Swept Away*, 1974). Gabriele Salvatore's *Mediterraneo* (1991) and Nanni Moretti's *Isole* episode of *Caro Diario* (*Dear Diary*, 1993) also come to mind. I will now turn my attention to one of the major Italian productions in recent years that deals with the subject of immigration in the Mediterranean, albeit in ways that contrast it to the previous film I have discussed: Marco Tullio Giordana's *Quando sei nato non puoi più nasconderti* (*Once You Are Born You Can No Longer Hide*, 2004) simplified to *Quando sei nato* in the rest of the book. The title of Giordana's film explicitly points toward three of the key concerns of this book: first, the importance of embodiment to the constitution of identity (you cannot hide once you are born because you possess a body), second, the cinematic representation of the body as a constitution of the nation, and finally, the centrality of the body to a politics of inclusion or exclusion in social-spatial-paradigms (you need to hide only if you are where you are not supposed to be).

Quando sei nato narrates the story of Sandro, an upper-middle-class adolescent from Northern Italy (specifically, Brescia). To further stress this cultural specificity, the characters speak with a strong accent, and Sandro's family name is "Lombardi." Sandro's father, Bruno, is a small-business owner. Sandro thus has superficial access to the migrant Other through Bruno's employees, who are mostly immigrants. Bruno treats his employees well, and is open, albeit paternalistic, in his relationship with them. Sandro and Bruno depart for Greece to undertake a yacht trip in the Mediterranean along with Bruno's friend Popi, while his mother, Lucia, stays at home. One night, as Bruno and Popi are asleep, Sandro leaves the yacht's living quarters and goes up to the deck, and leaning out into the sea, slips and falls. Bruno and Popi are unaware of Sandro's absence for a long time, and are therefore unable to locate him when they do find him missing. Sandro's fall into the sea radically changes the tone and rhythm of the film. He is miraculously rescued by a passing boat, filled with illegal migrants who are heading to Italy. Sandro meets and bonds with the boy who saved his life, a young Romanian called Radu, and his sister, Alina. The three children experience the horror and suffering of a long sea voyage in economic and hygienic circumstances that are a stark contrast compared to the conditions in Sandro's sleek yacht. Soon, all the migrants, including Sandro, are brought into a CPT. The CPT is a Centro di permanenza temporanea (literally translated as Center for Temporary Inhabitation), a euphemistic, oxymoronic, and awkward name for a space of detention of illegal immigrants, renamed by the media-savvy Berlusconi administration as CIE or the Centri di identificazione ed espulsione (Identification and Expulsion Centers). The CPT the migrants are brought to is managed by Padre Celso. After a few days, Sandro is united with his overjoyed parents, who ask Padre Celso if they can be of any help to Radu and Alina. Sandro begs his parents to adopt them. Lucia agrees immediately, and after initial hesitation, Bruno too, agrees to discuss the matter further. The *giudice di pace* explains that they must first establish if Radu is indeed a minor (they suspect that he might be lying that he is seventeen in order to not be expelled from Italy) before any adoption proceedings can begin. Sandro and his parents return to Brescia. Meanwhile, Radu's x-ray tests demonstrate that he has indeed lied about his age and is an adult. He escapes from the CPT, taking Alina with her, and they reach the Lombardi's house. Radu explains to Bruno that he could not wait for the adoption procedures because corrupt Romanian officials would most certainly foil them. In the middle of the night, Radu forces Alina to wake up, and they escape from the house while the Lombardis sleep, after stealing a few valuables. Sandro is dismayed by the betrayal, but he does not allow himself to judge Radu and Alina as quickly as his father does. After a few days, Sandro receives a call from Alina, who whispers that she is in Milan, in a place called "Corea." Sandro takes the train to Milan and finds that "Corea" (Korea) is an abandoned industrial complex in the outskirts of the city, completely overtaken by immigrants. After wandering in this surreal nether-world, a cityscape within the city of Milan, he finally locates Alina's room due to the Eros Ramazotti song he associates with Alina. He discovers that Alina is now a prostitute, forced into the trade by Radu. The final scene shows Sandro and Alina in an open piazza sitting by the road. Sandro offers Alina a sandwich and Alina accepts, while the camera goes out of focus to show the end titles.

The film's title comes from Maria Pace Ottieri's eponymous book, which is a journalistic account of marginalized immigrant communities in Italy. Indeed, her book is all about the lives of spatially marginalized individuals, as is obvious from the subtitle to her book: *Viaggio nel popolo sommerso* (*Journey to a Hidden People*). While the film titles mention that it is loosely inspired by the book, in actuality, only a few scenes shot in the CPT are directly derived from Ottieri's descriptions from chapter 3 (also entitled *Quando sei nato*). Ottieri's book is therefore not useful

Chapter Three

to us in order to make a direct comparison between a text and its cinematic adaptation, but it does, however, give us clues about Giordana's basic premises. *Quando sei nato*, indeed, is very much a film in the realistic mode rather than humoristic, and the close connection of the mise-en-scène to Ottieri's journalistic descriptions of immigrant "spaces" indicate a neorealistic sensibility of shooting "on location" in order to provide a certain integrity to the pro-filmic world. This aesthetic can be seen most clearly in the scene where the migrants are brought into the CPT, which, as the Director of Photography, Roberto Forza, explains, used a different style from the previous sections of the film:

> Abbiamo usato una tecnica quasi documentaria. C'erano queste luci naturali del porto—le ho solo rinforzate—e le fotoelettriche della polizia. Tutto il resto erano illuminazioni interne alla scena: i fari delle auto, i lampeggianti delle ambulanze e dei cellulari dei Carabinieri. [...] C'erano centinaia di comparse, veri poliziotti, veri carabinieri, veri finanzieri, veri addetti alla Capitaneria, della Croce Rossa, della Misericordia. Erano veri anche gli immigrati, tutti reclutati in zona. (Giordana et al. 57)

> We used a quasi-documentary technique. There were these natural lights of the port—I only reinforced them—and the police lights. All the rest were lights internal to the scene: car headlights, ambulance lights, the Carabinieris' cell phones. [...] There were hundreds of extras, true policemen, true Carabinieri, true finance police, true employees of the harbormaster, of the Red Cross, of the Catholic charities. Even the immigrants were real, recruited from the area.

This insistence on the "real" is akin to the neorealist zeal to "mummify" through the indexicality of the photographic image. While this particular section of the film exemplifies neorealism, and is indicative of Giordana's desire, a slightly expressionistic style does emerge in the other sections, lending the film a minimal hybrid quality, an "expressionistic realism," if one may call it thus. The film, like *Lamerica*, is shot in anamorphic format, which for Giordana, was the best format to shoot the central scenes in the open sea, and also radically "anti-televisive" (15), once again unveiling a central concern of many directors who have been trying to represent the immigration crisis in film. The scenes shot in the Mediterranean in anamorphic are thus more "real" than television formats, because the framing brings out the vastness of the horizontal spaces. The final sequence in the "Corea" immigrant complex, likewise, was a real, abandoned industrial location, meticulously, almost fetishistically recreated into the immigrant's "*un*-city" through the use of only materials found in the trash: "Abbiamo utilizzato solo la roba raccolta nelle discariche, la stessa che gli extracomunitari vanno a raccogliere per i loro alloggi. Alessandra Mura, la mia arredatrice, non ha noleggiato niente. Ha utilizzato i rifiuti presi da cassonetti. Un lavoro enorme" ("We only used things collected from the trash, the same that immigrants use to collect things for their lodgings. Alessandra Mura, my set designer, did not rent anything. She only used trash from the dumpsters. An enormous task)(48).[3]

The stylistic elements described above link Giordana to the realistic mode. It is especially in the director's explicit ethical alignment to the subject matter that we can spot his alignment with the ethos of neorealism. Giordana's style, which gained maturity especially in his previous film *La meglio gioventù* (*The Best of Youth*), is expressionistic, but his ethics ground him more securely within the tradition of the neorealism. Indeed, Giordana embraces but partly revisits and modifies the neorealistic humanism due to his awareness of the cultural turbulence of the intervening decades. This certain neorealism, as I have described it in my earlier chapter, concerns the possibility of rejuvenation through cinematically providing an "objective truth"; Giordana's use of the realistic mode being only slightly different in that the possibilities of approaching that truth are now more restricted. One of the key indicators of the persistence of such an idealistic and optimistic outlook is in Giordana's stated belief that it is still possible to procure an "innocent" gaze, possible through certain points of view, such as that of a child. Sandro Petraglia and Stefano Rulli, screenplay co-writers along with Giordana say:

> Con Marco Tullio Giordana non volevamo fare un film sul "problema dell'immigrazione" ma raccontare un incontro tra culture di adolescenti innocenti. L'innocenza permette ai personaggi di incontrarsi, mentre più in là con l'età diventrebbe tutto più complicato. (Giordana et al. 16)
>
> With Marco Tullio Giordana we did not want to make a film on the "immigration problem" but narrate a meeting of

> cultures through innocent adolescents. Innocence allows the characters to meet each other, while, once they grow older, everything would become more complicated.

Indeed, Giordana insists that it would be impossible for him, an Italian, to make a film about immigrants, because he does not have their experiences. He therefore decided to make a film through the point of view of an "innocent," i.e., an ideologically uncorrupted Italian, who experiences the embodiment of migration. Giordana insists the film is about Italians, "di noi non di loro"—in other words, a detourist film:

> I miei ultimi film erano tutti ambientati negli anni '70, Pasolini, I cento passi, anche gran parte de La meglio gioventù era ambientata in quegli anni che considero la preparazione, il "laboratorio" dell'Italia che ci ritroviamo oggi. Da un po' di tempo mi pongo altre domande. Cosa siamo diventati esattamente, in cosa ci rispecchiamo? Cosi di entusiasma e cosa ci fa paura? [...] [Con Petraglia e Rulli] abbiamo pensato che servisse un punto di vista per così dire "innocente," come di qualcuno che guadasse ai migranti fuori dagli schemi di razzismo puro o della solidarietà di maniera. Per questo il protagonista è un adolescente, anzi un bambino, un personaggio che non ha ancora consolidato i pregiudizi e che si ritrova esposto a qualsiasi suggestione. (Giordana et al. 6)

> My most recent films are all set in the seventies, Pasolini, *I cento passi*, also a major portion of *La meglio gioventù* was set in those years that I consider the preparation, the "laboratory" of the Italy that we have today. I have been asking other questions for a long time. What have we become exactly, what do we reflect ourselves in? What enthuses us and what makes us scared? [...] [With Petraglia and Rulli] we thought that we needed, so to say, an "innocent" point of view, as someone looking at the immigrants from outside the schemes of pure racism or forced solidarity. This is why the protagonist is an adolescent, or actually a child, a character who has not yet consolidated prejudices and is open to any suggestion.

Giordana's career, which has keenly explored the radical divisions of Italian society in the Seventies, cannot conceive a ready possibility of a "pure" gaze, in the sense of Bazin's "objective" gaze, but his neorealistic sensibilities push him to access that ideal gaze through the point of view of the child protagonist, Sandro. Indeed, *Quando sei nato* is fundamentally a morality story about Sandro's education and entry into a "corrupt" and ideologically divided adulthood through an accidental adventure that gives him a mistaken identity of migrant.

Giordana's viewpoint provides an interesting example of a different strategy of representing the marvelous with respect to some of the other examples of radical marvelousness we have seen in this chapter. This strategy of accessing the marvelous—through the child—is problematic, as the director must repress any wider possibility of ambivalence and hybridity by confining it to the privileged space of childhood. Understood in this way, therefore, this strategy can be seen as more cynical about access to the marvelous than that used in *Lamerica*, because it presupposes and accepts the universal existence of "fixed" political and racial ideologies in adult Italians. This conception, while sincere, risks imagining cultures as essential and separate blocs, "noi" and "loro," which are only now encountering each other in Italy. The sentimental use of pity in this film, used in relation to the use of a child, is also problematic for similar reasons. I believe that this attention to realism, while praiseworthy in its social commitment that is similar to the neorealism that I described in the previous chapter, has the unintended effect of creating sentimentality and therefore distancing rather than real compassion for the immigrant condition. The extreme attention to detail while showing the material degradation of the immigrants in the extended sea-voyage sections, the cityscape of Corea and the CPT creates a certain politics of sentimentality that simultaneously provokes a compassion that is slightly patronizing, and also creates safe voyeuristic distance between the Italian viewer and the immigrant bodies and landscapes. The *oikos* of the viewer, through his identification with the child-protagonist Sandro, remains firmly Italian, unlike in the films by Garrone and Amelio we have explored in this chapter. The temporary destabilization, or suspension of Sandro's body in the Mediterranean remains a *partial* suspension, as the viewer is always well aware that he has only been mis-identified as an immigrant. This "viaggio in un popolo sommerso" is in these ways structurally similar to Spackman's description of the representations of the harem I described in my Introduction—they serve, unintentionally, to consolidate Italian-ness rather than go beyond these conceptual categories. This risk of falling into stereotypical

Chapter Three

portrayals is slightly mitigated by the increasing subjectivity in the film, especially in the second half, to coincide with Sandro's point of view, thus giving the viewer access to an "innocent" gaze that goes beyond fixed identities. But this marvelousness is temporary, because Giordana's ethical and social framework also stresses that perhaps only children are beyond these identities, and can thus live within the zone of the marvelous. The best the director can do is briefly point to that marvelous by aligning his camera's gaze with that of the child.

Quando sei nato was a partial critical success and a commercial failure, partly due to its ambivalent and open-ended conclusion. The original script called for a confrontation between Radu and Sandro/Alina, ending in Alina's shooting of Radu, who had forced her into slavery and prostitution. Instead, the ending is left open, like the piazza in which the final shot is framed, with Sandro and Alina either entering the adulthood forced upon them through violence upon the body, or possibly maintaining freedom from such corruption, and a continued existence within the Marvelous. There is a hint of possibility in the final scene because both Sandro and Alina are silent. This indicates a central truth of the marvelous in the film: words are useless, the only "truth" being that of the body. Indeed, the futility of words and the centrality of embodied experience and gestures is a central theme, established right from the film's first scene. "Quando sei nato, non puoi più nasconderti" is, other than being the title of the film, also the name of a minor character who Sandro encounters in the establishing sequence (Figure 8):

Figure 8: Sandro's encounter with the Other. *Quando sei nato*

> ... there is a phone cabin. Inside, a colored man, in shabby shape and dressed badly tries in vain to place a call. He is confused, swears at the phone instrument in an incomprehensible language, hits the phone earpiece against the glass, speaks—it's not clear with whom in particular—with a tone of voice that increases in intensity until it becomes a scream.
> Sandro watches him hypnotized.
> The Man is coming out of the cabin, angry, restless ...
> SANDRO: (kindly) The phone does not work ... it says so right there ...
> The big black man does not listen. Slowly he takes off his jacket and lets it fall on the ground. He takes off his shirt, begins to unbutton his pants. Meanwhile, he murmurs ...
> BLACK MAN: *Soki obotami okoki komibomba lisusu te* ...
> He throws away his shoes, his pants, the rags of his underwear. He remains naked. He spreads his arms like a Christ on the cross, fixing little Sandro with desperate eyes ...
> BLACK MAN: ... *soki obotami okoki* ...
> [...]
> Sandro raises his arms as if to defend himself. But that man, who is not very close to him, places his head on the shop window and starts to cry. He cries and caresses his chest, points at himself with a moving sadness.
> BLACK MAN: (*shouting*) ... *soki obotami okoki* ...
> One hears, in the distance, the police siren. Sandro is alone and impotent in front of that desperation. But he does not run. He gazes fixedly at the black man as if he might be able to decifer the sense of his words in his eyes. Then ...
> ... a pair of policemen arrive [...] They take him away. (my transcription)

Sandro is greatly moved by this event, as is the viewer, whose gaze is aligned deliberately with the child's. Sandro will continuously try to find the meaning to the man's desperate chant. It is only in the CPT that he will understand the meaning—they mean the title of the film, but his own age and "innocent" gaze do not need the translation, while the viewer does. The man's undressing and Christ-like self-flagellation are compelling images in the film, understood by a child and therefore "performed" only for him. The black man's actions point toward the subject's inability to go beyond the body. In the words of the screenwriter Stefano Rulli:

> Già la scena iniziale del nero che si spoglia fuori dalla cabina telefonica suggerisce una specie di mistero della comunicazione

> che attraversa tutto il film. Non sono le parole che comunicano, ma gli sguardi, i gesti. E questo è vero soppratutto nel rapporto tra i tre ragazzi. Il lavoro di regia, in questo senso, è stato determinante. (Giordana et al. 17)
>
> The first scene with the black man who undresses in front of the phone cabin suggests a kind of mystery of communication that carries throughout the film. Words do not communicate, but gazes, gestures do. And this is true especially with the relationships between the three children. The work of the director, in this sense, was fundamental.

Sandro has access to this hyper-reality inaccessible to adults. He, like most children, chants indecipherable sounds very similar to the foreign-sounding chants of the black man, as he does while being shot by his father during their vacation on the yacht. When rescued by Radu, he keeps silent when asked about his nationality. When repeatedly asked what language he speaks, he only answers with the black man's chant "soki obotami ...," first whispering it, and then shouting at the top of his voice. Sandro does become a marvelous body, temporarily and problematically stripped of ethnic and national identity. It is important to note that his experience never does go beyond the duality of immigrant/Italian. While the intention may have been to override language and racialized bodies, the final product does otherwise. The politics of sentimentality of *Quando sei nato*, fueled by a creditable yet misguided view of multiculturalism that I described in my Introduction, creates a partial suspension, as it is one that can be carefully calibrated, controlled, and kept at a safe distance from the protagonist and his world, and therefore, from the Italian audiences. This film shows some of the possibilities for Italy's new migrant cinema in filming marvelous bodies in the realist mode, but crucially, displays its limits.

The Haptical Mediterranean: Crialese's *Terraferma*

As I have explored in the previous two films, the theme of the Mediterranean as a contact zone between Italy and the South has been treated on screen in a variety of ways, with the landscape-image of the sea and its relationship to bodies representing a promise of being a third space where identities can be suspended.

In the quasi-sacred rebirthing scene in *Quando sei nato*, Sandro's body is anointed by the sea, temporarily making his body marvelous.

This trope of suspension in/through the Mediterranean, used in one single sequence by Giordana, is developed into a far more sophisticated extended metaphor by Emanuele Crialese, who presents the Mediterranean as a complex locus primarily of fascination but also of unspeakable horror in *Terraferma* (*Terrafirma*, 2012). In this excellent film, the sea is configured as a privileged space of suspension, but because of this it is also a prime location of a fundamental contradiction. Indeed, visions of the sea-image provoke a split feeling in the viewer between fascination and fear. On one hand, the film presents us with a promise of surplus, as a third space where identities can be suspended. Yet, it is also a menacing location of suffering and death. This contradiction accurately reflects contemporary reality of the sea as an important passage for immigrants from Africa and the Middle East countries such as Albania and Greece. Not only are the arrivals of these immigrants on the coasts of Italy a dramatic event, but the number of deaths in unsuccessful attempts indicates the scale of the tragedy that continues to unfold: 6166 deaths have been confirmed in the Strait of Sicily since 1994, 1822 of which took place in a single year, 2011 (Del Grande). There is no doubt that the actual figures are much higher as most shipwrecks are not observed or documented, and most bodies are never recovered.

In *Terraferma*, the point-of-view shots of bodies immersed in the liquid world of the Mediterranean become sophisticated visual metaphors for suspended identities (Figure 9). In comparison

Figure 9: A haptical perspective of the SEA. *Terraferma*

to *Lamerica* and *Quando sei nato*, this film not only extends the scope of the metaphor of the sea by representing the marine environment's ability to suspend identity, but is also more complex due to its illustration of the ambivalent nature of this suspension. I have mentioned before that the Mediterranean has often been used as a trope and location for the renegotiation of Italian identities. In the case of *Terraferma*, two films come to mind, Visconti's *La terra trema* (*The Earth Trembles*, 1948), and Antonioni's *L'avventura* (1960). Visconti's neorealistic masterpiece was undoubtedly an important influence, as the film's title, setting, and subject of a family of Sicilian fishermen seem to pay direct homage to it. Nevertheless, I would like to ascertain how *Terraferma* presents the most visual commonalities not with Visconti's epic and theatrical realism, but with Antonioni's humoristic portrayal of islands as existential third spaces. Just like in *L'avventura*, the island is not only a geographical location, but a psychological, cultural, and ideological space. The island is therefore one of the principal characters in the film. Also, just like Giuliana's fable in *Red Desert*, set on the pink sands of a Sardinian beach, in *Terraferma*, formal aspects such as the manipulation of color, sound, and composition align the island and the sea with a different, non-normative psychological perspective. Crialese's style creates an analogy between the buoyancy, material viscosity, and boundlessness of the ocean to a possibility of release from the violent and repressive perspectives that are confined to characters that subscribe to a land-perspective view of the world. This view is far from a pure celebration of freedom from land-based customs, as the fascination with the sea and the promise it provides to characters is coupled with the horror of the very same waters being the gravesite for thousands of immigrants that fail to make a successful crossing from the shores of distant lands.

Crialese was born in Rome to Sicilian parents. All his films feature two main themes: human conflict and the sea. Rather than approach the tragic question of the thousands of refugees dying in the Mediterranean in the realistic mode, he lets his humoristic tone tackle representations of Europe's contemporary holocaust along with another troubling moral question, that of the European economic system and the underclass it has created in its own citizenry. These two problems are interrelated, but mediatic categorizations would prefer to keep them apart.

Crialese masterfully unites the humiliation and destruction of Sicilian fishing communities on the incredibly beautiful island (importantly, left unnamed in the film) to the suffering of the immigrant refugees arriving at its shores.

Terraferma recounts the story of the island through one family: the bearded quasi-mythical grandfather Ernesto and his grandchild Filippo, the son of widowed Giulietta. Ernesto refuses to sell his old boat that "is of more value if broken up and sold than if kept intact." The fishing industry is dead and the villagers are trying to make do by attracting tourists from the "land," as Ernesto calls the mainland of Sicily and Italy. When Ernesto and Filippo ignore official commands not to rescue a stricken raft of immigrants, their only means of livelihood is confiscated by the police. As an act of silent protest against the injustice of the confiscation of their boat, Ernesto secretly covers the entrance to the police office with fish (Figure 10). While the plot wonderfully fuses the economic and cultural suppression of a sustainable and humane community of natives as well as immigrants, the true value of this film is its representation of this repression through

Figure 10: The Sea symbolically invades the Land in protest.
Terraferma

a unique visual language that sets up an antithetical perception between the land and the sea. *Terraferma* visually establishes the SEA as the realm of the economic and cultural pre-industrial society where the code of the sea is to save people, while the Other is the industrial/bureaucratic state represented by the political/geographical LAND map with rigid borders. The rule of the land is to let abandoned immigrants die, while the code of the sea demands life-saving intervention. Taken in this context, Ernesto's fishy protest can be read as an apt symbol of the seafaring islanders' protest against the rules of the LAND establishment.

The filmic representation of the sea is not only visual or symbolic, but is *sensorial* in terms of its spatial treatment vis-à-vis the bodies of the characters in the diegetic world, and in consequence, the viewers of the film. El Hadi Jazairy describes how Antonioni makes use of the hapticality of cinema to immerse the audience into "being in the landscape" of the Lisca Bianca island, thus setting up a dialectical relationship between the enigmatic protagonists of the film and the landscape itself. In doing so, she argues, both human bodies and the landscape become parallel agents in the construction of emotional drama (Jazairy 349–67). Haptical qualities of cinema relate to the spatiality of the screen-images as opposed to their purely optical qualities. Walter Benjamin describes these haptical properties of film as opposed to the optical with a striking analogy where he compares the painter to a magician, but the cameraman to a surgeon:

> The magician heals a sick person through the laying on of hands; the surgeon cuts into the patient's body. The magician maintains the natural distance between himself and the patient; though he reduces it very slightly by the laying on of hands, he greatly increases it by virtue of his authority. The surgeon does exactly the reverse; he greatly diminishes the distance between himself and the patient by penetrating into the patient's body, and increases it but little by the caution with which his hands move among the organs ... The painter maintains in his work a natural distance from reality, the cameraman penetrates deeply into its web. There is a tremendous difference in the pictures they obtain. That of the painter is a total one, that of the cameraman consists of multiple fragments which are assembled under a new law. (Benjamin 731–51)

The key difference in Benjamin's description of the painting as representation versus film as simulacra is the distance between the object/body and the viewer of the picture. This closeness, where the viewer engages not only visually, but also spatially with the landscape-image or body-image, is crucial in understanding how filmmakers can potentially better engage with the haptical properties of cinema to make viewers "be" in the landscape. Crialese does exactly that in *Terraferma* in order to give his viewers a visceral and therefore emotional message represented by the

Mediterranean. The establishing shot immediately contrasts the image conjured by the decontextualized title "Terraferma" with the exact opposite of what the title signifies: instead of land, we are presented with a high angle *underwater* shot within the sea. It is not a shot of the sea from just above its surface, but a view that immerses the camera deep under. As important as the images in contributing to the haptical power of this sequence are the sounds the audience hears—the typical roar of the motor of the approaching boat is subdued, strange, and unfamiliar in the water-world in which we are immersed. We then hear what sounds like a human heartbeat, and the disorientation it creates further destabilizes and suspends rather than establishes a fixed space. The sound director was maniacal about wanting to record every motion of the seawater throughout the filming, illustrating the director's deliberate engagement with the haptical. Not only is this alignment of our view with the sea maintained, it is also made to remain with us once the action shifts to the characters inhabiting the land. The perspective of the sea is the point of view of Ernesto on land as well, and is shared by the camera's point of view. This sea-perspective on land can be seen in the first sequence on land, where we are shown Ernesto's fishing boat not filmed from the usual perspective but viewed once again with the upside-down perspective of a body suspended in the sea looking up at the underside of the boat, coated with algae and encrusted with limpets. Indeed, with these kinds of manipulations of point of view, even the island is filmed as if it were a liminal area with close, almost interpenetrating openness to the sea.

The perspective of the sea retreats only in the scenes where bodies of masses of tourists dominate the perspective, when the dwellers from the terra firma—the Italian mainland—crowd the beaches in search of "authentic" island cultural experiences, relaxation, and partying. The perspective of the land is fraught with problems, and the stereotyping of the fishermen as quaint touristic spectacles to be consumed is equated with the rigid delineation of political borders between countries that leads immigrants to be "illegal" in one place as opposed to another. The scene in which Titti, the refugee who has been rescued at sea by Ernesto and Filippo, explains her arduous journey from Ethiopia to Libya by using a globe as a prop reveals this land-based problem. It is revealing that Giulietta says that their island is too small to be even represented by a tiny dot on the globe, setting the island as being beyond political barriers that regulate the movement of people on the land. Their island is literally and metaphorically "lost" and claimed by the sea. The sea-based perspective that gives an almost surreal touch to everything in the film is, of course, a moral perspective and relates to the code of ethics harbored by the fisherfolk. Even Giulietta, who tries to see the rescued immigrants as a source of trouble, slowly accepts this perspective of ambivalence. Finally, the family decides to smuggle the immigrant woman and her two children to the mainland in order to save her from capture and deportation. While their first attempt ends in failure, Filippo, the grandson, finally decides to take things in his own hands. He steals his grandfather's confiscated fishing boat and heads out with Titti and her children into the night.

The ending of *Terraferma* represents Filippo's final escape to the realm of the sea rather than to Terra Firma. In a long duration slow zoom out, Filippo and Ernesto's boat, confiscated but now set free, is seen slowly crawling against an increasingly never-ending SEA that stretches out endlessly (Figure 11). As the boat is reduced to a speck/reverse stain on the screen, even the soundtrack slowly fades out from the anthropomorphic

Figure 11: Filippo's boat escapes into the SEA in the final shots of the film. *Terraferma*

Sicilian music to a fade-in of the natural sounds of the sea, wind and waves. I think this open ending is actually not as open as it might seem. Crialese's resolution points toward the only possible resolution in an Italy, a Europe, and a world that is increasingly a fortress—both physically, with highly controlled borders, and also, more damagingly, in representations and people's perspectives—through the continuous repetition of the stereotypes that create harmful dichotomies such as Europe/Orient, Western world / Muslim world. Crialese's haptic and poetic treatise on the sea is a highly innovative work, as it goes against the mediatic images not only of immigrants, which would be commendable in itself, but also of its own native Italian underclass. In fact, in order to better understand Crialese's vision, one must look at his collective filmography and include his representations of the Italian body and its connections to the ocean in *Respiro* (2002). Both films have strong visual and thematic connections.

Respiro, a seemingly realistic film about the life of an Italian family in Linosa, soon frustrates any expectations of narrative coherency and departs from realism by concentrating on the peculiar and unpredictable personality of Grazia, played by Valeria Golino. Grazia is wife to Pietro and mother to Marinella, Pasquale, and Filippo. Visually, Grazia's mental instability and her consequent unwillingness to conform to the expected gender roles of dutiful wife and mother in the claustrophobic community of islanders is directly linked to her close connection to the boundlessness of the sea. Just as in *Terraferma*, this film deals with the inability of individuals to integrate into society because of their nonconformity. In the case of Grazia, it is her specific nonconformity to gender roles assigned to women in the village of Lampedusa in the Seventies. While the rules of the land require her to be dressed and composed in public, Grazia's relationship with the world follows the rules of the sea, where she bathes naked. In the sea, Grazia's body becomes marvelous. She is filmed swimming naked with her children, and her unclothed body is also a welcome source of desire for her husband, Pietro. On land, however, Grazia's sensuality and compassion are only allowed expression strictly within private spaces, while her public nonconformity provokes transgression and quick repression. When the danger of institutional repression approaches, and Grazia is about to be deported far from the aquatic realm to the north of Italy in order to be cured, she runs away and lives in a sea cave, while her son Pasquale leaves the symbol of her imprisonment in society, her dress, on the shore as a ruse. The

Chapter Three

villagers assume she is dead, and indeed, her identity of mother and wife is.

As in *Terraferma*, Crialese's resolution of the inability of society to accept ambivalent gender roles in *Respiro* is poetic. Unlike several readings of film critics that assume an open ending, I believe that there is a decisive closure due to its visual connections to the rest of the film. Pietro finds Grazia, considered lost at sea, swimming in the sea just before the start of a religious festival, and her re-discovery is considered a miracle. It is very important to note that the festival is specifically the Feast of St. Bartholomew, held every year on August 24. Bartholomew, in Aramaic-Syrian, means "Gift of God, the one who moves the Waters." He is one of Jesus's twelve apostles, the patron-saint of the island of Lipari and the protector of the Eolian archipelago. St. Bartholomew is said to have either been cast into the sea or been flayed alive, and therefore famously represented by Michelangelo in the Last Judgement fresco in the Sistine Chapel holding a knife and his own skin. He is also frequently attributed in Lipari and other areas of the Sicilian archipelago to miracles related to the weight of objects. Indeed, it is said that his coffin, made of lead and thrown into the sea in the Middle East, miraculously floated and was carried to the island of Lipari ("La storia della cattedrale."). His body therefore has both supernatural properties related to the sea and is also a conduit between the East and the West.

This symbolic finale assumes a very specific meaning when taken in the spiritual context of St. Bartholomew and Crialese's visual representation of the aquatic realm as a space that suspends identities. The Grazia that is found again is her marvelous version, born like a Venus from the sea. The villagers' acceptance of this Grazia is complete due to her new origins from the sea, unlike the land-locked version that was split between the gender requirements of her society and personal desires. Only a leap of human comprehension, the categorization of the rebirth of Grazia as a Venus or a Madonna of the sea, protector of all fishermen, can cause a lasting suspension of her identity as woman, wife, and mother. Gender roles, that dominate society in both *Respiro* and *Terraferma*, are therefore given the possibility of suspension through the sea. Both films also represent adolescent boys as in-between figures, a commonality we find with *Quando sei nato*. Pasquale and Filippo, similarly to Sandro, are yet unformed by rigid societal stereotypes and potentially marvelous in their ability to understand their mothers.

The harm done by the representation of both the immigrants and the Sicilian fishing communities is grave, the wound almost mortal. Crialese presents an undidactic and humoristic stand against such images of both Italians and immigrants, and therefore allows for the possibility of a new perspective. While not an easy decision, like Filippo's escape into the realm of the sea, the resolution to this increasing rigidity of thought is a breaking away from the lure of the stereotype, and an entry into the realm of the ambivalent, the fluid, and the uncertain.

Chapter Four

Ambivalent Desires

Desiring Gazes: Bhabha and Mulvey

In Chapter 3, "Ambivalent Geographies," I was able to examine four films that used diverse approaches to understanding Italy's interstitial landscapes, populating them with marvelous bodies. This chapter, "Ambivalent Desires," explores five more films, but shifts the focus to teasing out the complicated ordering of positions of desire, both between characters in the various diegetic worlds, as well as between the viewers and the gendered bodies viewed on screen. I have earlier quoted Graziella Parati's description of how the immigrant's existence within the nation is measured through his or her productive and reproductive capacities. Italian cinema must therefore present interesting explorations of immigrants' influence on the nation's biology, culture, and economy, in other words, the Italian nation's oikos. This chapter's focus will accordingly center on the subject of desire, which has much to do with gender identity and sexuality as well as the potential for reproduction and miscegenation. The following final chapter, on the other hand, will focus more on the notion of the dubious legality and morality of the immigrant, which is a direct reading of his or her potential productive contribution to Italian economy and society.

The question of desire is indispensable to a study of cinema, power, and postcolonial identities. As Robert Young states, fantasies of desire abound in colonial discourse, as they are the location for the control and calibration of both biological and cultural hybridity:

> It was through the category of race that colonialism itself was theoretically focused, represented and justified in the nineteenth century, it was also through racial relations that much cultural interaction was practiced. The ideology of race, a semiotic system in the guide of ethnology, the "science of

Chapter Four

races," from the 1840s onwards necessarily worked according to a doubled logic, according to which it both enforced and policed the differences between the whites and the non-whites, but at the same time focused fetshistically upon the product of the contacts between them. Colonialism was always locked into the machine of desire [...] Folded within the scientific accounts of race, a central assumption and paranoid fantasy was endlessly repeated: the uncontrollable sexual drive of the non-white races and their limitless fertility. (Young 180–81)

For Young, colonial obsession over demarcation of minute degrees of mixed racial identity resulted in both an establishment of a discourse that miscegenation would result in degeneration of purer races and yet, by doing so, also brought fetishistic attention to the possibility of inter-racial unions. As discussed in the first chapter, Bhabha's description of the colonial stereotype-as-fetish provides a fruitful framework to understanding how discourses are "fixed" vis-à-vis the cinematic representation of the immigrant question in Italy. If cinema is indeed a "desiring machine" then the understanding of how the stereotype functions to regulate desire would be an important path to understanding the cultural work of new migrant cinema and how it might depart from or parallel the race and sex-obsessed "colonial desiring machine," as Young calls it.

As already noted, Bhabha's stereotype works like Freud's fetish. It is a contradiction, a split, in that what it substitutes (the phallus) is also the basis of the confirmation of its lack. The stereotype-as-fetish, in other words, sets itself up for its own failure just as it forcibly impresses identity. Its anxious repetition is therefore needed, yet that very repetition constantly undermines its stability:

> The visibility of the racial/colonial Other is at once the *point* of identity ("Look, a Negro") and at the same time a *problem* for the attempted closure within discourse. (Bhabha 115–16)

If visibility of the racial Other is a problematic yet universal point of entry into identity—and postcolonial discourse creation in new migrant cinema does function as a "machine of desire," as Young describes the colonial mentality—cinematic representations of inter-racial and intra-racial desire can be successfully analyzed to better understand how an Italian *oikos* is being negotiated through these films. Indeed, all the productions considered in this book, whether more realistic or humoristic in style, must confront the issue of the visibility of the national, racial, or sexual Other, complicated further by the national, racial, or sexual Self's own chronic ambivalence. What therefore is inevitable is a complex interplay of power between the subject and the object of the gazes. The purpose of this chapter is to examine these complex interactions in order to better understand the positioning of both immigrants and Italians, men and women, within the body politic of the Italian nation. What emerges from these explorations is, for me, both unsurprising and intriguing. All the films in this chapter represent visual vectors that perpetuate and/or subvert societal imbalances and inequalities of gender, race, and nationality. Some films, such as *Pummarò (Tomato)*, that initially seem to provide didactic messages of acceptance of Italy's new others, on further analysis turn out to show just how perniciously they continue to (consciously or unconsciously) perpetuate historical hegemonies. Other films, such as *Lezioni di cioccolato (Chocolate Lessons)* which only appear to present themselves as lighter forms of entertainment, sometimes contain far more interesting and unexpected moments of suspension of gender inequalities. What can be safely concluded is that most of the films studied here have until now not been closely mined within the existing scholarship to unearth all their hidden contradictions.

Laura Mulvey's seminal essay "Visual Pleasure and Narrative Cinema" still lends itself to productive explorations on the question of desire in film. Despite much subsequent work that has tried to dispute or depart from Mulvey's initial ideas (such as Cowie, Stacey, Klinger), I find that her essay still holds the most convincing arguments in understanding the complex interplay of gender and power in cinema. It would be useful to first summarize Mulvey's observations and then connect them to our examination of the films. The essay is quite remarkable in its density and succinctness. For her, men and women are unequal in society, and this inequality is mirrored by the mainstream film industry through two principal methods of ordering of the film's mise-en-scène: first, scopophilia is incited. *Scopophilia* simply means the pleasure that is gained by the act of looking. Mulvey then says that audiences are encouraged to identify with a male character (hero/narrator) on the screen (the character that almost always is the subject of the gaze, the one who holds the power and therefore access to the pleasure of looking). This is done by the alignment of the point of view of the camera with that of the narrator's gaze. The female character is the object of the gaze of the camera/male hero/narrator. The spectator, who is encouraged to identify with the male holder of the gaze, shares in the scopophilia entertained by the controlling gaze.

What complicates this scenario of gender division for Mulvey is probably the most interesting part of her essay. The woman in psychoanalytic theory is a sign of castration (she does not have what the male has, and therefore her existence symbolizes the possibility of losing the phallus). She therefore not only provides pleasure for the male through the scopophilia, but is also a source of anxiety (what Freud calls "castration anxiety"). This is where I believe Bhabha's understanding of the colonial stereotype and Mulvey's understanding of the woman's body as object of the gaze meet. Both mechanisms provide a split feeling of pleasure and anxiety, in that they are both fetishes. The way in which this contradiction is resolved (unsuccessfully) is, for Bhabha, through constant repetition, and for Mulvey, through two methods: what she terms *voyeurism* and *fetishistic scopophilia*. Both are ways in which the narrative forcibly "tames" the threat represented by the woman-as-object. Simply put, pleasure at looking at the woman-as-object creates a split feeling of pleasure/fear, which in turn instigates further domestication and constraint of the woman-as-object within the narrative, visually and thematically (voyeurism) and further depiction of the woman-as-object as extremely beautiful and desirable (fetishistic scopophilia). So the split feeling generated within the holder of the gaze leads the subject to further fuel the source of his own split feeling by even more looking of a certain kind.

I would like to point out here that the mechanism described by Mulvey is analogous to Bhabha's description of the colonial stereotype. As Bhabha mentions, the stereotype-as-fetish must be repeated anxiously to gain currency. Mimicry—where bodies that try to tame the contradiction provoked by the stereotype by providing a feeling of being "almost, but not quite" only serve to fuel the stereotype, thus perpetuating the repetition of the stereotype once again. Cinema, therefore, with its ability to visually provide means of both provoking and domesticating bodies on screen, lives up to its promise as a *desiring machine* that regulates the viewer's identifications with bodies on screen.

The Volatile Sexual Politics of the Gaze: *Pummarò* and *Lettere dal Sahara*

The desiring or desired body is an important element utilized by filmmakers to negotiate national belonging. Since the logic of Orientalism (the dichotomy of East/West) often reproduces the logic of sexual difference (the dichotomy of Woman/Man, heterosexual/homosexual), the study of how gendered bodies look, or are looked at, in films presents a productive path of exploring Italy's relationship to its Others.

Several scholars have engaged with Mulvey to show how women too can be the subject of the gaze. Others discuss how homosexual characters and audiences complicate the male/female dichotomy set out by the author. I do not disagree with these observations. However, Mulvey's argument rests in that—it is important to stress this—her description is not about spectator reception, but a critique of the way in which mainstream films are produced with an embedded encoded desiring machine that privileges the dominant (usually) white heterosexual male gaze. Her description is about how visuals are ordered within a cinematic product, and how this specific ordering mirrors imbalances in society. While spectator affect can be somewhat variable, the dominant visual "hints" in mainstream cinema push the spectator in a certain direction. If the immigration question is inserted into this mechanism, it can be shown how cinema systematically follows the pattern of aligning the dominant gaze with that of the Italian characters (of national or racial construction) while allowing even so-called immigrant heroes to fall into becoming objects (or even more intriguingly, oscillate between the role of subject and object) of the gaze. After carrying out this operation, cinematic products then align the spectator's gaze with that of the dominant gaze thus established, allowing the spectator a way to domesticate and limit and therefore have controlled access to the Other (woman, immigrant, homosexual, etc.) that is the source of the troublesome split feeling of pleasure and anxiety. In short, a cycle of fetishization (fixing) of the Other is set in motion. It is the creation of a gender-based postcolonial discourse through cinema.

Chapter Four

But enough of theory—let's go directly to two wonderful illustrations of these complex manipulations of the gaze as they intersect gender, nationality and race: *Pummarò* (*Tomato*, 1990), directed by Michele Placido, one of the very first full-length feature films to deal with the issue of immigration, and a more recent film, *Lettere dal Sahara* (*Letters From the Sahara*, 2006), directed by Vittorio de Seta. Both films can be said to be generally in the realistic mode but achieve different results. They can be termed immigrant "road movies," narrating stories of a young, attractive male African protagonist who journeys through Italy from the South up to the industrial North in search of something he has lost. They are cinematic travelogues, and thus, create a point of reference, an *oikos*, through which the immigrant's travel can be domesticated, and therefore, comprehended. In both *Pummarò* and *Lettere* the interplay and oscillation between fascination/attraction versus horror/disavowal of the gendered bodies on screen plays a central role in establishing the contours of the protagonists' *oikos*. Specifically, the normative male subjectivity in mainstream cinema is at times maintained or occasionally subverted or suspended, causing an unintended re-establishment of gender stereotypes or the creation of ambivalent/androgynous identities and non-normative sexual identities.

In *Pummarò*, Ghanian Kwaku Toré seeks his missing brother Kwalu, nicknamed "Pummarò," which means "tomato" in the Neapolitan dialect. The central event in this film involves a love affair between Kwaku and Eleanora, an Italian teacher he meets in Verona. On a first viewing, the intentions of the filmmakers seem quite simple—to present the viewpoint of the difficult life of a black immigrant in contemporary Italy. Yet, further analysis leads to a more complicated situation. David Forgacs, in an excellent analysis of this film, explains how Kwaku's body on screen is a "focalizer" rather than a narrator whose point of view is shared by the gaze of the camera. Therefore, Kwaku, while seeming like the protagonist who visually holds control over his actions, is not really such. He is almost a narrator, but not quite—a mimic-narrator. A focalizer, as opposed to a narrator, is seen on screen as he or she is looking. There are no strategies to reinforce the point of view of the focalizer as the holder of the subjective gaze in the film, such as voice-over narration. Being a focalizer, therefore, allows Kwaku to "be looked at as he or she looks," making the look extremely volatile (Forgacs 87). Visually then, he is a marvelous body—neither subject nor object.

Forgacs explains that this dynamic, where the black immigrant protagonist is a focalizer for a white Italian viewer, results in an ambivalent and conflicting identification; the viewer can fantasize vicariously and empathize with Kwaku's plight, and *also* distance him/herself from him by viewing his attractive body as an eroticized object of the gaze. This oscillation, Forgacs concludes, makes the viewer's relationships of power vis-à-vis the immigrant body an unusually unstable one. I would like to argue that this volatile relationship with the body on screen, as described by Forgacs, is emblematic of many Italian films of immigration, and is rooted within the nation's conflicting identification with the immigrant other (its chronic ambivalence). In other words, Italy's ambivalence toward its self-identity as a nation translates into ambivalent and volatile representations of and relations between bodies on the screen.

Kwaku and Eleonora's relationship becomes possible only at a crucial moment in which traditional gender hegemonies (Man/Woman is to West/Orient) are subverted. This occurs primarily through Kwaku's becoming a scopophilic object with regard to Eleonora's gaze rather than a marvelous focalizer, which is his primary positioning in the rest of the film. Kwaku's racial Othering allows the female subject to temporarily inhabit a dominant role. This temporary subversion is abetted through the context of a Catholic missionary/colonial mise-en-scène that places Kwaku in a relatively fixed visual position as racial Other compared to other sections of the film. In fact, it is important that the primary sight/site of seduction occurs at an "African" party that is held in a Catholic church-owned building containing a small museum full of African ethnographic objects, dioramas, maps, paintings, and photos. Images of these artifacts populate the screen and frame all bodies in this seduction sequence. The camera establishes the party scene with a long shot that frames a gigantic mural depicting a map of Africa, framed by two coconut palms and the logo that boldly states "*Nigrizia, o morte!*" This statement is a motto made famous by Italian missionary Daniele Comboni, who was canonized by the Catholic church for his unending commitment to the evangelization of principally the Sudan region, and his defense of black men during attempts to justify slavery through

Chapter Four

church doctrine in the First Vatican Council in 1864 (Vecchi). After the camera dwells upon this image that explicitly recalls Italian involvement in Africa in a comforting way to the Italian viewer, indoor shots inside the building lead us slowly to the actual moment of seduction. Kwaku has invited Eleonora to attend the party, which features traditional music and food from Africa. The first indoor shot is a long tracking shot that destabilizes the viewer's geographical bearings. The screen is completely filled with an image of the African savannah rather than that of Italy. This fixed image is then revealed to us by a long tracking shot to be a diorama rather than a real landscape. Yet, the image fixes the viewer in a simulated exotic Orientalized cultural setting. The stage is set for a postcolonial re-enactment of colonial desires.

Kwaku invites Eleonora for a dance, and after initial hesitation, she agrees. The next shot establishes Kwaku and Eleonora's romantic intentions and interestingly, it occurs over a conversation about communication. Eleonora asks, "Is it true that you can communicate with the drum? Sentences? How?" This question leads to an extended moment of multicultural spectacle where Kwaku performs African-ness for the viewer (and Eleonora, whose point of view the viewer shares) by displaying a virtuoso drumming performance. This spectacle of the virtuoso performing black man (viewed with fetishistic amazement by Eleonora and through her, by the viewer—Figure 12) is the culmination of a series of visions of artifacts and objects, all visual citations that allow viewers to engage in fetishistic scopophilia and thus form a stable, safe and reassuring Orientalist discourse that momentarily

Figure 12: Kwaku performs "African-ness" for Eleonora and the viewer. *Pummarò*

stabilizes Kwaku into a subverted economy of desire where racial Otherness trumps masculinity. Eleanora is able to assert a dominant position vis-à-vis this visual and cultural operation as racial and colonial history trumps normative gender hierarchies.

While Otherness is important for the woman on screen to establish a dominant position of desire, this otherness is tempered in order for the seduction to lead to a sexual tryst. This happens in the scene that precedes Kwaku and Eleanora's lovemaking scene, when the now dominant Eleanora takes Kwaku to Juliet's balcony—one of the most important romantic touristic spectacles in a country marketed globally as a romantic destination. The viewer hears a pre-recorded narration of the historical and cultural importance of Shakespeare's drama playing in the background as the characters approach the balcony. This further emphasizes the touristic nature of the location and frames Eleanora and Kwaku's parallel courtship. As Eleanora looks upon the presumed sight/site of Shakespeare's doomed star-crossed lovers, Kwaku disrupts her authority as the agent of access to the site by reciting lines from *Romeo and Juliet* in English. Eleanora is incredulous, and asks, "You went to high school?" betraying her stereotypical assumptions of immigrants as poor and undereducated. Kwaku replies that he is a graduate of medical school and is on his way ultimately to Canada so that he can complete his specialization. With this final piece of information, the filmmakers complete the puzzle of negotiating Kwaku's problematic acceptance as a possible sexual partner for Eleanora. The respectability his impeccable academic background combined with his stereotypically fixed African exoticism allows Eleanora to take the final step. She tells him: "Take me home."

While Kwaku and Eleanora do get temporary access to a transgressive inter-racial relationship that further suspends Kwaku's identity, a forceful assertion of the racial stereotype puts an end to all possibilities of long-term happiness and/or procreation of mixed-race children. Eleanora is a divorced mother, and as news about her transgressive relationship spreads through gossip, her temporarily dominant position is forcefully disrupted by a phone call. Eleanora's ex-husband tells her that since she was seen with a "colored man," he would not be sending her their child, although both parents have joint custody. The woman's maternal role is thus threatened, which can only lead to the disruption of her empowering sexual role. Indeed, Kwaku and Eleanora's relationship is doomed after this event, and a series of violent, racially motivated attacks force Kwaku to leave Verona for Germany.

Pummarò's unintended complicated politics of subjectification versus erotic objectification are handled more deftly in a similar migrant travel film, *Lettere dal Sahara*. Assane, a Senegalese immigrant, arrives on the island of Lampedusa and works his way up the boot of Italy to Florence via Villa Literno in the Campania region, and finally, to Turin. This *voyage en Italie* in reverse once again results in a relationship with an Italian language teacher, Caterina. As in *Pummarò*, this potential relationship is disrupted by a dramatic event of racial violence. Unlike the former film, however, De Seta is able to lend a little more final authority to Assane as the immigrant subject of the look. Indeed, Assane's status as narrator rather than focalizer or object of the erotic gaze is established in the final section of the film. In an extended coda to the main story, which lasts for almost a third of the film, Assane returns to Senegal, meets his mentor and teacher, Thierno, and must debate whether to return to Italy and become culturally hybrid, or remain in Senegal and retain his traditional values.

It would be rewarding to look more closely at this very interesting film. Assane's ascent to the role of the narrator has been interpreted as a move that goes against narratives that perpetuate liberal multiculturalism—films that under the guise of acceptance actually perpetuate difference and Western superiority (Lerner 368). Indeed, De Seta's film does exhibit a "provocative attempt to subvert this position [of multiculturalism as racism] by allowing the protagonist to tell his own story and assert his right to difference" (368). While I agree with many aspects of Lerner's assertion, I believe that the film presents a more complex dynamic that shifts back and forth between Assane's positioning as a subject versus an object of gaze (and therefore between his positioning as Self versus Other). To a large extent, this is very much Assane's story. I agree with Lerner's observations that the filmmakers bravely subvert canonic rules of Italian cinema by allowing the majority of the dialogue to be improvised and spoken in Wolof and French instead of Italian, as well as allowing the immigrant actors a great degree of freedom to shape the dialogues within sequences. However, I would like to demonstrate that it would be more interesting to explore possibilities that go beyond the conclusion that "De Seta effectively gives the last word in the film to Assane's teacher, thus empowering the other with speech" (Lerner 376). The relationship between the coda of *Lettere* and the remainder of the film is complex, with many stylistic and thematic threads that serve to bequeath power to the Senegalese voice, while at the same time, to complicate the Italian viewer's position with respect to the immigrant body on screen. Instead of looking at the film in terms of how the "Other" is given a voice, or is able to "talk back," as Parati describes it, a study of how Assane's journey leads him to become a marvelous body, gradually suspended between (and beyond) Italian and Senegalese national, cultural, and even sexual identities, might present us with an even more fruitful approach. This exploration can be undertaken by shifting the focus of the analysis to its central theme—that of desire and its relationship to the search for domesticity. Assane's pursuit of this literal and figurative home (and in consequence, homeland), or *oikos,* allows the film to regulate and define the limits of the immigrant and the Italian's personal and collective identity within the Italian nation by modulating his subjectification or erotic objectification and keeping it within acceptable bounds.

As the title of the film suggests indirectly, domesticity, the sense of space and place as home, is a central theme of the film. This is because the "letters" of the title are familial missives. First and foremost, it is a family letter that instigates Assane's migration across the Sahara and the Mediterranean. This is the letter Assane reads in the opening sequence of the film from his cousin, Makhtar, inviting him to travel to Italy as a first step toward reaching Canada or America to complete his studies. The next correspondence is Assane's own letter to his mother, which describes in detail the various domestic comforts that he has found in Italy—electricity, running water, etc. These material elements, which constitute Assane's primary objects of desire that push him to immigrate to Europe, make up the basic representative objects of what can be said to be a dignified living. These basic elements are sorely lacking in Assane's reality, as is evident in the marginalized spaces and conditions in which he finds himself throughout the first half of the film. He is first presented to the viewer as he travels in a mini-bus transporting migrants to a CIE in Lampedusa (the same Centers for Identification and Explusion that appear in *Quando sei nato*). The vehicle-as-*oikos*, a contradiction in itself,

Chapter Four

once again makes an appearance in Turin, when Assane is forced to find shelter against a violent thunderstorm in an abandoned van, as there is no space available in the local homeless shelter. Assane is also continuously shot in trains, where long takes show him seated and viewing an endless stream of landscapes, towns, and homes. These medium shots and shot-reverse shot pairings occur frequently enough, and for a duration that is long enough for them to send a clear visual message of Assane's longing for and lack of a stable home. Yet it is the elaborate mise-en-scène of the Villa Literno[1] section of the film that firmly establishes Assane's precarious condition in terms of his ideal of domesticity. As he lies to his mother about the wonders of his cousin Makhtar's home in his letter, he is living in a badly lit, decrepit abandoned structure. This location is in such bad condition that it is unclear to the viewer whether it is an old farmhouse or chapel. Bodies of sleeping immigrants lay strewn around in every possible available space. There are no doors or windows, no water, heat or electricity, and no recognizable furniture.

A touching humoristic scene that features a casual evening get-together of immigrants serves to highlight their remarkable marginality. The extended sequence also introduces women in the film for the first time and therefore establishes the interconnection between desire and domesticity. The group first sings and listens to a song about marriage "Mom, I do not want to marry, please wait." This song introduces the theme of attraction between the sexes and its relationship to traditional norms on its regulation through arranged marriage. The group then dances to Senegalese music and partakes in the elaborate preparation and drinking of tea together. These rituals of domestic stability, through the demonstration of hospitality toward a visiting group of guests, are coupled with flirtatious glances between the men and women guests as well as a dance. The party sequence is humoristic in style and intent, as we watch a typical youthful ritual, which is familiar and yet alien to the Italian viewer. It is disconcerting because of the discrepancy between the actions of the bodies enacting domesticity and the dismal mise-en-scène of material poverty in which it takes place. The setting directly contradicts the emotional joy and abundance unleashed by the immigrants' performance of desire. The comfort of "almost-domesticity, but not quite," a domesticity that Assane yearns for in his letters and that allows for the flow of desire at the makeshift party, is further visually contradicted by the characters' clothes (they cannot take off their heavy and bulky winter coats as the makeshift home has no windows or heat), the cluttered temporary nature of the props that surround them, as well as the tiny proportions of the room in which they are dancing, visually rendered even more miniscule by the kerosene lamps that illuminate the room.

At every point in the film, when even a semblance of domestic stability is established, there is a moment of rupture that frustrates the formation of a stable *oikos* and instigates yet more travel. Assane's mimic-home in Villa Literno must be abandoned when a bomb placed by the local organized crime syndicate destroys Mahktar's friend Safil's makeshift home nearby. Assane decides it is too dangerous to stay and goes to another familial point of reference, his cousin Salimata's home in Prato, near Florence. The episode with Salimata is crucial to understanding the film's politics of subjectification of the immigrant body and its relationship to gender. Salimata has successfully established herself in Italian society. She is a physically attractive woman, works as a model, and lives with her Italian boyfriend, Vanni. Salimata's physical desirability is established via Assane's first gaze that is set upon her: he searches for her in the crowd at the Florence station, and when he finally finds her, his words call out her name repeatedly, in an incredulous way, "Salime, no! Salime? No!" He then says, "You've really grown up, I didn't recognize you!"

Salimata is the film's marvelous body. Her in-betweenness, both visually and culturally, create a feeling of desire and unease in both Assane and the viewer, whose gaze upon the woman is aligned to that of Assane. Not only does Salimata visually and linguistically suspend national identities (she shifts rapidly between French, Wolof, and Italian, even mid-sentence), but this suspension is also visually linked to the possibility of the creation of a new *oikos* for the ever-wandering protagonist. She is framed with the church of Santa Maria Novella as she leads Assane to her car. This association between Salimata's body and one of the iconic façades of the Italian Renaissance is further stressed by her descriptions of the history of the church. Salimata's precarious suspension between cultural entities is witnessed further in the next scene as they drive to Prato. Assane asks what a cupola is, and Salimata explains that it is "that round thing, like the one in Rome on Saint Peter's. I went to see it." She then adds a hasty caveat to this information, stressing to Assane that she only went to the center of Catholicism to view it as a tourist. She says, "I did not pray. Don't worry, I haven't become Christian!" followed by nervous laughter. The viewer, at this point, realizes that Salimata might have to play a balancing act that establishes her hybrid status vis-à-vis national, religious, cultural, and most importantly, gender without threatening Assane, who is a male family member.

Salimata's home is a complete contrast to Assane's previous mimic-homes, and yet, while it provides all the comforts to which he aspires, it also provokes unease in him. Her home is a Bhabhian third space just as Salimata is a marvelous body—it has contemporary Italian interiors and furnishings, and is at the same time decorated extensively with traditional Senegalese art. This hybrid mise-en-scène further compounds Salimata's marvelous status. She is shown selecting a dress to wear for a typical Senegalese dinner she is cooking for Assane, and then is framed within the hybrid home in a traditional yet modern Senegalese-Italian dress. The parallel editing in the next sequence switches between Salimata's display of hybrid feminine domesticity (she cooks, does Assane's laundry, and irons his clothes) and Assane's increasing unease with his surroundings (he lies on the bed after a shower and stares into empty space, in a stupor, as if disoriented). The rhythm of the editing leads to a crescendo of tension, which finally explodes in the next scene when Assane confronts Salimata. He declares his gratitude for her welcome but states that he cannot stay and must leave immediately. After being asked for a reason, Assane reluctantly mentions that he is not comfortable with Salimata's choice of living with Vanni, which goes against his religious and cultural principles. Salimata counters this with an argument that establishes her steady awareness of empowerment, pointing out the hypocrisy of Assane's viewpoint. Salimata's superiority is also established visually by the high-angle shots with which this dialogue is filmed (Assane is seated and Salimata stands over him, gazing down upon him). Furthermore, her display of authority is strengthened by her removal of the traditional turban, a visual symbol of her traditional gender role as she stresses her financial independence. This gender-reversal of roles, both in the content of the dialogue and visual framing of bodies, leads the narrative to another major point of rupture. Assane leaves the home in a hurry, followed by a distraught Salimata. The final scene of this important section of the film concludes with a shot of Assane boarding yet another train, this time bound for Turin. The last frame of this scene depicts Salimata covering her face in shame and anger for the humiliation meted out to her by Assane's rejection of her lifestyle and violent assertion of native gender stereotypes.

Salimata is rejected, but I believe that it is precisely this rejection that shows the importance of her marvelousness for Assane's search of a new *oikos*. The rupture created by his encounter with his cousin stems not from an empowered postcolonial rejection of imperial Western culture that Salimata, a mimic-woman, represents, but arises from the disorientation caused by the temporary suspension of the dichotomy provoked by her hybrid status that goes beyond national, racial, and perhaps most importantly, gender roles. The climactic statement in the scene that leads to the point of rupture is when Salimata exclaims, "You can have a European woman, who is not of your religion, your culture. And I not ... why? I do not understand!" This display of authority and the annexation of male sexual privilege by the woman, with the resulting emasculation of Assane, who plainly sees his disempowered status both financially and culturally, is too much for Assane to bear. He leaves, but is now touched by the disorienting experience that has temporarily suspended his established norms of evaluation that every economy of travel requires in order to comprehend (delimit as well as understand) the wandering.

This event leads us to the final "Italian" third of the film. This section focuses on the relationship between Assane and Caterina—his Italian teacher—in Turin, and brings together themes and elements of the previous two sections set in Villa Literno and Prato. It serves to solidify and fully explore Assane's search for domesticity through a romantic relationship. As I previously mentioned, domesticity is used in the film to delineate and tame the possibility of sexual and cultural miscegenation to culturally acceptable limits. Indeed, the fact that Caterina is introduced to us as a teacher allows her to inhabit a privileged position. Also, the first time we view this character, she is teaching a class of immigrants the vocabulary of the home (*casa*). Utilizing illustrations on the classroom board, she elaborates on the words for various rooms in a home, the appliances and furniture found in the rooms, and finally, the people that inhabit a home, thus becoming a representation of everything that Assane has been looking for in his journey. Even Assane's entry into Caterina's intimate personal life occurs as a result of a gender-reversal and the role of a domestic. It turns out that the only way for him to get a resident permit is to be hired as a *badante* ("caretaker"). The viewer is told that a special law in Italy allows inclusion for immigrants who are caretakers. In other words, they are included if they can fulfill the role of a mimic-family member (a caretaker who is an almost-relative, but not quite). Assane must therefore become a caretaker for Luca, Caterina's troubled younger brother. The immigrant is finally included within the family, but only through a suspension of his masculinity. He confides in Luca, gains his trust, mothers him. When Caterina returns home from work, she finds the table set and a home-cooked meal awaiting her.

I have tried to demonstrate, through my reading of *Lettere*, the presence of a logical pattern of repetitions that create a map, an *oikos*, of a new Italy through Assane's search for a domestic life. The romantic relationship between Assane and Caterina is the culminating step in a journey that constantly promises and then frustrates Assane's assumptions of what that new domesticity might look like. The first step of the journey, a fledgling attempt at the creation of a new *oikos,* happens in his cousin's mimic-home in Villa Literno. A bomb must literally explode on that attempt, and leads to a redeployment of wandering. Salimata's representation of a marvelous body that goes beyond defined roles of what a Muslim and Senegalese man must and can perform provokes an even stronger existential crisis. Finally, Assane's relationship with Caterina, rendered acceptable only by a gender subversion, provides a possible answer for stability.

The final evidence of the use of domesticity to circumscribe transgressive sexuality comes from the most important point of rupture in the film. This scene begins with a representation of Assane's performance of African-ness through an erotically charged dance with drummers playing traditional music. This scene is remarkably similar to Kwaku's display of African-ness through a drumming performance in *Pummarò*. A local Italian gang of hoodlums witnesses this public display of sexual attraction between Assane and Caterina. They confront Caterina and Assane as they leave the venue and question Caterina's transgressive choice of partner. That the already unacceptable bounds of domesticity have been transformed into the even more transgressive realm of sexual desire is stressed by one of the men's comment to Caterina: "Little girl, you enjoyed yourself tonight, eh? Doing it with these negroes here!" In this way, racial and gender transgression is verbally announced by the fixing of Assane into the colonial stereotype of the black man with unbridled sexual appetite. While this scene represents the oppressive environment immigrants must face in Italy, there is a slight complication to the creation of a strict dichotomy between the subaltern immigrant and the oppressive Italian. This is because viewers have not forgotten that the humiliation of Caterina by the Italian men echoes Assane's own sexist denunciation of Salimata in the previous section of the film. The words used by the patriarchal Italian moral-police to publicly shame Caterina echo Assane's judgment toward Salimata in the previous section. Discrimination toward women parallels injustice toward the immigrant Other, creating a subtle, but definite suspension of racial caricatures.

The transgression of acceptable limits placed upon the threat of miscegenation thus results in an act of violence. Assane and his friend are beaten and are saved only by their fall into the river Po'. Water, representing a crossing of cultures, brings Assane's journey full circle. His journey across the Mediterranean and reverse journey in the Po' river lead him back to his origins. The extended coda of the film, which takes place in Senegal and is spoken in Wolof with Italian subtitles, does to a large extent definitively place Assane and Senegal into a position of being the subject of the film, rather than simply the erotic object. However, as I have shown through my analysis, it would be reductive to interpret this return to Assane's point of departure as a confirmation of postcolonial nativism. This is because all the series of searches for an *oikos*, followed by ruptures, have led Assane to a point of suspension. Back in Senegal (Figure 13), he says, "Non so più a chi appartengo. Mi sembra di aver perso le mie radici, la mia cultura. Scusate ma non riesco più a pregare. [...] Mi sento di andare alla deriva" ("I don't know to whom I belong anymore. I feel as if I have lost my roots, my culture. I am sorry but I am unable to pray anymore [...] I feel like I am wandering"). Thierno, his mentor and teacher, mentions the various ways in which the Europeans have oppressed them, but he also says "non dovrete mai sentirvi

Chapter Four

Figure 13: Assane's (temporary) return. *Lettere dal Sahara*

migliore dei bianchi. Questo non deve mai accadere. Rimanete umili" ("you should not ever feel that you are better than the whites. This should never happen. Remain humble"). I would therefore hesitate to interpret this coda as an affirmation of native superiority or of negritude. It is rather a far more open-ended, and therefore a confirmation of suspension, of the opening up of a third space where disorientation and openness to new possibilities is the norm. Assane cannot stay back in Senegal, he must return to Italy for the moment, and perhaps always navigate the third space that is beyond the jurisdiction of racial, national, and gender boundaries.

Guess Who's Coming for an Italian Dinner?— The Palatable Immigrant in *Bianco e nero*

In both *Pummarò* and *Lettere dal Sahara* various visual and narrative tensions pull the immigrant body in opposite directions, creating a volatile representation as the subject and/or the erotic object of the gaze. Kwaku and Assane are both gradually suspended within this interplay of desire. Their relationships with the viewer and with Eleanora and Caterina respectively are managed carefully, which allows for a negotiation of a new *oikos* their unions represent and brings them within defined and acceptable limits. I would now like to discuss a film that presents a contrast to these two works, in that the immigrant body is presented in a more stabilized rather than hybridized manner. Cristina Comencini's *Bianco e nero* (*White and Black*, 2006) differs from the previous two films for a variety of reasons. The first major disparity is that of budget and genre. *Bianco e nero* is a mainstream, relatively big-budget, romantic comedy film. It is in many ways a pioneer due to the courage of its producers to invest in a usually non-commercial subject such as immigration. All films, especially mainstream social cinema, have dual aims, to entertain as well as inform. In this particular film, I would like to demonstrate that in the contest between these two primary concerns, entertainment wins out and pushes the film into a light crowd-pleasing (in this case, meant to be understood as "non-threatening") representation of the race rather than a thought-provoking or destabilizing realm. Aiming to entertain, in itself, is not a reason to debunk a film; I tend to believe the opposite, and as I have frequently mentioned, the Italian comedy is for that very reason a genre that needs to be re-evaluated by scholarship as it succeeded in blending the commercial and entertainment functions of the film industry with a nuanced and original critique of society. The by-line to *Bianco e nero* proudly reads, "Nella vita non è tutto bianco e nero ... esistono le sfumature" ("Not everything in life is black or white ... shades [of grey] exist"). Despite this caveat, I would like to demonstrate that the film irrevocably slides into a comforting re-determination of racial difference for its Italian audience rather than truly explores ambivalent racial and gender identities. There are no marvelous bodies in this film, as it circumspectly maintains its distance from any subversive representation of in-betweenness. Essentially, it seems as if the filmmakers would like to have their cake and eat it too—Comencini makes an earnest and admirable attempt to overturn the stereotype of the uneducated, dirty, and criminal immigrant, and yet, also visually presents the black woman immigrant as unequal, as a passive, Orientalized, female object of desire in order to provide pleasure and entertainment to the audience. *Bianco e nero* is therefore quite an interesting addition to the films studied in this book in that it provides us with a good illustration of how a cinematic product can (intentionally or unintentionally) reproduce the very discourse of "separate but equal" it is attempting to dismantle.

Bianco e nero is a "rom-com" that centers on an Italian male protagonist, Carlo, and his growth and coming-of-age through a romantic relationship with a Senegalese immigrant, Nadine. Both Carlo and Nadine are married and have children, Carlo to Elena and Nadine to Bernard. Elena works in a non-profit organization that fundraises for various humanitarian initiatives in Africa, and Bernard, also of Senegalese origin, is her co-worker. Carlo and Nadine meet at one of the association's meetings and begin a passionate affair. When their secret is discovered almost immediately, they both move away from their respective spouses and children, and continue to see each other. At a crucial moment when they both decide that such a relationship cannot be sustained, they break up and return to their previous lives. However, the film ends with them meeting again by chance (or destiny) and they realize that they still love each other. The idea one gets from this summary is that *Bianco e nero* is a "chick-flick," a colloquial term that A. O. Scott describes as "a demeaning name applied mostly to cynical and threadbare rom-coms trotted out with dreary regularity every spring." However, despite similarities to that ubiquitous Hollywood genre, *Bianco e nero* is declared to be very much a *commedia di costume* in the most Italian tradition by its makers. In the DVD's extras, everyone involved in the film's making stresses the innovative choice of the genre in which a subject like immigration has been tackled. They frequently refer to the film as a *commedia*, intending it as a part of the *commedia all'italiana* tradition. The actors playing the roles of the Senegalese couple, Nadine and Bernard, are French, because few Italian black actors have extensive professional experience. Both actors exclaim and wonder at the absence of a comedy in French cinema on such an important social issue, in a nation that has a far longer history of immigration in contemporary times.

As I have tried to demonstrate in earlier chapters, there is nothing spontaneous or original about comedy films' engagement with vexing social issues in Italy. Viewed in this historical context, Comencini's attempt at exploring race and immigration continues a legacy of the *commedia* being an integral forceful voice in the creation of the nation's cultural discourse. *Bianco e nero* could be understood as an *Italian* comedy in its insistence on an exploration of social mores through stereotypes. Many of the superior comedies of the golden age of Italian cinema that I have spoken about crucially engaged in reflection upon social stereotypes through Pirandellian deployment of humor, rather than mere *comicità* ("comicality") in their plots and aesthetics. *Bianco e nero* lies in a more unsubversive zone in its exploration of the relationship of the Italian with the immigrant Other. Laughter becomes consensual rather than transgressive, mostly through the visual representation of Nadine's erotic body. None of visual modes used by the genre to instigate "reflection" as described by Pirandello occurs in this film as messages of racial harmony are directed toward accepting difference rather than understanding that difference itself is a social construct. Therefore, a "feeling of the other" that is so important in the *commedia* is missing, as all the important distortions of the *commedia* genre are avoided to present a picture-perfect immigrant and Italian society. Ainé O'Healy's assessment of the film gives some important clues as to how the fraught immigration question is glossed over:

> *Bianco e nero* ultimately constructs the black protagonist's "difference" as largely epidermal. Far from presenting a real threat to social order, Nadine [...] constitutes what Katarzyna Marciniak describes as a "palatable foreigner"—an immigrant who is expected to enhance rather than to impinge upon, the wellbeing of the nation. (O'Healy, "'[Non] È Una Somala'" 195)

I would like to build upon O'Healy's observation and suggest that the regulation of Nadine's "palatability" for the mainstream Italian viewers is undertaken both through the character's racial, sexual, and social attributes, as well as through certain stylistic choices that firmly position the female/Oriental body as the object of the gaze of the male/Western subject.

First, the palatability, and the next step, desirability, of the Other is achieved through voyeurism toward the attractive female body on screen by the presupposed hetero-normative male audience. I would like to term the film as a "dude-flick," as it departs from the Hollywood chick-flick genre primarily in that it places at a man as the undeniable protagonist of the film rather than a woman. Unlike in *Pummarò*, the "dude" in this film is white, Italian, and not a focalizer but a narrator. The audience is therefore almost always unequally aligned toward a voyeuristic experience of the woman's body through Carlo's eyes. Very little oscillation of the gaze occurs throughout the film, with an exception of some moments, as I will explain later. Fabio Volo, who plays the role of Carlo, is also a successful prolific writer of male-centered coming-of-age romantic novels in real life. Volo's off-screen persona as a contemporary "professional romantic"

Chapter Four

parallels and influences his screen characters, who are similarly identifiable by the average Italian male middle-class professionals in their mid-twenties to early-thirties. Director Comencini makes a very deliberate and important choice of actor, because I believe that the easy-going and readily identifiable "every-man" image of Volo is key to the effectiveness of the viewer's access to the "prohibited" inter-racial male-onto-female voyeurism in which the film engages.

In contrast to Carlo's average looks and social position is Nadine's incredible attractiveness. Elegant, poised, educated, and as importantly, well-heeled, Nadine is an updated version of the desirable and domesticated black woman of colonial times. The viewer is first introduced to Nadine when Carlo meets her at one of Elena and Bernard's fundraisers. Carlo steps out of the room to avoid yet another discussion about Africa's problems (specifically, Bernard is giving an in-depth lecture on the caloric intake of children in Burundi) and to smoke a cigarette in the building courtyard, which features a dimly lit swimming pool. The pool's waters reflect dim waves of light that create a visually striking *chiaroscuro* pattern that sets up the viewer's interest. On a musical cue, we see Carlo look up and stare at the camera. A reverse-shot reveals what he is looking at—a body slowly emerging from the darkness. It is a revelation, but a slow one, allowing the viewer to ponder the implications of what he is seeing through Carlo's point of view. The body that is seen is a black body, and this blackness causes the viewer to initially confuse the contours of her face and body with the darkly lit surroundings. However, her facial features are slowly unveiled as she walks toward the camera, creating a scopophilic effect that is extended in time. The image concentrates on Nadine's epidermal difference, and simultaneously establishes the viewer's and Carlo's complicity in this moment of racy/racial voyeurism through a point-of-view shot. The metaphor of consuming food is paired with this image as the first words said by the gorgeous Nadine are "Ora chi a voglia di andarsi ad abuffare!" ("Now who feels like gorging!"), referring to Bernard's depressing lecture about famine in Africa (Figure 14). In the same shot-reverse shot pairing, Carlo even describes her entrance as "Certo ... è un approcio un po' ad effetto" ("an approach that has a certain effect"; Figure 15). While overtly he is speaking in the context of a conversation belittling the fundraising speeches, and

Ambivalent Desires

Figure 14: Nadine's entrance as viewed by Carlo. *Bianco e nero*

Figure 15: Carlo's amazement at Nadine's beauty. *Bianco e nero*

therefore describing the approach of the speakers inside the room to convince their audience, it is a double-entendre that also refers to the opposite kind of spectacle in which he and the viewer are complicit: the viewing of the erotic rather than famished African body that inspires consumption rather than compassion. If the stereotype-as-fetish must work through visual or other types of citations ("Look, a negro"), then recalibrating the Italian viewer's gaze from the suffering body of the African Other to its erotic body in the first sequences of *Bianco e nero* can only be understood as an operation of substitution rather than addition.

After establishing this firm visual relationship with Nadine's body, the viewer visually possesses the female object of the erotic gaze with continued examples of fetishistic scopophilia. Other narrative elements of the film also work to enhance and maintain this visual power imbalance. O'Healy mentions how Nadine "scarcely represents the average immigrant, but could be more accurately classified as a cosmopolitan sophisticate" (O'Healy, "'[Non] È Una Somala'" 195). Her disinterest toward Elena and Bernard's earnest humanitarian interest in Africa allows her to become an apolitical and unengaged character that steers into palatability rather than undesirability. Hunger is neither entertaining nor sexy, and Nadine offers a very different approach to understanding Africa—via the erotic rather than the abject. It is highly unclear whether her disavowal of the abject stereotypes of Africa stem from a need to provide a more complete and vital alternative to a stereotype or from a need to disassociate her identity from the poor lower classes of immigrants that typically feature in the Italian stereotype of African immigrants. However, for the purposes of the narrative, Nadine's attractive body and its visual treatment certainly create a strong Orientalized citation that provokes an engagement with erotic stereotypes.

While indulging in postcolonial fantasies that mirror colonial ones, humor is used in one instance to demonstrate the fallacies of the colonial mind. This is done principally through the antics of Alfonso, Carlo's father-in-law. Alfonso's fetishization of the black woman is extreme and almost grotesque, in the perfect tradition of the various "masks" of the *commedia* genre. He obsessively pursues Nadine when she attends Giovanna's birthday party and waxes eloquent about the joys of his amorous relationship with a Namibian woman during a business trip to Africa. Alfonso's wife, Adua, cannot restrain her anxiety generated by this threat from the exotic competitor, and tries to cover this anxiety through her polite condescension toward Nadine. The name Adua is of course of great colonial significance for Italians, as it represents the historical defeat of the Italians in Adwa in 1896 by the Ethiopians, and this crucial party scene therefore serves as a way to draw parallels between colonial discourses and contemporary mechanisms of representing the black other. As Shelleen Greene observes in her analysis of the film:

> The name "Adua" not only suggests colonial nostalgia, but also an inability to fully process on the psychic level the legacies of Italian colonialism, the rapid demise of Italian East Africa and the shame of Italian fascism. The fact that Italian colonialism

> is never explicitly mentioned in *Bianco e Nero* points to how the name "Adua" signifies an absent presence in contemporary Italy. (111)

Indeed, while this farcical scene replete with colonial imagery allows for some very tepid humoristic reflection by the viewer upon the constructedness of the colonial stereotype, this reflection is only temporary. This is because Alfonso's colonial hangover and its criticism is negated and annulled by Carlo's own postcolonial obsessive shadowing of Nadine and the viewer's complete complicity with Carlo in this pursuit. The historical wrongs of colonial stereotyping are not corrected but reappropriated and legitimized by Carlo's own interest in Nadine, and by proxy, the viewer's interest in her.

Epidermal difference is established from the first few scenes even before the viewer sets eyes upon Nadine. In one of the opening scenes, Giovanna, Carlo and Elena's daughter, is shown playing with two Barbie dolls, one black and the other white. She is represented as a person who has already absorbed racial stereotypes, as she casts the black Barbie as the white Barbie-princess's maidservant in a role-playing game. When Giovanna calls the black family "quei negri di colore" ("those negroes of color"), Elena laughs, kisses her, and says "Amore no, non si dice così. Non si dice né negri, né di colore. Come si dice?" ("Oh no my love, one does not say that. One says neither 'negro' nor of color. What does one say?"), upon which, Giovanna gives her mother the correct terminology, "Neri" ("Black"). Rather than admonishing the daughter for her racism by problematizing the very notion of racial categories, the mother permits her daughter to access visible difference and place importance on this visible, thus reinforcing the entry into other fantasies of the colonial stereotype of the other via epidermal difference. As Greene observes, the Barbie doll playhouse scene "identifies the home as the site for the reproduction of normative values, including traditional gender roles, heterosexuality and racial endogamy" (107). She follows with another important observation:

> Elena teaches Giovanna that difference between behaviors is acceptable with public and private places. At a young age, Giovanna is learning to harbor racist attitudes towards blacks, and black women in particular, but to mask these

> sentiments when speaking in public. Thus, *Bianco e Nero* registers a cognizance of colorblind racism, or the assertion of the irrelevance of racial categories that results in a reassertion of racial hierarchy and inequity. (107)

While I fully agree with the excellent points made in Greene's analysis of the film, I would differentiate my conclusions slightly by arguing that *Bianco e nero* is not even *partially* successful in highlighting the performativity of race, or lingering on racial ambiguity, due to the various reasons discussed here. In an analysis of the landmark 1967 film that explores the topic of mixed-race couples, *Guess Who's Coming to Dinner?*, Anne Gray Perrin notes that the film "reduces racial politics to who has the power over white womanhood, and argues that complicated political conflict is resolved between elite black and white men. Therefore, the movie's simultaneous depiction of the class and gender hierarchy is the means by which the social category of race is preserved" (846). Not unlike Sidney Poitier's character Dr. Prentice, Nadine in *Bianco e nero* is served up to the Italian audience as the perfect, palatable Ms.-Perfect-Immigrant containing an abundant amount of reassuring upper-middle-class familiarity with just a pinch of a (non-threatening, slightly titillating) dose of the exotic *Other*. The racial politics of the film are reduced to who has power over the Orientalized black immigrant woman, the black husband or the white lover, and argue that transgressive opposite-race-attraction can be resolved by romantic love. The social categories of Italian race and nationality are, in this way, strengthened and preserved at the expense of a strict delineation of class and gender hierarchies.

If progressive access to the taboo female immigrant body is the central driver of the film's plot, then it is also important to note that for its effectiveness to be sustained, any hint of a parallel romance between the African man and the white Italian woman must be blockaded. Bernard (Nadine's husband) does try to kiss Elena (Carlo's wife) in one scene, yet the action results in failure to make an erotic connection. Their temporary attempt to become lovers stems from their common pain and frustration of being the affected spouses of the affair rather than a genuine erotic and romantic connection. The containment of any possibility of sexual attraction between the black man and Italian woman is the final piece of the puzzle. It is yet another aspect in the sequence of visual and thematic elements described above that successfully allows *Bianco e nero* to stabilize the stereotype of the erotic Orientalized black female body. Nadine's body is packaged for easy visual and cultural consumption on screen, her status preserved and maintained by upholding other gender, class, and epidermal hierarchies.

Marriage, Bengali-Style: Vittorio Moroni's *Le ferie di Licu*

Comencini's *Bianco e nero* maintains palatable stereotypes through a politically correct screenplay while visually providing a comforting mechanism to tame the split feelings of desire and anxiety provoked by the female Orientalized body on screen. The mechanism is textbook Mulvey, and is comprised of unmitigated voyeurism (visually and thematically restricting Nadine as the object of the gaze of the male protagonist Carlo) and fetishistic scopophilia (depicting that object of the gaze as desirable and attractive). I would now like to contrast this film with a far more original endeavor in the creation of a marvelous body— Vittorio Moroni's *Le ferie di Licu (Licu's Holidays*, 2006). This film masterfully deploys Pirandellian humor to directly confront rather than gloss over the uncomfortable feeling of in-betweenness that cultural hybridity provokes. The split feelings of desire and anxiety the colonial stereotype tries to resolve through mimicry can be witnessed most directly in this film through the marvelous body of the protagonist, Md Moazzem Hossain, "Licu."

The film can be divided roughly into three separate "acts." The first revolves around Licu's life in Rome, the arrival of the engagement proposal from Bangladesh and his preparations for departure. The second act takes place wholly in Bangladesh, and is filmed in Bengali with Italian subtitles. This section focuses on Licu's family and their complicated negotiations with Fancy's family and the wedding itself. The third act is substantially different in both style and mood, and primarily focuses on Fancy's life in Rome as a new bride. The film project began with the idea of creating a documentary on Licu's life as a Bangladeshi immigrant in Rome. This part is now only the first act. In an interview, the director, Vittorio Moroni, describes that he initially planned on recording Licu's everyday life, the difficulties he faced at work, and his precarious living conditions, etc.

Chapter Four

However, a letter from his family in Bangladesh, inviting him to meet his chosen bride, Fancy Khanam, changed the focus of the film, which now became the very opposite of the original intention—focusing on Licu's reproductive rather than productive life. Sexuality, gender, and desire become the principal focus of the film, rather than descriptions of work and the daily grind. The title of the film highlights this specific focus and deploys Licu's body in a different direction from audience expectations of a typical social film on immigrants portraying a stereotypical fetishized productive immigrant-body for easy consumption by Italian audiences. Rather than describing Licu's work life, the film redirects the audience to his holidays.

Licu manages with some difficulty to obtain a four-week vacation to travel to Bangladesh to wed the girl chosen for him by his family. He inhabits the role of producer/worker while simultaneously fulfilling the function of voyeur/consumer. Moroni is very capable of demonstrating the contradictions that emerge from the coinciding presence of these two opposing roles within the same character: in essence, Licu becomes an archetypal mimic-man through his embodiment of "an almost Italian/male/voyeur—but not quite" qualities. He is neither Italian nor Bangladeshi and is alternately a voyeur and an object of the Italian female gaze through Moroni's deft editing and the entertaining humoristic screenplay. While this film could be labeled as a documentary, it actually cannot be easily categorized, as it inflicts a "classificatory confusion": it is at moments realistic, at times comedic, and especially in the final third of the film, claustrophobic and melancholic. The end result, though, through the deployment of humor, is undeniably humoristic. The director visually and thematically undermines the pernicious unequal logic of Orientalism (West/Orient) that mirrors the logic of gender (Man/Woman) encoded within mainstream cinema by asking much more interesting and difficult questions: what happens when the typically (ef)feminized Oriental is also the holder of the privileged white male gaze? What happens to the typically empowered male when he is deprived of that position becuase of his race or nationality? Through these explorations, the film demonstrates how gender and desire are integral to the construction of race and nationality.

The act of looking and being looked at is both visually and culturally central to the film. Moroni's meta-cinematic reworking of the cultural value of the gendered look into the formal aspects of *Le ferie di Licu* provides it with a satisfying complexity. The importance of the gaze is most directly established in the scene when Licu takes two Italian women friends/colleagues (one is named Giulia) out for a drink in Rome to celebrate his long-distance engagement to Fancy. At the bar, a discussion ensues on what Muslim men can and cannot do. Licu says, "Non puoi bere alcol, non maiale …" ("You cannot drink alcohol, no pork …") and then when prodded on other rules, he laughs nervously and says, "Non posso vedere la donna, è haram" ("I cannot see woman, it is *haram*"). His Italian female friends do not understand this formulation of the rule because of Licu's uneven Italian. He explains "non posso vedere e pensare 'mamma mia che carina!'" ("I cannot look and think, 'wow, she's cute!'"). While regulating the act of looking at a woman is by itself logistically difficult, it also lies in a morally ambivalent zone for Licu, but when it is connected to thinking and conscious desire, it becomes surely taboo. He finally adds, "Se donna passa per strada devo girare" ("If woman passes by on the street, I must turn away"). As he says this, he mimics the act of turning away by actually turning away from the women he is talking to.

If a discussion about the cultural/gendered look has been included in the film in such an explicit way, then the very act of looking and/or being must certainly present a heavy significance throughout the film. Indeed, I would like to demonstrate that looking and being looked at has direct implications upon gender and cultural/religious identity in the film. Licu's in-between status as "almost Italian / almost male—but not quite" is established primarily through a careful editing of almost 125 hours of footage, and revolves primarily around the tensions and the ability or inability to look in public and private spaces.

Moroni was attracted to Licu for his "look." Licu's contradictory physical and cultural traits are indeed one of the most interesting aspects of the film. He says:

> Mi interessava sia il suo aspetto esteriore, il suo ciuffo, le sue camicie, il suo modo di parlare ma mi interessava anche la sua profonda contradizione che c'era nel suo tentativo di costruirsi un'identità di bengalese che abita in Italia. (Moroni)

> I was interested in both his exterior looks, his hairdo, his shirts, his way of talking but I was also interested in the deep

Chapter Four

contradiction that lay in his efforts to construct an identity of a Bangladeshi living in Italy.

Moroni's understanding and depiction of these contradictions of identity are Pirandellian. It is telling that while referring to Licu, he says "his efforts to construct an identity" rather than "his identity." Indeed, the first third of the film focuses on Licu's heterogenous physical and cultural attributes in a humoristic rather than realistic mode. The inherent contradictions that lie beneath Licu's in-between status come to the forefront.

The establishing shot of the film is a medium shot of Licu walking down the street, wearing stylish sunglasses, a striking black and white striped shirt with a "Yves Saint-Laurent" label. The shirt is obviously not an original, but a cheap spinoff of the famous brand, most probably taken from the garment factory staffed by mostly Chinese immigrants where he works. He is slightly built and his general appearance is vaguely androgynous. The heavily tinted sunglasses already prevent the viewer from establishing a definite power relationship vis-à-vis the protagonist as he cannot meet that gaze eye-to-eye, further complicating the viewer's identification with Licu (Figure 16). He enters a clothing store, and speaks to the shop owner, Giulia, who is standing high

Figure 16: Establishing shot of *Le ferie di Licu*

above his line of sight on a pedestal and is clothed only in her undergarments. Licu seems to have a relatively informal relationship with Giulia, rather than a more hierarchical boss-employee rapport. Giulia and the other lady assistant ask him to bring them two coffees (Figure 17). The first few seconds of the film already establish a tenuous relationship both between viewers and Licu as

Ambivalent Desires

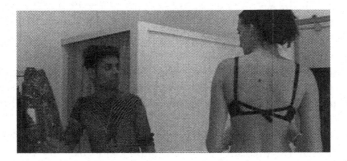

Figure 17: Viewing gendered bodies. *Le ferie di Licu*

well as between Licu as a gendered body and the other women on screen. A successive scene shows Licu bringing Giulia her coffee. As he sits down to drink his own coffee, Giulia asks him to look at the dress she is trying on and say if he likes it. The camera is aligned with Licu's gaze as he sits in the background, while Giulia's body is in the foreground and therefore a little out of focus. The effect of this shot is disorienting when analyzed on both racial and gender perspectives; on one hand, the viewer is firmly aligned with the male subject of the gaze (Licu) as he carefully evaluates Giulia's body for her level of attractiveness (Figure 18). Licu himself is being viewed as he views, thus establishing him as a focalizer. While we participate in this scopophilic moment, our voyeurism through Licu's gaze is disrupted as it is not accompanied by fetishistic scopophilia—Giulia's body is out of focus, and more

Figure 18: Licu views Giulia's body as the viewer gazes at both bodies. *Le ferie di Licu*.

161

importantly, she is standing on a raised platform (looking down at Licu), and too close to the camera for the viewer to gaze at completely. The resulting overall feeling generated by this shot is simultaneously pleasurable and a source of frustration. It is empowering because it allows the viewer to align his gaze with Licu. At the same time it disempowers Licu/viewer, because the female object of the gaze (Giulia) is placed on a higher level than Licu and is looking down upon him. The woman object of the gaze is therefore in a position of relative power within the mise-en-scène. The final result of this complex interplay of gazes is that of suspension—Licu, and the viewer whose gaze is aligned to that of the protagonist—are neither subjects nor objects of the female gaze.

Other instances in the first act of the film continue to destabilize Licu's masculine identity in a variety of ways. While he is undeniably male, he is often emasculated and feminized by Italian women due to his race and culture. At the convenience store where he works, an Italian couple joke when they hear about his impending wedding, saying that the "girl got a bad deal, that *he* should be the one wearing a burka rather than her when they walk down the street." The storeowner then says that Licu "takes twenty minutes to fix his hair each day" as Licu protests and tries to reestablish his male identity by focusing on his productive role in society: "I have to work, how can I have so much time to fix my hair?" A scene in which Giulia and another friend choose perfumes and other gifts at the Chinese store is yet another example of Licu being suspended in an in-between gender role. The scene shows stereotypically female camaraderie through participation in shopping for women's products, including bras (they discuss Fancy's cup size), perfumes, skin/beauty products, jewelry, and clothing. This scene represents not only Licu's suspension but also Giulia's, who seems to gain a masculine role just as Licu gains a more feminine one. Indeed, Giulia begins to admire Fancy's beauty as she looks at her photograph. She assumes a male point of view, saying "Of course you like her, look how beautiful she is." Giulia's partial suspension vis-à-vis gender parallels her subsequent suspension between the West/Orient dichotomy. There is a long sequence in the store where she dresses up and masquerades as a Bangladeshi woman, wearing jewelry and a sari as Licu admires her. She even does a short Bollywood dance step. The suspension created by Licu's partially feminized role and Giulia's partially Orientalized body is yet another example of racial/sexual uncertainty in the first act of the film. Besides considering himself "half Italian," Licu also performs Italian/Western-ness in other ways: he plays *calico balilla* (table soccer), a favorite young Italian pastime and discusses details about the Hollywood *Terminator* films like any young adult. In one scene, he effortlessly transplants made-up Italian lyrics to a Bengali love song, switching back and forth between the languages.

Act One of the film, set in Rome, establishes Licu as a marvelous body, suspended in an ambivalent zone of "almost, not quite." The second act set in Bangladesh stabilizes it somewhat. Most of this section of the film is divided between outdoor shots of the courtyard in front of Licu's home, and tense negotiations to conclude the agreement between Licu's and Fancy's families. As Licu inhabits the defined cultural and visual space of the dominant male groom-to-be, there are still moments where his dominance is threatened. In terms of plot, negotiations seem to come to a standstill when the bride's father says that Licu and his family should wait for a few more days until the bride's family comes to a decision. This is seen as an affront to Licu and his family's honor, as they have already welcomed thirty of Fancy's family members in an elaborate feast, assuming it had all been decided. Family pride must be reestablished, and Licu "performs" his masculinity in a following scene where he declares "I will not agree to marry Fancy, even if they say yes now." His rejection of the bride before the bride rejects him is a way of preserving his position in a patriarchal system. Once again, the act of looking establishes his authority, and through his authority, the honor of his extended family. All family members discuss the affront and as they do, the camera focuses on repeated shot/reverse-shot couplings of Licu and his family passing a photograph of another prospective bride and gazing at it (Figure 19). Licu fetishizes the image of the second prospect in public, thus reasserting his authority:

> "Not bad, she's pretty. Her skin is a pretty color, light like Shilpi's. She only has one defect: maybe her two front teeth are too long. Let me explain! She can have them fixed in Italy. It's not very noticeable plus it's not a big problem. Shilpi says she has a nice face, but she has some pimples. Sure everyone gets some at certain times."

Chapter Four

When asked about her height, he says "The perfect height. She's not even too plump." The verbal fetishizing of the woman's body is effectively emphasized by fetishistic scopophilia through the repeated shots of the girl's photograph as it is looked at by everyone in Licu's family.

Figure 19: The public viewing of prospective brides.
Le ferie di Licu

The first meeting with Fancy at her home once all negotiations are completed is an important moment, as it establishes Licu's identity as the dominant/male subject of the gaze at the expense Fancy's position. A relevant moment to our discussion is the moment when Licu tries to break the ice with Fancy. Several family members closely watch the couple as they sit in a separate room, and a child is sent into that room specifically so that they may not remain alone. As Fancy and Licu perform their established gender roles (Fancy is shy and submissive and does not speak initially, while Licu is gentle, mildly patronizing, and far more upfront), it is a photograph, once again, that establishes the nature of their relationship. Licu brings out his cell phone, which contains a camera, and asks Fancy to look at him. He takes a picture of Fancy, which temporarily brings her out of her performance of a submissive woman (Figures 20 and 21). She does not like the photo that has been taken, and Licu explains: "You're pretty in person, but it doesn't show in pictures. I'm ugly in person, but I look good in pictures." It is not difficult to arrive at the meta-cinematic ramifications of this scene, as it questions the main characters' relationships between their physical bodies/identities to their simulacra/desiring or desired identities. The physical contradictions embodied in Licu's in-betweenness gain further significance through the viewer's realization that he undertakes an active and complex evaluation of the way he sees himself versus the

Ambivalent Desires

Figure 20: An image recording becomes the mediator.
Le ferie di Licu

way he is seen by others in real life as well as in reproduced images, either photographs or videos. The power residing in his possession of the tool for recording images allows Licu to dominate Fancy and exert authority over her body and her identity. Indeed, just before this first meeting, Fancy's mother says: "You are now my son-in-law. [After the marriage] you'll take Fancy to Tangail and do as you please, hang her from the ceiling, make her eat *pura barir chomchom*. We hand over all our rights." Visual possession of Fancy's body is in lieu of possession of her actual body.

Figure 21: An image recording becomes the mediator.
Le ferie di Licu

After the wedding, the third act of *Le ferie di Licu* abruptly brings the audience back to familiar territory, as there is a jump cut from the Bangladeshi environs to an image of the Colosseum. Licu and Fancy are in a taxi. It is apparent right from the start of this act that Licu will transition from his suspended gender identity in public in the first act to a far more radicalized dominant position in the private space of his home in the final act. This change is immediately highlighted by his discussion with his friend Mario, the Chinese taxi driver, about Fancy's attractiveness:

165

Chapter Four

> LICU: When I left Bangladesh she was even more attractive. Now she is a little thinner, a little blacker.
> MARIO: But you'll see, in about two months her face will be whiter.
> LICU: Yes, yes, I've seen that. Before, when I left her, she was whiter, like an Italian woman. Now she is black like me.
> MARIO: It's the fault of the airplane.
> LICU: Ah, yes, maybe it's the airplane's fault.

This exchange brings all the pressing issues of Licu's suspended identity with regard to his gender, race, and nationality to the forefront. Obsession with color and the color-line demonstrate the importance of the visual fetishization of the woman's body in order to relegate her to the reproductive/domestic sphere and exclude any productive/communal functions. Licu's friend warns him about the dangers of women losing their traditional place in the family and urges him to assert his authority over Fancy: "When our women come here, they become free. They feel free. They lose respect for their men."

Indeed, the third act of the film revolves almost completely on Fancy's experience of alienation and privation from the outside world of Rome. Visually, all the charged looking and being looked at that the audience experiences in the first two sections of the film are completely contrasted with the impotence of the look in the third act. More than thirty minutes of the film concentrate on Fancy spending the day waiting for Licu to return from work and staring out of her top-floor apartment window at the Italy that she cannot access. Extended sequences of this section of the film are dedicated to shot/reverse-shot pairings of Fancy's profile in close-up or extreme close-up shots looking out of the window alternating with shots of what she is seeing: passing clouds, different people walking on the street, a couple playing with a ball inside an apartment (Figure 22). This section most closely resembles Zavattini's dictum of "waiting" extolled in his writings on neorealism. The problem here, just as in Garrone's *Terra di mezzo*, is that the waiting and looking all result in nothing dramatically. Fancy's impotent gaze is further magnified by her glazed look, reflecting a pervasive *ennui* that stands in great contrast to her expressions of spontaneous curiosity in the second act. The mise-en-scène of this section is almost completely restricted to the things found in one room and the kitchen of the

Ambivalent Desires

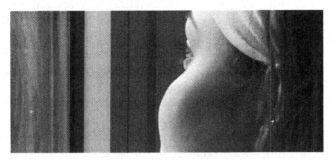

Figure 22: Fancy gazes out of the window. *Le ferie di Licu*

apartment. A few sequences of Licu working at his usual places end every day with a tracking shot of him climbing the stairs to his apartment complex and greeting Fancy, who is waiting for him just within the threshold of the home.

The third act of *Le ferie di Licu* is depressing and claustrophobic, and provides a powerful combination of thematic and stylistic elements that accurately represent the complex gender and cultural negotiations that immigrants must deal with upon displacement. It is to Moroni's credit that he has created a work of great subtlety and lightness provided by Licu's comic-mask and a deft editing that captures gazes in telling and effective ways. The film ends, literally, on thin ice. The final scene, shot on New Year's Eve, shows Licu and Fancy holding hands and trying to skate in a public ice rink. As they try to navigate their new lives and the contradictions between what they desire personally and what they are required to desire by society, Moroni presents us with a more optimistic yet open-ended final image that represents the difficulties and opportunities of inhabiting an in-between, hybrid cultural space.

Immigrant-as-Masquerade: Sugar-Coated Fantasy in *Lezione di cioccolato*

The previous films in this chapter have demonstrated the great variety of ways in which ideological inequalities between gender and sexual identities and bodies mirror racial and national inequalities. My analysis of *Le ferie di Licu* also describes how these inequalities are partially or momentarily suspended through a

Chapter Four

particular ordering of images within a finished cinematic product. A departure from the typical cycle of voyeurism and fetishistic scopophilia in Moroni's film creates a suspension of fixed order in the desiring machine aligned to satisfy the dominant gaze. I will now concentrate on a far more popular big-budget film that tackles the question of immigration.

Cupellini's *Lezioni di cioccolato* (*Chocolate Lessons*, 2007) is a commercially successful comedy film that narrates the adventures of a young Italian building contractor, Mattia Cavedoni (played by heartthrob Luca Argentero, who entered the film industry after winning an edition of Italy's Big Brother reality television series). Mattia is a self-employed construction contractor living in Perugia—a beautiful town in the region of Umbria known as, among other things, the headquarters of the famous Perugina chocolate company. Mattia poses as a suave golfer to entice the rich Dr. Ugolini to hire him (Figure 23). The doctor insists that he will only hire Mattia if he can build a home with a cutthroat budget, leaving Mattia no option but to illegally hire low-paid immigrant laborers, use substandard materials, and permit hazardous working conditions. As a result of a lack of the required scaffolding, Egyptian immigrant Kamal Hawas Guaib (Hassani Shapi) falls from the roof and is badly injured. Mattia begs Kamal to lie to the police to cover up his noncompliance

Figure 23: Mattia posing as a golf player. *Lezioni di cioccolato*

with building and employment regulations. Kamal insists that Mattia can only repay him by impersonating him and attending the Chocolate School run by the Perugina company to celebrate its 100th anniversary, for which he has won a coveted spot. Kamal was a pastry chef in Egypt and his dream is to learn how to use chocolate and win the final prize in the Perugina competition so he can start his own pastry shop. Unwillingly, Mattia undergoes a physical transformation to resemble a believable Egyptian immigrant (Figure 24) and begins to attend the school during the day as Kamal while continuing to work on his construction business at night.

Figure 24: Mattia's transformation into Kamal.
Lezioni di cioccolato

Lezioni di cioccolato is heavily contoured around the traditional *commedia all'italiana* genre, where exaggerated physical traits and cultural stereotypes are used to reflect on societal norms. I have often mentioned that mistaken identities or impersonation is a primary theme/feature of the *commedia*. Since the motor of the film is a masquerading of Other-ness by the Italian Self, leading to an in-between identity of "almost Egyptian, but not quite," I believe it would be interesting to explore more in depth the mechanism of fantasy as it pertains to impersonation. While I have used Mulvey in most of this chapter, I find the descriptions of the workings of fantasy by Elizabeth Cowie to be the most appropriate "entry" into this interesting film. Many readers will know Cowie's work just as well as Mulvey's, as she stands in some ways as Mulvey's counterpart due to the importance of her work on feminism and film. Her work on fantasy in film, found in a revised version in her book *Representing the Woman* (1997), presented the field with a different Freudian and post-Freudian approach to understanding how fantasy works.

For Cowie, unlike Mulvey, spectators do not identify with characters on screen as much as with *the situations in which these characters find themselves*. If, for Mulvey, identification is based on a fundamental misrecognition by the spectator, for Cowie, fantasy is a way in which we express deep wishes. We imagine ourselves in a particular situation in which a character finds him/herself and this maps out a possible access to pleasure. Typical fantasies are ones in which there are changes in social position, wherein relationships with other people change due to a transformation. This is of course highly pertinent to *Lezioni di cioccolato*, where Mattia is given the possibility not only to have an encounter with the immigrant Other, but also to impersonate it. It is important to understand that this change is not a transformation, but an impersonation, and Mattia must oscillate back and forth between his Italian and Egyptian personae to maintain the lie. Cowie is particularly interested in how a spectator is urged to "enter" the situation of the film, the fantasy:

> This is not a cognitive mistake, we are not deceived or deluded by the fiction, we have not misrecognized or disavowed the otherness of film fiction … we do not take the character's desire as our own, but identify with the character's position of desire in relation to other characters. (Cowie 140)

In the case of Mattia/Kamal, I would like to posit that the entry point into the fantasy of impersonation occurs through his situation of being in a difficult position in life, where he must compromise and discard his principles in order to please an overbearing and demanding client in an economy that provides very few opportunities for young aspiring professional white-collar Italian men. Mattia's willingness to bend the rules in order to get ahead in society allows the mainstream Italian spectator to identify and commiserate with his ethnical quandaries and economic desires.

The function of this impersonation is to enter into a situation in which an economy of desire can be explored and re-negotiated. Specifically, Mattia's impersonation as Kamal and the oscillation between the Italian and Egyptian selves allows for a renegotiation of masculinity. I would also like to posit here that Mattia's impersonation of the Egyptian immigrant allow him to partially shed the masculinity associated with his Italian and aspiring upper middle-class identity and become more accessible as an object of romantic affection for women. It is telling that in the scene when Mattia transforms physically in order to look like Kamal, the latter's reaction is to commend him on his increased masculinity "Sembri più maschiale" ("you seem more masculate [sic]") demonstrating this direct link between national identity and gender performance. Mattia's masquerading as the oriental Other allows him to also masquerade as a "softer," more romantic man with a mixture of stereotypically masculine and feminine qualities. The deep wish, then, that is satisfied by this fantasy of impersonation, is not that of becoming an immigrant other, but the typical romantic fantasy of the "chick-flick" genre of finding a physically desirable heterosexual male who is also "sensitive" to the woman's emotional needs and has interest in long-term commitment to family rather than simple sexual intentions.

Mattia/Kamal's negotiation of his masculinity occurs through and for the female interest in the film, Cecilia Ferri. Cecilia is his classmate in the school who begins to become attracted to Mattia precisely because he is unlike her previous Italian partners. She tells Mattia/Kamal how she has gone through multiple relationships that have floundered because her psychologist told her that she is "attracted to men who lie, just like my father." So the cute girl with daddy-issues seeks someone who will be a committed and trustworthy long-term companion, and Mattia, posing as Kamal, turns out to have just those characteristics. Before being completely desirable emotionally, Mattia/Kamal must first negotiate the rules of sexuality, romance, and love with Cecilia, who is attracted by some features of Arab sexuality and wary of others.

A principal worry for Cecilia is Mattia/Kamal's stance on polygamy. This question is approached in a scene where Cecelia decides to go to a Middle-Eastern restaurant with Kamal and their other classmates. A general very awkward discussion of Egyptian culture leads up to the question of polygamy. Cecelia asks, "But there is something about your culture that I do not understand—polygamy. Why don't you explain it to us?" Mattia is of course at a loss of words, but he makes up an excuse to leave the restaurant and finds an immigrant flower-seller, who mentions he is Pakistani. Mattia, in a typical *commedia* situation of misrecognition, then calls the flower-seller an "Arab" and asks if he can explain the deeper meaning of polygamy. It turns out the flower-seller is of course, not Arab, but he is also not Muslim, but

Chapter Four

a Pakistani Hindu. Armed with an answer from this mimic-Arab, Mattia re-enters the restaurant and explains: "Women do not have sex in certain days, if she is pregnant, or just tired, or the baby is crying. But a man, he wants sex every day."

Upon hearing these words, the other Italian men at the table look up with far more interest than before and listen attentively to Mattia/Kamal's explanation. He goes on to say, now with an expression of conviction: "So where is the respect for woman? With lover, screwing in motel? Or better with second wife with house? Where is the respect for woman? Go with whores? […] Yes, it is *best* concept in my culture." The fantasy of sexual surplus of the Arab male, as opposed to material surfeit of the society, is a typical feature of orientalist discourse. Mattia, by becoming "almost-Arab" has been able to not only perform, but also appropriate this typical orientalist fantasy of sexual agency and surplus and through him, allow the Italian male spectator to indulge in it as well.

The negotiation of masculinity continues when Kamal discusses Mattia's sex life as they fight over who created the best recipe for a new chocolate:

> KAMAL: Why nervous? Wife angry? Make no more love with you? Eh? (*Winks knowingly*)
> MATTIA: Listen, you who have girlfriends without having sex. How do you manage?
> KAMAL: I don't remember. Too long ago. I old, 42.
> MATTIA: You are only 10 years older than me?
> KAMAL: You are 32 years old? You seem like child! Do fuck-all, have smooth skin! How many children?
> MATTIA: None.
> KAMAL: (*Concerned*) You like men? (*Angry*) You go with men, with name Kamal!
> MATTIA: (*calming Kamal*) We are not in Egypt here. You can have many women without marrying.
> KAMAL: That is wrong! Woman is to be married and loved. (*Looks in other room to check if they are alone, then whispers to Mattia*) How many did you have?
> MATTIA: (*Thinking*) Fifty, sixty, I don't know!
> KAMAL: Oh! (*Dazed and amazed, sighs. Then he takes on a confused look.*) But I not understand. If you have many woman, many money, why not many children? Oh … I understand … not much "masculinism" … (*sighs*) Want Egypt magic?

> MATTIA: No no! I don't want kids, it's different.
> KAMAL: But nature says "Man plus woman equals children!"
> Or, what use is your money? What use is your life?

It is important that even the word "masculinity" in this exchange is only used by both Kamal and Mattia in its made-up hybrid migrant-Italian linguistic form (*maschialità*), rather than the proper *mascolinità*. When Kamal repeatedly upbraids Mattia's looks by saying "Tu non sei maschiale!" ("You are not mascoline") the linguistic slip points at a slip of the seemingly fixed category of what constitutes male gender identity, besides of course thematically introducing and reiterating Mattia's typical Latin-lover posing when in his Italian persona as a sham. The dialogue above between the two protagonists indicates the most important plot point as well as thematic moment in the film, as it creates a bond of camaraderie between Mattia and Kamal through a discussion of their sexuality together with the discovery of what will become the prize-winning chocolate recipe. The analogy of food, which reflects an important aspect of culture in the film, is also tied into this camaraderie, as the two friends finally discover a winning recipe for the upcoming Perugina chocolate competition. Just as a negotiation of gender roles suspends Mattia/Kamal in an in-between position of desire vis-à-vis the female interest in the film, a negotiation of Egyptian and Italian tastes in chocolate, which is a metaphor in the film for desire, results in a hybrid, a winning recipe that combines the sweetness of dates and the nuttiness of hazelnuts from the Italian region of Monte Acuto. The fantasy of being able to work with chocolate, which their chocolate maestro calls "little moments of ecstasy," is a whimsy of being able to go beyond the day-to-day drudgery of difficult work, complicated women, needy families, and other such responsibilities and indulge in the luxury and freedom of literally "time standing still." In his introductory lecture to the class, the Maestro points to this special, magical quality of chocolate:

> I see a man in a café. He has problems at work, at home. Small broken dreams. He takes one [chocolate] and eats it. In an instant, time seems to stand still. It is a small moment of ecstasy. If you are here to learn how to make chocolate, you might as well leave. You are here to create small moments of ecstasy.

Chapter Four

Lezioni di cioccolato is a fantasy that allows the Italian spectator, through an imagined impersonation of the immigrant Other, to indulge in a daydream where his (the man at the café is a man, not a woman!) economy of desire that regulates and limits his choices is given a momentary chance of suspension and re-negotiation. Following Freud's musings on "Creative Writers and Daydreaming" (Freud and Gay 180), Cowie claims that fantasies are wishes for a change in the circumstances of social reality. Mattia/Kamal, whose in-between physical and cultural traits present a quintessential impersonation in the tradition of the *commedia all'italiana*, represents a path to diffusing the tensions and ambivalence of the Italian spectator toward a mix of fascinating cultural taboos that promise sexual surplus (such as polygamy) and more conservative "family values" (such as a nostalgic return to a more traditional patriarchal nuclear family) presented by the Arab Other. As in other films in this section, the positioning of desire vis-à-vis a marvelous body results in a negotiation of Italian-ness with the disavowed Other, creating solutions that are at times pat, and at times challenging and original.

Chapter Five

Ambivalent Moralities

As I have elucidated in the first chapter, Bhabha's concept of cultural hybridity depicts it as an "in-between" space, the space where culture forms and "works." It is far from celebratory, focusing instead on tropes such as the stereotype-as-fetish and mimicry to describe a creative yet difficult situation that creates a "menace" due to its unstable nature (Bhabha 131): The idea of menace provoked by mimicry resonates powerfully in this chapter that explores films that deal with the subject of immigration and criminality. I believe that audience distress toward ambivalent characters on the screen demonstrates Bhabha's description and mechanism of the "menace" that accompanies mimicry. Mimicry is, for Bhabha, a "metonymy of presence" (129). The situation of being "almost, but not quite" of the mimic-body creates a menace, which results in what I would like to call a *suspension* of fixed identities that eludes secure dichotomies like Us/Them, Good/Bad, Italian/Immigrant. Forced upon the colonized, mimicry has the unintended consequence of forcing the colonizer to see traces of himself in the colonized, as sameness begins to slide into otherness. The colonized subject's sudden realization of inauthenticity, of being ideologically constructed and fixed in representation, is the menace of mimicry:

> The ambivalence of colonial authority repeatedly turns from mimicry—a difference that is almost nothing but not quite—to menace—a difference that is almost total but not quite. (131)

The criminal-minded citizen has been a frequent subject of exploration in post-war Italian cinema. One has to go no further than the canonic masterpiece of neorealism, Vittorio De Sica's *Ladri di biciclette* (*Bicycle Thieves*, 1948) to understand how the question of the national body's productive versus destructive capacities would become a central theme in post-war Italian cinema. Neorealism's many thieves often came from the poor lower class citizens who were the focus of the filmmakers, and the discussion of poverty, marginalization, and crime become not only about moral issues belonging to individual characters in films, but about a collective ethical and existential problem facing the entire body-politic. This interest in thieves and outcasts continues in post-neorealist traditions. In *Rocco e i suoi fratelli* (*Rocco and His Brothers,* 1960), which famously narrates the story of the Parondi family emigrating from the South to Milan, Luchino Visconti tracks the moral dissolution of the second brother, Simone, and his descent into homicide due to his inability to reconcile with the new economic, social, and cultural environment of Northern Italy. But perhaps it is in Pasolini's characters—in the marginalized subproletariat figures such as *Accattone* (1961)—that Italian cinema's complex obsession with the depiction of criminality in the lower classes is most evident. The moral outcasts of the national social fabric have been studiously examined, with ideological readings of the Leftist-leaning traditions seeking to find solutions to the social inequalities of their time that were considered the root cause of a chronic malaise. While mostly realistic depictions of criminals seem to be the norm when thinking about Italian cinema's representations of lower class criminals, thieves and other moral outcasts have been even more interestingly depicted by the more humoristic modes, such as the *commedia all'italiana*. In *I soliti ignoti* (the title in the English language releases is *Big Deal on Madonna Street*, but a better translation would be *The Usual Suspects*, 1958), Mario Monicelli transforms a tragic subject—theft resulting from hunger and poverty—into a farcical caper where several stereotypical characters representing regional and class archetypes bungle a seemingly infallibly planned heist, ending up with only a pot of pasta e ceci (pasta with chickpeas) as the prize for their efforts. The study of moral dubiousness in society becomes far more cynical and bitter when criminality becomes associated with the middle and upper classes, such as in Dino Risi's *I mostri* (*Monsters,* 1963, Figure 25) and its episodic follow-up *I nuovi mostri* (*The New Monsters,* 1977), made by the masters of Italian comedy, Mario Monicelli, Dino Risi, and Ettore Scola.

Ambivalent Moralities

Figure 25: The debased crime-fighting authority figures in *I mostri*.

In these humoristic post-neorealist traditions, moral ambivalence is represented through a Pirandellian understanding of doubling, where characters rely on double standards, lies, and hypocrisy to gain advantages in life for selfish reasons, at the cost of societal betterment. Characters in this *Monster*-style of films, for example, are stereotypically represented. Often, a single group of extremely talented actors such as Vittorio Gassman and Ugo Tognazzi wear metaphorical masks in different episodes, transforming like chimeras into different twisted forms of morally debased characters. In most instances, as is typical with the *commedia* genre, moral deviance is highlighted by literal "masks," exaggerated physical deformation through extensive makeup. This doubling and warping effect of the national body and repetition of class and regional stereotypes demonstrates perfectly a method of representing the menace of mimicry on screen, and lends the comedic depiction of these characters a heavy dose of bitterness.

I will now explore four fascinating films that continue Italy's cinematic tradition of the investigation of the nation's moral sicknesses in the context of immigration. Just as Italy's own chronic ambivalence has spawned numerous soul-searching works that seek to represent Italy's ethical heart of darkness, a new range of interesting films has turned to the stereotype of the Italian migrant-as-criminal as a source of inspiration and examination. As the immigrant becomes a more integral part of Italian society in the second half of the period between 1990 and 2010, especially due to the expansion of the European Union toward the East to include countries from the former Soviet bloc such as Romania and Bulgaria, more complex explorations of cinematic bodies emerge that focus on the stereotype of the foreigner-as-criminal. I will now focus on an in-depth examination of these varied films that delve into the interior moral and psychological ambivalence of characters in the contemporary Italian city. My central argument in this chapter is that the realist tendency in Italian cinema, as seen in some of the films (or notably avoided in others) actually reasserts immigrant stereotypes (in this case, that of the criminal). Humoristic treatments, on the other hand, explore far more ambiguous situations, placing the audience in the uncomfortable position of not being able to completely identify the innocent versus the malign elements.

Ambivalent Affect: Double-Visions in *La sconosciuta* and *La doppia ora*

La sconosciuta (The Unknown Woman) is very different from the much-loved *Nuovo Cinema Paradiso* (1989), Giuseppe Tornatore's best-known film. *La sconosciuta* captured the nomination in the category of Best Foreign Film in the 2007 Academy Awards, but it did not win. I believe this is partly due to the relentlessly uncomfortable thematic and stylistic aspects of the film, which present a great contrast to the style that is expected by most American audiences of Tornatore—the bittersweet nostalgic and melancholic melodrama such as *Cinema Paradiso*. *La sconosciuta* narrates the story of Irena (played by the Russian actor Ksenia Rappoport, who won the David di Donatello for this role). The narration flows in a style that is deliberately spatially and temporally disorienting. In the first hour of the film, Irena arrives in a gray-tinged northern Italian city (actually Trieste) and slowly but resolutely starts making her way into the home of the Adacher family, who are goldsmiths. The Adacher household is made up of an estranged couple and their four-year-old child, Tea. We do not know much about Irena, but we slowly start to get glimpses of her past through a highly stylized and subjective series of flashbacks that interject abruptly from within the present. We discover that she was a prostitute, forced into slavery by Muffa (played by Michele Placido). Irena acquires the trust of the doorman and manager of the apartment building where the Adachers live, and is thus able to secure the job of cleaning the lobby and staircase of the apartment building. She then gains the trust of the old maid who works for the Adachers. Although we follow Irena closely, and experience the world from her viewpoint, the intent and direction for her actions are completely unknown to us. Suddenly one day, she trips the old maid, who falls down the spiral staircase and is almost killed. Irena is now in the position of becoming the Adachers' maid. Once within the home, Irena slowly but surely manages to break into the safe, possibly where the gold is kept. What are her intentions? Where will this story lead us?

La sconosciuta is a mix of several cinematic genres, the features of which all aid in maintaining a characteristic mysterious mood throughout the film: the detective film, *il poliziesco*, the *noir*, the melodrama, the splatter, the psychological thriller, and the Hitchcockian suspense film (there is even a scene where Irena stabs Muffa with a pair of scissors, as in *Dial M for Murder*. Also, her spying on the Adachers from her dark apartment across the street is reminiscent of *Rear Window*). This film is a highly innovative work that, like other films explored in this book, departs from dwelling on the issues of immigration in Italy through the realist mode by an extremely successful stylization. Mystery, rather than mere exposition of discrimination and injustice, is central to this film, and this presence of mystery is key to my argument on Tornatore's affect of ambivalence, which, I will argue, is a device that effectively questions the moral standpoint of the viewer without being didactic. Even the subject of the film written by Tornatore highlights the importance of the mysterious nature of Irena/Ksenia and her intentions. The first lines of the subject for the film are:

> Tutto è misterioso nel comportamento di Irena. Sopratutto il passato che si lascia alle spalle. Un passato che vuole dimenticare ma che in qualunque momento nel giorno, qualunque cosa faccia, affiora inesorbilmente alla sua memoria. (Giordano 217)

Chapter Five

> Everything is mysterious about Irena's behavior. Especially the past that she has left behind her. A past that she wants to forget, but that in any moment of the day, whatever she may do, it inexorably flowers in her memory.

At the center of the film's theme, therefore, lies a *menace*. There is the menace felt by the protagonist, of a past that she is trying to both escape from and affront and change. There is also a constant menace felt by the audience, who feel the disquiet generated by the unknown nature of Irena's incessant drive to become a part of the Adacher household. All these sources of menace are, in a general way, associated with an *ambivalence*—a non-resolution that generates disquiet. Tornatore's mastery, as I will try to demonstrate, lies in the creation of a new style that visualizes and embodies this theme of menace and ambivalence. I call the prevailing result of Tornatore's assemblage of stylistic and thematic choices in *La sconosciuta* its *affect of ambivalence*. What do I mean by this term? William Hope describes Tornatore's ability to "activate affective mimicry within viewers" (7), a process created by specific stylistic choices:

> [The affective power of Tornatore's films] emanates not only from genre manipulation but also from techniques which include an overdetermination of subjective character perspectives, an engendering of the sublime and the lyrical to overwhelm the senses, and the use of purely technical methods such as the extreme deployment of camera close-ups to activate affective mimicry within viewers—a process that involves the perceptual registering and reflexive stimulation of another person's emotion through bodily and facial cues. (7)

Quoting Carl Plantinga, Hope describes affective mimicry as a process of the creation of a bond of allegiance through facial and bodily cues on screen:

> We "enter" the fictional world in part through developing a bond of allegiance with one or more characters. This orients us toward the narrative events and is essential in eliciting the desired emotional response. Whether we laugh or cry or feel suspense during a scene often depends on our estimation of its significance for characters. (13)

Tornatore uses all the above-mentioned means once again in *La sconosciuta*, but they are perverted to create a bond of allegiance that is ambivalent, specifically with the leading character Irena. The allegiance is uneasy, leading to a disorientation, rather than a stable orientation. The disorientation caused by the affect of ambivalence leads to a feeling of *menace*. Bhabha's concept of hybridity, and its related concept, that of mimicry, are once again useful keys to a better understanding of Tornatore's film. The centrality of ambivalence in Bhabha's understanding of the condition of hybridity and his fusing of the identities of "colonizer" and "colonized" into a common entity—that of the "colonial subject"—is useful in determining the positioning of the viewer vis-à-vis the characters in this film. Tornatore's deliberate obfuscation of Irena's identity and motives, her mysterious biological and hence, racial link to Tea, and the various methods described above create an affect of ambivalence in the viewer. These thematic and stylistic choices all point toward the development of a cinematic language that masterfully conveys a feeling of what Bhabha describes as the "third space" where culture forms. When viewed through the lens of Bhabhian hybridity, Tornatore's *La sconosciuta* can be understood as a prime cinematic example of a film that is invested in exploring the new frontiers of the often repressed kinds of social collective narrative. *La sconosciuta* carries out this exploration through the manner in which the subject matter tackles "in-between-ness" and the means by which the director creates an innovative hybrid style that not only visually conveys information on Irena's hybridity, but also generates within the viewer that exact affect of ambivalence, that sense of menace that is a sure symptom of Bhabha's hybridity.

Mimicry, in particular, is an excellent trope that explains the underlying menace felt by the viewer that experiences Tornatore's affect of ambivalence. Suspense, or mystery, was considered key to generating menace in both the diegetic and the extra-diegetic realms of *the film*. Coming after a break of five years since his previous film *Malena* (2001), Giuseppe Tornatore's new film release was a highly anticipated event. Alberto Crespi of *L'Unità* says in his review: "Era uno dei film italiani più attesi dell'anno. Non si può dire che non si sia fatto notare" ("It was one of the most anticipated Italian films of the year. One cannot say that it did not make itself to be noted") (19). Living up to its title, the nature of the film was kept secret until its release. Indeed, the subject matter of the film was kept tightly under wraps, while the leading role was to be played by an unknown actor from Eastern Europe. These moves were highly calculated by Tornatore. In an interview with Mario Sesti, he mentions that he chose Ksenia Rappoport for a few solid reasons, one of them being that while she is well known in her native Russia, she was an "unknown" face in Italy (Sesti). The director stresses the importance of this choice as a key factor in the potential success of the film, saying that he further highlighted the unknown quality of the lead actor by hiring more or less well-known actors to play the supporting roles (a physically perverted but nevertheless instantly recognizable Michele Placido, who plays the role of the sadistic Muffa, Margherita Buy, Claudia Germi, Pierfrancesco Favino, Alessandro Haber, Piera Degli Esposti).

Tornatore's obsession with getting the correct actor for the central role in the film is understandable, as she would be present in almost every sequence of the film, but his attention to the visceral impact of Ksenia Rappoport's face and body are nevertheless exceptional in this case. The director, speaking about the auditioning process, says that he was instantly attracted by Ksenia's face due to its "qualità sfuggente" ("enigmatic/unfathomable quality"), its "mutevolezza" ("ability to transform") (Sesti). He was seeking a face that would have a haunting quality and would be able to transform and convey diverse and often contradictory emotions, but at the same time, hide a secret. Tornatore also refers to the same qualities in Irena/Ksenia's body, saying that:

> La deformazione del suo fisico era importante. Non doveva essera troppo esplicita, troppo mostrata, ma lo spettatore doveva avvertire che il fisico di questa ragazza gradualmente deformasse, diventasse un'altra cosa. (Sesti)
>
> The deformation of her physique was important. It had to not be too explicit, too obvious, but the spectator would have to be able to realize that the physique (body) of this girl was gradually deforming (changing), becoming something else.

What is the reason for this almost obsessive attention upon Irena/Ksenia's body? Tornatore answers this question by drawing a strict relationship between the immigrant and gendered body of Irena/Ksenia and the plot and theme of the film: "il concetto proprio di … possedere carnalmente, è il concetto chiave del film" ("The concept of actually … possessing carnally, is the key concept of the film") (Sesti). Irena's past is revealed to the audience in startling and violent jump cuts, which disclose that she is a prostitute forced into sexual slavery. Her body is literally violently possessed and consumed for pleasure. Not even her reproductive rights are left free. Indeed, we discover that Irena has been forcibly impregnated repeatedly, giving birth to babies that are then immediately taken away from her and sold. The link between power, pleasure, and reproduction is made even more explicit when we discover that probably not all her pregnancies were a result of forced sex. Jump cuts into the past now also reveal a lover, who represents the one moment in her life where sexual desire and romantic love are brought together. The result of this relationship is, possibly, another baby. The centrality of the theme of the body is made more obvious also through the mysterious illness that inflicts Tea, Irena's possible daughter. Tea is affected by a syndrome that inhibits her self-defensive reflexes. When she falls, she does not block the fall with her hands. If something were to fall on her, she would not have the instinct of protecting herself. Irena, stepping into her maternal role, educates Tea to protect herself through a torturous process in which she binds her and repeatedly pushes her to the floor.

I have discussed how Tornatore uses the tortured body within the plot and the aesthetic of the film to generate menace. He also uses his trademark visual strategy of melancholy, well known to Italian and international audiences through *Nuovo Cinema Paradiso*, to contrast, and thus heighten this affect of ambivalence. The flashbacks to Irena's only positive memory, of her time spent with her lover, are the ones in *La sconosciuta* that are bathed in a wholesome golden light (Figure 26). The rest of the film is destined to the stifling blue-gray tints of the Italian north, or the naked hot electric lights of a seedy den in an undisclosed location. William Hope, quoting Fredric Jameson, describes Tornatore's dominant visual strategy in *Nuovo Cinema Paradiso* that creates an "ambience of melancholy" (Hope 14) and nostalgia to evoke a sentiment in his viewers:

Chapter Five

> Jameson cites Marville's photographs of Parisian streets and houses during the epoch of Napolean III, and concurs that Newhall's suggestion that a sense of somber beauty may be derived from their views of a vanished past. (12)

Figure 26: A rare nostalgic escape.
La sconosciuta

Similar techniques of creating audience affect used in *Nuovo Cinema Paradiso* are also used in *La sconosciuta*, but the visual instances of melancholy are rare and fleeting, evoking a haunting sense of loss, especially when these sequences then jump back to the violent and alienating present of Irena's life. Due to the abrupt nature of the flashbacks into a violent, or sometimes melancholic world, the present within the diegetic world becomes suffused with a desperate yearning for repossession of the body and its associated memories of maternal and sexual pleasures. Despite these brief moments of humanity in the past, the audience is presented mostly with only a violent and enigmatic present. The viewer is split between its fear and mistrust of the unknown woman and her intentions, and the slowly increasing allegiance generated by her desperate attempt to repossess her body. This split creates a sense of a disorientation and hence a feeling of menacing ambivalence. The disorienting and fluid camera movements that slide the frame precariously over high windows and spiral staircases, the arrhythmic and fast-paced editing set to Ennio Morricone's Hitchcockian soundtrack, and most importantly, the centrality of Irena/Ksenia's Delphic face throughout the film all serve to create the affect of ambivalence. The difference and innovative quality of *La sconosciuta* from Tornatore's previous works lie in the perversion of the usual way in which affective mimicry is used by the director to create empathy for the character. In this film, the audience is not given an easy character to trust, such as the child protagonist Totò in *Nuovo Cinema Paradiso*, or the adolescent Renato Amoroso in

Malena: the face that dominates the screen throughout the film, the only face/character that the viewer can readily create a bond of allegiance with, is a mysterious face which is hiding its intentions. The director limits allegiance toward other characters in the film, thus forcing the viewer to grapple with Irena, and Irena only. The minor characters are mostly devoid of substantial time on screen or sympathetic qualities. Michele Placido, the other substantial character, is completely dehumanized and bereft of any positive qualities. His face is completely devoid of any hair (even his eyebrows are shaved off) resulting in a monstrous apparition that seems to reek of sex and sweat. The viewer hence concentrates on the haunting Irena, but Irena produces disquiet. Even when her laudable intentions become clear in the second half of the film, the violence of her actions to know if Tea is really her biological child, juxtaposed upon the grotesque and sadistic nature of the violence we see inflicted upon her by Muffa, tug the viewer in opposing directions of allegiance and repugnance. Even in the crucial opening sequence of the film before the credits, Tornatore establishes the viewer's instinctual want for allegiance, creating an ambivalent feeling instead. He does this by showing the viewer four semi-naked women standing in a line under harsh electric lighting, rather than Irena's now identifiable face (Figure 27). All four women are not recognizable because their faces are covered with sinister masks. One of these women is Irena, but which one? The uncomfortable nature of this graphic scene is heightened by

Figure 27: Masked women being viewed from a secret peephole (Establishing sequence). *La sconosciuta*

the fact that the viewer is placed in the perspective of the voyeur, enabling him to participate visually, and hence morally, in the dehumanizing yet titillating world of anonymous flesh trading.

Chapter Five

Behind-the-scenes footage of Tornatore directing Michele Placido shows him insistent on an extremely violent and fetishistic treatment of the body of Irena by Muffa, to the point of becoming grotesque. Tornatore, in these sequences, seems to almost relish the role-playing as he directs Placido. The viewer of the film, similarly, is placed in the extremely uncomfortable position of both being moved by the dehumanization and suffering of Irena/Ksenia's body, and being an active participant in that process.

I have highlighted some of the ways in which Tornatore creates an audience affect of great ambivalence through specific stylistic choices. These choices are a result of a maturation of a personal style that originated in *Il camorrista* (1986) and developed in *Una pura formalità* (1994). The resultant creation of an affect of ambivalence, when placed within the thematic context of the film (that of the economic and sexual commodification of the migrant woman's body), creates a very interesting alternative to the didactic and somewhat overwrought sentimentality generated by realist films that dwell upon the immigrant condition in Italy and elsewhere, such as *Quando sei nato*, discussed in Chapter 3. In *La sconosciuta*, Irena's immigrant face/body is initially looked upon by the mainly Italian viewer with suspicion, generated by the affect of ambivalence. The viewer then unwillingly participates in the visual dehumanization of Irena's body, but also creates a hesitant allegiance with Irena due to the almost positive plot developments, such as when Irena resolves Tea's mysterious illness that causes her to be defenseless in protecting her body through a seemingly cruel education. Finally, the viewer comes to reflect upon the horrors inflicted on Irena, and reaches some kind of resolution. He, however, does not get a satisfactory answer to whether Irena is truly Tea's mother or not. Her will to "carnally possess" Tea as a mother therefore leads to a dead end of sorts, while her past as an object of sexual possession constantly threatens to catch up with her hopes of a more integrated future with her own body. Tornatore, however, does give Irena a possibility of peace at the end of the film. She goes to prison for her role in the death of Valeria Adacher, but upon her release, finds a now grown-up Tea waiting for her at the prison entrance. Apart from this final possibility of grace, however, Irena/*la sconosciuta* is provided only with mystery and violence. Even the cultural/architectural environment of Trieste contributes to the disorienting feeling in the viewer. Tornatore chose Trieste, because, in his own words, it is "la piu straniera delle citta italiane, e la piu italiana delle citta straniere" ("the most foreign of the Italian cities and the most Italian of foreign cities") (Sesti). The name of the family, Adacher, is also tellingly Austro-Germanic, further stressing the hybrid culture of Trieste.

Bhabha's mimicry, and the menace it constitutes, forces the problematic question of what it is to be the "original" in the first place (to take an example from the film, who is the "true" mother of Tea?). The menace, the threat, posed by the mimic-character (Irena, and to a lesser extent, Tea), or the mimic-city or mimic-nation (in our example, it would be the non-Italian Italian city of Trieste) comes from his/her/its partial resemblance, from a revulsion and fascination that such a kinship suggests. The differences constructed by colonial discourse are thus threatened by resemblance, creating, in effect, a double vision: "The menace of mimicry is its double vision which in disclosing the ambivalence of colonial discourse also disrupts its authority. And it is a double vision that is a result of what I've described as the partial representation/recognition of the colonial object" (Bhabha 126). Mimicry is a repetition that is "almost but not quite the same" and thus questions not only the definition of the original, but also its self-identity. As we have often seen in this exploration of cinematic migrants to Italy, the nation often becomes a prime mimic-nation due to its capacity to generate and repeat multiple such "double visions" of identities. It is to Tornatore's credit that he masterfully invents a new style that captures and conveys the disquiet of being both the Self and the Other at the same time (this includes being both immigrant/citizen, sexual victim/voyeur, mother/assassin, judge/criminal), thus creating an original film with great visual and moral impact and most importantly, of subtle cultural relevance to the situation in contemporary Italy.

I have tried to explore some of the innovative mechanisms Tornatore uses in *La sconosciuta* to create an affect of ambivalence in his viewers. Tornatore's mixing of thematic and narrative genres and his corresponding stylistic choices all serve to deliberately prevent Irena/Ksenia from being readily understood and becoming a focus of the viewer's allegiance. The aesthetic result of the overall mix of genres cannot be called an eclecticism, since the result is a style that generates a consistent characteristic mood throughout the film. Tornatore's choices are deliberate and cohesive as a whole, rather than a mere "collage." He creates an innovative visual and narrative style that conveys the sense of menace and disquiet that characterizes the chronic ambivalence of migrants in Italy. Irena's generation of an ambivalent affect within viewers mirrors the reception of the figure of the immigrant in Italian society today. If the body on the Italian screen has a tradition of reflecting the national social self, then Irena's ambivalent body is a significant indication that the migrant condition is now a mature and integral part of the Italian national cultural discourse.

In *La sconosciuta*, Tornatore creates a split/double vision of the primary protagonist, thus playing a twisted game of shifting allegiance and suspicion with the viewer. I would now like to explore another beguiling film in which literal and metaphorical double visions become the principal concept and theme. Giuseppe Capotondi's directoral debut, *La doppia ora* (*The Double Hour*) masterfully portrays ethical ambivalence in the migrant/hybrid character. This film earned Ksenia Rappoport, once again playing the lead character, the Coppa Volpi for Best Actress and Filippo Timi the Pasinetti Award for Best Actor at the Venice Film Festival in 2009. *La doppia ora* presents us with an interesting pairing and complement to *La sconosciuta*, not only due to Rappoport's double-act, but also based upon its similarly effective use of the psychodrama/thriller/horror genre in portraying the migrant as morally dubious and therefore chronically ambivalent. In contrast to the previous film, though, Capotondi's thriller takes audience affect in a directionally opposite trajectory—we are first made modestly comfortable in our affective relationship with the immigrant protagonist, and then gradually, this bond begins to fall apart as ambivalence takes hold.

La doppia ora is set in yet another border city, and this time it is Turin rather than Trieste. Turin is simultaneously the heart of the Italian nation as well as its periphery. While geographically it lies in the northwestern extreme of the nation, politically it played a central role in the Risorgimento as it was one of Europe's principal cities and the heart of the Kingdom of Savoy. So Turin is both the colonizing power that usurped power from the other cultural and political entities of the Italian peninsula and became the first capital city of a unified Italy, and is also a geographical border city.

Ambivalent Moralities

Indeed, one could argue that Turin truly represents a concrete example of how hybridity dwells within the heart of the historical cultural center of the Italian nation.

The story begins with a seemingly chance meeting of Slovenian immigrant Sonia with an Italian ex-cop Guido at a speed-dating session. Guido, intrigued by the shy/diffident, blonde, and enigmatic Sonia, asks her out on an actual date. At this juncture, he looks at his watch and notices that it is 23:23 on the 24-hour clock, or 11:23 p.m. Guido declares that double hours like this are special, moments when wishes can be made: "23:23. It's a double hour. Like when you see a shooting star, one must make a wish" (Capotondi).

Guido works as a private security guard in a palatial villa in the countryside and invites Sonia to his workplace. As they take a walk in the woods surrounding the villa, they are ambushed by thieves, who bind and gag them and proceed to strip the villa of the objects that are emblematic of the upper class, such as precious paintings, gold candelabras, etc. As the gang loads their truck, one of the masked hoodlums threatens Sonia with rape. In a bid to protect her, Guido attacks the thief, thereby setting off the thief's gun. The scene slowly fades out at this point, without offering a clear indication of the consequences of the gunshot. The viewer is next presented with a slow fade-in of Sonia back at her job as a hotel cleaning lady. She looks dazed and peers into a mirror. She touches a healed scar on her forehead, a mark demonstrating the passage of time since the attack. We then see Sonia visiting Guido's grave, confirming that he died in the scramble to help our vulnerable protagonist.

For a long section of the film, the time after the fade-out that follows the gunshot, we grapple with Sonia's psychological disorientation (deterioration?) as Guido's ghost haunts her. He appears to her in the hotel security camera exactly at 14:14 hours, and then also speaks to her or appears in her apartment at other such "double hours." Capotondi films these ghostly appearances by utilizing some of the quintessential techniques of the contemporary supernatural thriller, with a suspenseful soundtrack, sudden sounds, abrupt jump cuts. Things that go bump in the night abound.

I would like to posit that the titular "double hour," when the hour matches the minutes, becomes not only a literal moment

Chapter Five

of supernatural resonance, but can be actually interpreted as a metaphorical "third-space," a metaphysical moment when identities and possibilities converge and become hybrid. Sonia's past, present, and future events and identities merge in these special moments, and haunt her, leading the audience to abandon their allegiance with her as a reliably intelligent, positive, and vulnerable character and look upon her with suspended, contradictory, and unresolved emotions. The most interesting aspect of the film is how Capotondi parallels Sonia's mistrust of what her own eyes see and her ears hear with the viewers' increasing mistrust of what they have seen. The ambiguous version of events that occurred during the heist and of our protagonist's role in these events allows us to begin to mistrust our own eyes and ears, just as Sonia begins to lose her grip on what is real and what is a figment of her guilt-concocted imagination.

In a nod to the magical quality of the double hour, the biggest plot twist is revealed at exactly one hour and one minute of screen time. As will be revealed to the viewers, Sonia is not innocent as we first imagined, but is involved in the plan to lure Guido into deactivating the villa's alarm system so that her lover can steal. We often listen to Sonia practicing her Spanish through language-learning tapes at home, and we then come to discover that this is because she and her lover/thief plan to escape after the heist to Buenos Aires. Double hours thus become marvelous moments of suspension when Sonia must confront her guilt in the participation of a major theft. Yet, she is also vulnerable and produces empathy in the audience due to her own inability to fathom the visual and aural world that she is plunged into after the incident, which caused a bullet to be lodged in her brain.

Sonia's present guilt is also associated with her past. Guido's friend and ex-colleague Dante does some research on Sonia's background and discovers that she is half-Italian. Her Italian father, who had met Sonia's mother in Slovenia and then abandoned her because he already had a family in Italy, refuses to recognize her as his daughter since the day that she escaped from the house, stealing cash and jewelry. Dante is convinced that Sonia's past actions are indicative of a criminal deviance, and proceeds to question her on several occasions, but she maintains her silence. Throughout the section of the film that provides a mounting suspicion of Sonia, the audience experiences a split feeling of simultaneous allegiance with our underdog protagonist and suspicion of potential betrayal of trust resulting from our inability to understand or explain her physical and mental disorientation from reality. Our steadfast connection to Sonia is given a final deathblow in the very effective sequence that begins with Sonia being led away from the funeral of her best friend and colleague, Maria, by a predatory hotel guest, Bruno Caminiti, who has already demonstrated an excessive sexual predisposition toward hotel maids. As Sonia attends Maria's funeral, she hears the priest recite her own name instead of the dead person's, which leads her to panic and interrupt the ceremony. Bruno whisks her away in the car, and drugs her. As the film has been firmly aligned with Sonia's visual point of view until this point, the audience experiences her visual disorientation as she succumbs to the drug, is carried into the woods, laid on the ground on a plastic sheet, dragged on the leaf-littered ground and dumped inside a newly dug grave. Our suspension of allegiance toward Sonia becomes total as our link to the protagonist is severely threatened by literally participating in her (and therefore our own) burial alive. As the plastic sheet is wrapped around her head and eyes, the viewer too only sees her point of view, through the semi-transparent sheet. Our vision of reality, which is so closely associated with Sonia's own vision of the world, has been continuously questioned due to the various supernatural happenings. Our allegiance is finally put to rest through a blurred shot that disallows clarity. As Bruno shovels dirt on Sonia, our vision of the diegetic world is slowly and completely buried. We are radically suspended between reality and fantasy, life and death, and our understanding of Sonia's dubious positioning in space and time.

Those Damn Earrings: Latent (?) Orientalism in Franceso Munzi's *Il resto della notte*

While *La sconosciuta* and *La doppia ora* both play on the audience's fears with respect to the stereotype of the dangerous immigrant-as-criminal, they elegantly stop short on the slippery slope toward stereotyping the immigrant as a perilous entity within the body politic without seeming pat or politically correct. Both films play a careful game or balancing act, effectively suspending the body of the Eastern European woman in between the oppositional feelings of desire and fear that the colonial subject incites. This suspension, managed in no small part by the generic/stylistic choices of the filmmakers, questions the Italian audience's affective relationship with the imagined immigrant Other, leading to an emotional questioning of the viewer's preconceptions and prejudices without falling into patronizing didacticism. The next film that I would like to explore also engages with the subject criminality in the world of the Slavic immigrant community in the industrial North, but as I would like to demonstrate, in contrast to the previous two films, Francesco Munzi's *Il resto della notte (The Rest of the Night*, 2008) fails in maintaining the balance required to create a marvelous body that is suspended in a third space where established values attributed to collective identities are suddenly and momentarily abandoned. Knowingly or unknowingly, this film re-establishes the stereotype of immigrant-as-criminal, thus reassuring the Italian audience that it is perhaps not always mistaken to be suspicious of Italy's external Others. This film therefore provides a wonderful opportunity to illustrate Edward Said's description of how Orientalist discourse works and also of Bhabha's explanation of how mimicry often switches into the stereotype-as-fetish in colonial discourse.

Il resto della notte describes the lives of three families that live in a bleakly photographed Turin. The Boarin family lives in a swanky contemporary villa in the hilly countryside outside the city. They are represented as a quintessential rich and dysfunctional nuclear family to the point of cliché—for example, the father, Giovanni, is emotionally absent and, as we are shown later in the film, having an affair with a woman half his age for whom he purchases expensive jewelry. His wife, Silvana, seems to be a highly derivative character from one of Antonioni's films: she is perpetually anxious and has psychological problems of the undefinable kind that stem from a general existential malaise typical of the various characters played to perfection by Monica Vitti. Their daughter, Anna, seems to be relatively happy and has a positive relationship with their housemaid, Maria, who is a Romanian immigrant (played by Laura Vasiliu of the Romanian film *4 Months, 3 Weeks and 2 Days* fame). The second "family" is composed of Maria and her on-and-off-again boyfriend, Ionut, who lives with his sullen younger brother, Victor, in a grimy apartment within a ramshackle immigrant ghetto in the city center. The third and final familial conglomeration is that of Ionut's partner-in-crime, Marco, who comes from a relatively poor Italian family. Marco is a mercurial drug addict who takes part in petty thefts along with Ionut to finance his addiction. He is divorced from Mara, who now lives with an Arab man. Marco is enraged that Mara should live with a "negro" and actually allow their son, Luca, to be reared by an Arab stepfather.

When a set of pearl earrings disappears, the viewers get to participate in a seemingly unfair at-home trial tinged with racism. Silvana is convinced that Maria is the thief and then convinces Giovanni to fire her. Anna, mirroring viewer sentiment, is unhappy with her parents' irrational decision. Maria, who does not know where to go, reluctantly returns to her ex-boyfriend Ionut's apartment and seeks his forgiveness. She had previously left Ionut because she did not approve of his petty but undoubtedly illegal activities. Victor is quite unhappy with Maria moving in, but Ionut is delighted and celebrates the occasion with an instant romp in the sack. After a few days of inhabiting together in cramped quarters, an angry and jealous Victor demands that Maria pay her fair share of the domestic expenses or leave. At this point, Maria indignantly produces a pair of pearl earrings and hands them over to the brothers. The viewer, who previously assumed that the laconic Maria was innocent, thus realizes that she did indeed commit the theft at the Boarin home. Meanwhile, a subplot shows Ionut's sidekick Marco's efforts to establish a fatherly relationship with his son Luca, who he is allowed to see for short periods as established by the divorce settlement with his ex-wife Mara. Marco tries but fails to control his bursts of anger, thus driving the angelic Luca away from him, but at one point he manages to have a fleeting bonding experience when he illegally takes his son out of his elementary school and takes him for a swim. Once Maria admits to Ionut that she did steal the earrings from the Boarins, Ionut plans a heist as a desperate attempt to improve his family's future prospects. As Ionut and Marco enter the Boarin villa in the night, Giovanni and Silvana are at a classical music concert, leaving only their daughter Anna and her boyfriend—Southern-Italian Davide—at home. Silvana has one of her frequent panic attacks and demands that they return home immediately. As Ionut and Marco enter the villa and Victor stays outside as the watch, Silvana and Giovanni arrive, provoking a dramatic shootout that leaves Giovanni, Ionut, and Davide dead. Victor, shaken to his core, drives off with a wounded Marco, who subsequently succumbs to his wounds on the banks of a river. Victor leaves the body and walks home, where he must confront Maria. In the final scene, the still shell-shocked Victor and Maria leave their apartment, the final long shot framing them walking up the street and exiting on a side street as they make their escape.

Like Monicelli's heist caper comedy film *Big Deal on Madonna Street*, *Il resto della notte* is primarily inspired by the *cronaca nera* (news reports of criminal activity) by the society's more underprivileged sections. However, the genre and tone of this film could not be more different from Monicelli's masterpiece, nor its final message. The film was released in 2008, a significant year, as by then the consequences of the European Union's enlargement to include Romania and Bulgaria on January 1, 2007 were starting to become evident to the Italian public, thanks to an unending mass-media hype about their wide-spread presence in Italian communities. The Giovanna Reggiani murder that I discussed in my Introduction, and several disparate but dramatic incidents were used as propaganda tools by political entities to stir up a mass hysteria about a Romanian invasion in Italy. Parties such as the Northern League began to include, and have continued to include, the *emergenza rumena* ("Romanian emergency") within the conglomeration of other typical security threats to the nation:

> L'emergenza criminale per i rumeni, i problemi per i campi rom, la malavita albanese, oggi le retate che hanno portato agli arresti dei componenti di una cellula terroristica jihadista islamica presente e attiva sul nostro territorio. Sono tutti allarmi che la Lega Nord, purtroppo, aveva lanciato da anni, ma che sono rimasti inascoltati fino ad oggi. (Calderoli)

> The crime emergency due to the Romanians, the problems with the gypsy camps, the Albanian criminal organizations, today the operations that led to the arrests of components of an Islamic jihadist cell that was present and active on our territory. These are all alarms that the Northern League, unfortunately, had sounded for years, but have been ignored until today.

Such rhetorical and discursive strategies demonstrate perfectly the mechanism of the creation of the Orientalist stereotype in the age of post–9/11 globalized immigration. While the details may have changed, the strategy is similar and quite effective. As Edward Said mentions, the citationary aspect of Orientalism is important for its effectiveness—that it frequently must cite from "real" events, facts, and material truths to gain currency:

> Philosophically, then, the kind of language, thought, and vision that I have been calling Orientalism very generally is a form of radical realism: anyone employing Orientalism, which is the habit for dealing with questions, objects, qualities, and regions deemed Oriental, will designate, name, point to, fix what he is talking or thinking about with a word or phrase, which is then considered either to have acquired, or more simply to be, reality. (*Orientalism* 72)

This citationary quality of Orientalism is also explained by Bhabha with his notion of the stereotype-as-fetish, which I described in detail in Chapter 2. The stereotype-as-fetish must be anxiously repeated ad infinitum in order to gain currency, just as Said's Orientalist obsessively cites by naming, pointing to, and fixing in order for it to be treated as reality. Perhaps more importantly than simply demonstrating obsession with citation, Said fleshes out the psychological effects of the resulting Orientalist stereotype, which we will find quite relevant to our subject of the immigrant-as-criminal:

> Rhetorically speaking, Orientalism is absolutely anatomical and enumerative: to use its vocabulary is to engage in particularizing and dividing of things Oriental into manageable parts. Psychologically, Orientalism is a form of paranoia, knowledge of another kind, say, from ordinary historical language. (*Orientalism* 72)

In other words, Said really shows how pernicious the stereotype is due to its functioning as a radical form of realism. Like Calderoli's statement about Italy's security emergency, the stereotype acquires its "claws" from its citationary quality ("scientific," "real," and "based on facts") that establishes it as a legitimate form of knowledge (*This* Romanian is untrustworthy as he was caught stealing), and yet, the very same stereotype also functions psychologically as an irrational force akin to paranoia

(*All* Romanians/Rom/Muslims/etc. are out to steal from me or harm me). The menace generated by citation is the opposite of the systematic and logical mechanism it rhetorically works as. Orientalism, as a discursive form, has the potential to connect both the "real" and the "fantastic" realms of knowledge, and encompass and connect with what we consider as "fact" and "fiction/fantasy."

With this formulation of Orientalism as radical realism in mind, it is curious that the director of *Il resto della notte*, Francesco Munzi, should celebrate his obsessive search for realism in the "making of the film" documentary in the DVD's extras. In this feature, Munzi is shown repeatedly delaying the production of his film as he insists on getting the right non-professional Romanian actors and also the right locations that actually existed in Italy. His location-hunting trips show a fetishistic attention to detail while searching for marginalized immigrant communities. He enters one of these self-proclaimed "ghettos" and films the living conditions of the immigrants. Munzi's producers are shown to be frustrated with the director's failure to find the correct locations and actors after years of dallying. Munzi mentions how he "even travelled to Bucharest" to find the right faces and bodies to play Maria, Ionut, and Victor after failing to find them amongst the immigrant communities in Italy. Watching the feature, one is tempted to interpret this zeal as an indication of a drive toward profound objectivity on the part of the filmmaking team to provide a vision of a Bazin-like "reality as is." However, I would like to demonstrate that Munzi's crafting of the film does not result in an innocent and idealistic mirroring of reality as document, but is in fact (consciously or unconsciously) a film that follows Said's textbook formulation of selective yet extensive citation to create a psychological effect of irrational paranoia, or at least suspicion, toward the Romanian Other.

The most direct indication of how careful and deliberate Munzi's selection of bodies and locations is to the creation of a stereotype of the Slavic woman as an Orientalized menace is in his description of his selection of actress Laura Vasiliu for the role of Maria. Munzi finds himself in a conundrum when he finds two possible actresses for the role and must choose between them:

> Tutte e due avevano un'insieme di dolcezza e di mistero. La mia incertezza era dovuta dal fatto che una mi spostava il film su temperature piuttosto noir. Era più enigmatica, più Dark Lady,

> e l'altra aveva il mistero, ma che era più da popolana, quindi mi portava più a dei film, per dire, neorealistici. Quindi questo dubbio ... per dire, certe volte la scelta dell'attore può cambiare il registro del film. (Munzi)

> Both had a mix of sweetness and mystery. My uncertainty was due to the fact that one shifted the film toward noir-ish temperatures. She was more enigmatic, more *Dark Lady*, and the other had mystery, but she was more a common working-class type, so she would lead me to, let's say, the neorealistic kind of films. Therefore this doubt ... this is to say that, sometimes, the choice of actor can change the register of the film.

Munzi's revelation indicates how his stylistic intentions ("register") are actually far removed from a typical realism, but it is the *claim to realism* caveat that convinced me that *Il resto della notte* does indeed slip away from the gray areas of suspension meticulously maintained in *La sconosciuta* and *La doppia ora* into an establishment of an Orientalist stereotyping of the Romanian Other. The generic boundaries of the film, which are that of an unrelenting noir-like characterization of events, landscapes, and bodies, however, had sufficient citationary aspects, sufficient claims, and intentions of realism that allow it to present viewers with a pretense of filming the reality of a very present Romanian menace in Italy today. Maria's Delphic qualities (which Munzi contrasts to the more "everyday, working class" characteristics for the actress he did not choose) are not utilized to a humoristic effect as with Ksenia Rappoport's enigmatic face in the previous two films in this chapter. Her initial characterization is that of a mimic-body, an almost Italian, but not quite. She is part of the Boarin household, but not really. Very importantly, she is also racially ambiguous, which does not allow immediate stereotyping visually. The viewers cannot and do not immediately associate Maria with the immigrant/racial other. As I have discussed while exploring Bhabha's understanding of the colonial stereotype, just as the visual recognition of the point of identity ("Look, a Negro") fixes identity, so does it also set up the seeds for its own failure, as the visual basis upon which this fixing is based is also the problem for its attempted closure. Maria's ambivalent racial and national identity suspends her identity at the very beginning of the film. Her name is also a quintessential symbol of Italian motherhood and Catholic piety. Despite these characterizations, this principal character's marvelous body only serves as a first step rather than an end point. The second step after suspension is fixing into stereotype. When the plot reveals that Maria is indeed the thief of the pearl earrings, the mimic-body is effectively fixed into the stereotype of the Slavic-woman-as-criminal. The menace caused by the mimic-body's ambivalent and suspended racial/national identity provokes a psychological reaction to "domesticate" and normalize the menace through the stereotype-as-fetish. As Bhabha explains: "The fetish or stereotype gives access to an 'identity' which is predicated as much on mastery and pleasure as it is on anxiety and defense, for it is a form of multiple and contradictory belief in its recognition of difference and its disavowal of it." (115) The mimic-body, so effectively suspended in the characters of Irena and Sonia in *La sconosciuta* and *La doppia ora* respectively, cannot maintain this balance in *Il resto della notte*. The viewer is initially menaced by questions: is Maria Italian or Immigrant? Is she a nurturing substitute for an absent mother or a dishonest thief? Her uncertain positioning vis-à-vis stable reassuring dichotomies triggers the mechanism that will fix her identity as a criminal mind—the revelation that she did indeed steal the pearl earrings. A film critic mentions the importance of this revelation in tilting the film away from depicting a complex immigrant reality to a one-dimensional stereotype of delinquency:

> Bastava semplicemente tagliare una sola scena, lasciare lo spettatore con il dubbio che quei maledetti orecchini non si sapeva che fine avessero fatto, se fossero stati davvero rubati o semplicemente persi, per dare un quadro totalmente differente. Ma quella scena è stata girata e montata, Maria quegli orecchini li aveva davvero rubati, e anche l'immagine della colf rumena ladra ha finito per arrivare in faccia allo spettatore, stordito dalla messa in scena di così tanti negativi stereotipi.
> Peccato. (Boni)
>
> It would have been sufficient to cut out one single scene, leave the viewer with a doubt as to what happened to those damn earrings, that they might have really been simply lost, to give a completely different result. But that scene was shot and edited in, Maria did indeed steal those earrings, and now even the image of that thieving Romanian maid has ended up in front of the spectator, who is dazed by the depiction of so many negative stereotypes. Too bad.

Ambivalent Moralities

While I agree with Boni's description of the importance of this event in determining the message of the film, I would differ slightly with his characterization of this one single plot twist as being the *only* aspect where Munzi and his team is guilty of stereotyping in the name of representing "slice-of-life" reality. As I have been trying to demonstrate, the process of stereotyping is gradual, and is weaved into the film not via any one particular plot point, but more importantly through its claims and visual positioning as a thematic and stylistic representation of immigrant "reality" in urban Italy today. The fetishistic attention to the real by the filmmakers lends itself to providing the stereotype its efficacy and currency. For example, the photography of the film, where even the few daylight scenes are shot in dismally dark and bleak fashion by cinematographer Luca Servino provides a noir-like, stylized look. On the other hand, viewers could also interpret this very stylistic decision that is governed by a generic delineation as a geographically and seasonally realistic and appropriate representation of locations beset by *Torinese* winters, and therefore quite "realistic." The snatches of Arabic music that haunt the viewer's ears during scene transitions into Ionut's apartment complex are exactly what many viewers would assume is being played in the "real" immigrant ghettoes throughout Italy, when in actuality, it is equally possible to listen to generic Italian pop or even regional Italian music in areas dominated by immigrants. One has only to consider how different Matteo Garrone's sensitive approach to filming the Neapolitan apartment complex in *Gomorra* to see how a filmmaker can be thoughtful yet incisive in his approach to fact-based storytelling without descending into precarious ethnic and regional stereotypes. In *Il resto della notte*, the Arabs seem to be perpetually praying while facing Mecca (Figure 28) (in reality, Munzi obliged the actual film extras to pray facing in a different direction due to lighting and other practical filming needs, which caused many of them to refuse and leave the set), the Italian bourgeois couple spend evenings listening to German *lieder* in an opulent opera house and—of course it naturally and convincingly follows—that the Romanians and Italian drug-addict-sidekicks spend their nights plotting and executing heists. The strength of the film lies in its ability to build a mounting suspense, a menace, that a Greek-style tragedy is about to unfold. Yet its very dramatic fatefulness is tied to the

Chapter Five

Figure 28: The view from Ionut's apartment: Muslim men praying. *Il resto della notte*

way in which viewers are led to a long series of banal and expected characterizations of identities related to class and wealth (the rich come complete with pearl earrings, private swimming pools, and pitch-perfect existential crises), to gender (the women on the verge of an existential nervous breakdown or posing as angelic-yet-conniving mysteries), and finally, to nationality. These small repetitions of confirmations of stereotypes lead the viewer by the hand to a mounting feeling of menace, like a trail of bread crumbs that leads to a final doom, exemplified by Silvana's conviction that something bad is surely about to happen.

Good intentions about depicting the complexity of immigrant lives in Italy teem on the surface of the film. There are sufficiently honest portrayals of the trials and tribulations facing the perpetrators of the theft, Maria, Ionut, Marco, and Victor. Yet, despite these surface complexities, those damn earrings and their implications provide a clear conservative message to the viewer. It is also difficult to ignore the establishing scene of the film, one that in many ways decisively frames the film and sets the tone and approach of the discourse. The scene begins as a voice-over during the opening credits and it merits a detailed analysis as it is the key to understanding the slippery approach of the filmmakers to the immigrant question in Italy:

(Opening credits roll on the screen, soft piano notes, then fade in to a male voice-over): Western man has been able to obtain all the riches that humanity has always dreamed of. The West has been able to become materially rich. But now he is tired, weighed down. The journey has robbed him of his soul.

Ambivalent Moralities

(At this point, we are shown the first shot in the film, a middle-aged man in a medium shot, talking directly to the viewer as he stands in front of a lecture dais. We see the man talking directly facing the camera) (Figure 29): This man is exhausted. Everything that he needs is within his reach, but Man, as such, is not there anymore.
(Cut back to film credits, Man, still addressing the viewer): Now is your time. You have the possibility of being informed. Informed of the fact that behind these false truths …
(Cut to shot of man, this time he seems to address not the viewer of the film, but people to his right, within the diegetic world of the film, not the viewer): … there is a precise purpose. A bad purpose. That of making you weak and insecure. Slaves of fear.

Figure 29: The framing discourse on Western society.
Il resto della notte

(Reverse-shot reveals he is talking to a blonde middle-aged woman—Silvana): There is only one solution.
(Back to shot of man): Surrender.
(Reverse-shot, Silvana): Surrender yourselves.
(At this point, Silvana's gaze lowers, she laughs nervously, but it is uncertain if it is an anxious response to the man's words, or an action that represents her disregard for those words. Perhaps it is a mix of both.)
(The Man continues): For some time now I have stopped trying to become something different …
(Cut to film credits): … from what I am. Today is another precious day on the Earth and therefore let's look around us at each other, with love. All together …
(Foreground, long shot of the man's audience, a community-meeting room, filled with around fifteen to twenty Italians): Joy is with us! *(Repeated by the audience)* Inside us! *(Repeated by audience)*.

Chapter Five

> *(Shot of Silvana as she looks around at the people chanting.)*
> Man: We ARE! *(Repeated by crowd)* Yes, we ARE! *(Repeated)* We live! *(Repeated)* We are unique, irreplaceable, perfect! *(Repeated)* *(Silvana leaves the room. Camera follows Silvana, in the background, the lecture/pep talk continues. End scene.)*[1]

An analysis of this scene provides a simple conclusion: it provides the viewer with a simultaneously direct, explicit yet ambivalent ideological frame toward approaching the story of the three families in *Il resto della notte*. The words of the man, given a certain authority as it is through a voice-over and also that of the first body we see on screen, suggest to the viewer that the imagined geography of the Western and Eastern worlds is a fact. It then demonstrates, in a professorial way, that the history of the West is dominated both by success and guilt. It discusses this imaginary civilizational history as fact, outlining the myth of the West's rise and decline as common knowledge. It conjures up another false dichotomy, that between the material and spiritual economies of culture that define these imagined civilizations. The elaboration of this dichotomy then allows the discourse to move between pseudo-facts into the realm of the psychological and spiritual, cleanly making the shift between two seemingly opposite forms of knowledge—the "official" or the historical and the "phantasmatic." The second half of the man's speech therefore lends a different tone, where the professorial role shifts into that of a priest who seeks to salvage souls, or a leader of an alcoholics-anonymous session where a chronic malaise needs to be cured. What might Munzi possibly mean by framing his film with this interesting and arresting scene?

It is important to note that the scene functions as an introduction to one of the main characters, Silvana, who, as we have discussed, is most representative as a victim of the principal menace that seems to pervade this suspenseful film. The undefinable dread that Silvana feels is initially something that the viewer is unable to completely accept, yet in the subsequent scene, the viewer is instructed to note that the fear of Western decline as discussed by the lecturer and the multitudinous terrors that accompany it are justified. As Silvana walks home from this foreboding lecture under Turin's elegant porticoes, she is assailed by a group of Rom (gypsies), who beg for alms but then start to manhandle her (Figure 30). A male passer-by comes to her rescue and distracts the gang of rabble-rousers, and Silvana runs to her car, enters it, slams the door shut, and bursts into tears.

Figure 30: Silvana is assaulted by Rom children.
Il resto della notte

The prologue I have described in detail above functions as an underlying message that frames the bigger fantasy drama of "the fact of immigrants-as-criminals" that the film ends up becoming. The currency that allows this drama to become legitimate is not Maria's race, as she is not visibly different, but it is those damn earrings, which act as the visible fetish-object with which a primal encounter with the feared/desired Other can then be staged and executed. What allows this primal staging of colonial stereotypes to bypass more obvious forms of racism is the explicit declaration by the filmmakers about objectivity through radical realism, and it therefore "works" as a palatable depiction of reality in the same way as citationary Orientalist discourse works. The slippery intentions of the filmmaker are difficult to understand, but the message of their product is undeniably clear. "Look, a gypsy gang, troubling a well-to-do yet vulnerable Italian woman." The frame of the film sets the scene by allowing us to see. It points and cites in order to gain legitimacy without explicitly presenting a racist discourse.

A film critic who vehemently supported the film during the controversy that surrounded its reception seeks to sidestep the complex political issues of representation I have discussed in this section:

> La vicinanza della storia con fatti di cronaca, soprattutto quelli che coinvolgono persone di nazionalità rumena, ha portato non pochi commentatori a parlare di film che porta acqua a tesi

Chapter Five

> "leghiste" o nella migliore delle ipotesi [...] di ingenuità goffa e controproducente: pur non volendo "dare addosso" a stranieri e clandestini, lo avrebbe fatto senza nemmeno accorgersene. La cosa curiosa è che per alcuni critici che scrivono queste cose, "Il resto della notte" è "tecnicamente" un bel film ... Tipico modo di ragionare scisso: della serie, il regista è bravo, sa raccontare, i personaggi sono credibili ma politicamente si presta a strumentalizzazioni; insomma, fa il gioco del nemico.
>
> Non condividendo questo modo di ragionare, ci limiteremo ad analizzare il film. (Autieri)

> The fact that the story is similar to actual events, especially news stories that involve persons of Romanian nationality, has resulted in many commentators to speak about a film with a "Northern League" [Italy's main anti-immigration party] thesis, or, in the best of cases [...] of clumsy and counterproductive naiveté: even though he did not want to "go against" foreigners and illegal immigrants, he did it without even realizing it. The curious thing is that for many critics that write these things, *The Rest of the Night* is "technically" a good film ... Typical split way of reasoning: of the kind that the director is capable, he knows how to tell a good story, the characters are believable but the film could be instrumentalized politically, in short, it plays the enemy's game.
>
> As we do not share this way of reasoning, we will limit ourselves to analyzing [the technical aspects of] the film.

Autieri here carries out a classic evasive action that seeks to neutralize any complicated questions about social responsibility by claiming to not be interested in discussing those aspects of the film and limiting himself to judging the film's technical aspects. Yet, if anything is certain about new migrant cinema as explored in this book, it is the fact that the aesthetic qualities of these works are inextricably tied to their cultural, social, and political qualities and consequences. Even if filmmakers may deny, downplay, or overly exaggerate their socio-political and cultural *impegno*, a better understanding of Italy's cinematic history and a resulting *contextual* analysis of contemporary films certainly allows us to unveil unsaid or explicit connections to ideology. Francesco Munzi's personal intentions while planning and filming *Il resto della notte* do not interest me, and it would be counterproductive to interpret a film based on the filmmakers declared or imagined intent. The deciding factors lie within the final product, its images, editing, and other elements of the film itself. Those damn earrings were indeed stolen by Maria, and this connection leads the viewers to a realization of their worst fears about the immigrant other, however sympathetic or desperate their plight, due to the other generic and stylistic choices made by the filmmakers that I have described here. To employ a metaphor that Fanon uses in *Black Skin, White Masks*; it is these *seen* elements that create the *scene*, the replaying of a primordial scene or nightmare. The film, as in the other films I have examined in *Marvelous Bodies,* thus becomes a site of fantasy and desire and also a site of subjectification and power.

It is no surprise therefore that Autieri, after claiming to only analyze the aesthetic elements of the film, completes his review by making a political statement and declaring that the "fact" of immigrant criminality exists:

> Ma i fatti che raccontano esistono, innegabilmente. Conforta almeno l'assenza di pregiudizio ideologico e di buonismo da quattro soldi. (Autieri)

> But the facts that [the film] narrate exist, without doubt. What comforts is at least the absence of ideological prejudice and of a hypocritical liberalism (*buonismo*[2] *da quattro soldi*).

The facts exist. As my analysis of *Il resto della notte* illustrates, the selective yet extensive citationary quality of Orientalism, represented in cinema in the realist mode, has a power to persuade and provoke fantasy and fear that are indeed difficult to resist.

Radio as Koran: The War on Terror in Mohsen Melliti's *Io, l'altro*

Munzi's *Il resto della notte* demonstrates the pernicious way in which the citationary nature of Orientalism invades and overpowers cultural texts. The mechanism with which the immigrant becomes an undesirable element in society through film can be clearly described by Bhabha's understanding of the workings of the stereotype-as-fetish, a major feature of colonial discourse. In contrast to *Il resto della notte*, the final film to be explored in this chapter exposes the violence of the stereotype through a humoristic portrayal of marvelous mimic-bodies rather

Chapter Five

than indulging in it through fetishizing the real through the realist mode. In *Io, l'altro* (*I, The Other*, 2006) director Mohsen Melliti explores the process of stereotyping of the Arab-as-terrorist. This relatively short film exposes the links between Italy's historical past as a colonial power and its current role as an ally of the American-led "War on Terror" initiated by the George W. Bush presidency after the September 11, 2001 attacks on the World Trade Center in New York. The Afghanistan and Iraq wars loom in the background of a morality play that features only two characters, Sicilian Giuseppe (Raoul Bova) and Tunisian Yousef (Giuseppe Martorana). It is not insignificant that Italian actors play the roles of the two protagonists. The film brings together some of the principal themes that have been explored in this book, that of cultural hybridity and its visual manifestations of marvelous, suspended bodies on screen, and also that of the opposing mechanism of stereotyping and the creation of an Orientalist discourse that "fixes" identity.

An example of the hybridity revealed by the detourist nature of new migrant cinema can be found in a key scene that involves the sudden discovery of a body of a Somali immigrant woman, drowned at sea and caught in Yousef and Giuseppe's nets. On one level, this discovery can be read as a way to highlight the treacherous and tragic reality of desperate immigrants seeking to cross the Mediterranean into Europe from North Africa. Yet, there are several other layers of meaning to be peeled back and considered. Áine O'Healy presents a stimulating interpretation of this scene by positing that this gendered and racialized body is a symbolic representation of Italy's own suppressed colonial history in the Horn of Africa:

> I would argue, in fact, that the uncanny presence of the black woman's body in Melliti's film signals a return of the repressed memory of Italian colonialism, and at the same time obliquely draws attention to the relative absence of this figure elsewhere in contemporary cinematic imaginary. (O'Healy 177)

O'Healy unpacks the significance of this reinscription of a body that has often had great representational value in the past since the erotically attractive figure of the Somali woman is an often-repeated feature in the imagination of the Other during Italy's colonial presence in Africa. The re-exhumation of the nation's repressed past is also simultaneously an opportunity for re-interpretation. The body of the Somali woman is not the typical erotic image of the past, such as that presented in mass-produced images of Africa during colonial times, but is a maternal, unerotic body, fully clothed and wearing a necklace representing her Islamic faith. Her motherhood is confirmed explicitly as the two fishermen find a photograph of a child when they search for any documents to identify her (Figure 31).

Figure 31: Yousef and Giuseppe view the photograph carried by the dead Somali woman. *Io, l'altro*

I would take O'Healy's interpretation a step further. As she states, the Somali woman's body is a symbol and denunciation of Italy's repressed past and its connection to the contemporary crisis of immigration. In addition to this, I believe that it is also important to note that the agents of this exhumation are not two Italians or two immigrants, but an Italian and a Tunisian. The hybrid identities of the two agents of re-exhumation is further compounded by the fact that they are both purposely de-racialized to the point of being inter-changeable in their visible and cultural identity (both protagonists are played by Italian actors). My interpretation of this scene, which in the film is left unexplained and open to different readings, is that the body's exhumation from the buried depths of the sea was only made possible due to the hybrid nature of the two agents who bring about the discovery. In other words, detourism into Italy's complicated relationship with its disavowed other, caused by the exhumation of the dead and hidden body, is therefore sparked by the unstable *oikos* of the agents that institute the wandering through their discovery.

Chapter Five

Another important feature of hybridity in the film, as has frequently been noted in other films in this book, is the "third space" of the Mediterranean Sea, which becomes a prime metaphysical location where fixed identities are at least temporarily suspended. When Yousef and Giuseppe (both the Arabic and Italian versions of the same name, Joseph in English) are resting between chores on board their small fishing boat, Medea, they have a short conversation about the sea:

> Yousef: Quante volte siamo usciti al mare. E ogni volta mi lascia a bocca aperta.
> Giuseppe: A me piace perchè non lo conosci fino in fondo. È per questo lo devi rispettare. (Melliti)
>
> Yousef: How many times we have been out at sea. And every time it leaves me open-mouthed.
> Giuseppe: I like [the sea] because you cannot know it completely. And it is for that that you have to respect it.

Ultimately, the vastness and the mystery that represents the sea, but also its physical qualities of buoyancy yet viscosity, transparency yet opaqueness, all make it an excellent metaphor for the "third space" described by Bhabha, a space of hybridity where identities dissolve and mix. It is crucial here that the mirror image presented by the two friends, Giuseppe and Yousef, and the suspension of racial and cultural specificity that mirror image connotes, could only occur due to their intrinsic connection with the realm of the sea. Indeed, in the first half of the film, Giuseppe often expresses racial and Oriental biases, but they are in jest, as Yousef's Arab identity is perceived as secondary to the almost-familial connection the two friends have. Giuseppe mentions some of the typical Orientalist images of Arabs: he describes the messy work area on the boat created by Yousef as a "campo nomadi" ("Gypsy camp")—the term frequently used by the mass-media to describe the chaotic settlements by the Rom in Italy's urban areas. He chides Yousef's mongering toward their local Mafia-boss Rosario Troina by alluding to the taboo characteristic of homosexuality frequently attributed to Arab men. Giuseppe and Yousef harmlessly compete to declare their favorite singers as the best, with Giuseppe extolling the virtues of Neapolitan singer Gigi D'Alessio and Yousef praising Algerian star Khaled.

This suspension—where the sea plays the role of catalyst—is disrupted by the land. This is a move similar to one employed by Crialese in *Terraferma,* although in this film the domain of the land, where the politics and news events seek to revoke suspension and demand clear distinctions, is represented primarily through the boat's radio and wireless communication. Around fifteen minutes into the film, the viewer is presented with the first primary disruption of suspension, as Giuseppe hears that a certain Yousef Ali has been implicated as the protagonist of the terrorist bombings of the trains in Madrid. This actual event occurred on March 11, 2004, killing 191 people and wounding approximately 1800 ("Spain Train Bombings Fast Facts"). The first announcement inserts a kernel of suspicion in Giuseppe's mind about his Yousef's true identity and nature, and sets off a sequence of events that ends in tragedy. The process is typical of the fixing of identity described by Bhabha, in which metaphor (the Arab as terrorist) and metonymy (This Yousef is every Arab) work to their inevitable conclusion (This Yousef is the Arab terrorist they are seeking). The process of fixing of the stereotype is gradual, as Yousef is Giuseppe's friend. The most potent kernel of suspicion arises from another technological medium of communication—the boat's wireless radio communication. Nello, a colleague who is also fishing in the vicinity, warns Giuseppe of the news story, which he too has heard. As Gloria Pastorino explains in her detailed analysis of the film:

> The news is not presented as a possibility by Nello: "They say Yousef is a terrorist," no argument about it. The radio said it, it must be true. The idea that it could be a case of homonymy does not even enter Nello's mind. (Pastorino 316)

The importance of the "fact" in the creation of Orientalist discourse is evident here, as Said says:

> Rather than using all the figures of speech associated with the Orient—its strangeness, its difference, its exotic sensuousness, and so forth—we can generalize about them as [...] they are all declarative and self-evident; the tense they employ is the timeless eternal; they convey an impression of repetition and strength; they are always symmetrical to, and yet diametrically inferior to, a European equivalent, which is sometimes specified, sometimes not. For all these functions, it is frequently enough to use the simple copula is. Thus Mohammed *is* an

> imposter [...] No background need be given; the evidence necessary to convict Mohammed is contained in the "is." [...] Finally, of course, such categories as imposter (or Oriental, for that matter) imply, indeed require, an opposite that is neither fraudulently something else nor endlessly in need of explicit identification. And that opposite is "Occidental," or in Mohammed's case, Jesus. (Said, *Orientalism* 72)

This declarative quality of Orientalism as described by Said is the primary motor of the film. Nello declares that Yousef is a terrorist, and therefore he is. The repetition of the declaration only serves to provide more power to Giuseppe, who starts to build a case that, to him, seems solid, but is flimsy at best in reality. The most interesting aspect of *Io, l'altro* is that representation of the link between the declarative violence of mass-media and other such "documents" of reality and the other form of knowledge that is so important for the power vested in the stereotype; the fantastical and the imaginary realm of knowledge where desire and fear imagine and substitute for the real.

Melliti has created an ingenious way to represent the stereotype as if it were a hallucination or madness, una *follia*, as Giuseppe himself describes it. The suspension of identities so carefully maintained through friendship breaks as the madness of the stereotype forces Giuseppe to suspect, and then become convinced that Yousef is indeed the terrorist responsible for the Madrid bombings. He asks Yousef is he has ever been to Spain, and Yousef says: "Yes, only one time." This innocent statement becomes yet another "citation," yet another piece of evidence that builds Giuseppe's case. The other important document that confirms Giuseppe's suspicions is yet another news story, this time in print form. Searching Yousef's pockets, Giuseppe finds a newspaper clipping on Al Qaeda's Al Zarkawi. This turns out to be a mis-reading, as he is looking at the wrong side of the clipping (the other side contains a news clipping of the *Acireale* football match, which was the reason why Yousef had clipped it). It is important to note is that the revelation of this "fact" does not make a difference or convince Giuseppe that he is wrong. Even when faced with this new fact by Yousef, he is insistent on his suspicion, or rather, certainty, as the stereotype is fixed by this point and is only anxiously repeated, as if it were a form of paranoia. The radical realism, citation of news "facts" is not needed anymore.

Ambivalent Moralities

The very facts that should cause Giuseppe to pause in his drive to find Yousef guilty become the very reason for him to judge him: that Yousef was treated as a part of his family, that he eats lunch at Giuseppe's home every Sunday and is included within the *oikos* of the home, becomes yet another "fact" to demonstrate how well he was able to hide his true identity. The radio news update describes the terrorist as someone who "worked and lived integrated within the social fabric for many years" becomes a point against Yousef rather than a reason to rationally rethink unfounded suspicions. When he is betrayed by Giuseppe, who locks him up in the ice locker of the boat, and brings up the radio as his source of authoritative information, Yousef screams at Giuseppe: "Has the Radio become the Koran? Now the Koran is the Radio?" Yousef's outburst points directly to the flaw in Giuseppe's thinking, and to the mechanism with which the stereotype of the Arab-as-terrorist was fixed in his mind. When the citations become cyclical, every exception only confirms the rule rather than challenges it. The migrant is the criminal, as the words of the radio are sacrosanct as if they were those written in the Koran. The final murder of Yousef is also represented as a hallucination or a bout of madness on Giuseppe's part. The scene is shot in a sequence of both disorienting slow motion and quickly edited images of the objects that "prove" Yousef's guilt (the radio, the newspaper clipping). A blurry point-of-view shot represents Giuseppe's extreme stereotyping of Yousef's identity—it is a visual representation of the paranoia brought about by the menace generated by his inherent physical and cultural hybridity (Figure 32). This final image of threatening hybridity leads to Yousef's murder.

Figure 32: The double vision caused by hybridity. *I'o, l'altro*

Conclusion

Inside the Paradise of Marvelous Bodies

The previous chapters flesh out a plethora of marvelous bodies that provoke suspension and stupor: "Ambivalent Geographies" describes Garrone's Nigerian prostitutes, Albanian laborers and Ahmed/Amedeo, the Egyptian gas attendant; Gino and Spiro/Michele in *Lamerica*; the lost-at-sea Sandro (momentarily) in *Quando sei nato;* and Crialese's disempowered Sicilian fishermen and migrant bodies, all suspended in the marvelous realm of the SEA. "Ambivalent Desires" illustrates several unstable visual positionings of characters, both Italian and non. Through these volatile locations of desire on screen, roles embodying masculinity and womanhood are occasionally subverted. Examples of these suspensions were: the problematic representation of Kwaku as a focalizer rather than a narrator in *Pummarò*; the conflicted and delimited romance between Assane and Caterina in *Lettere dal Sahara*; Mattia/Kamal's suspended nationality and masculinity in *Lezioni di cioccolato*; and finally, Licu's humoristic representation as an "Ital-Bengali" by Moroni. Finally, "Ambivalent Moralities" discusses suspended identities vis-à-vis their productive and destructive roles in society; Irene and Sonia's enigmatic Eastern-European *femme-fatales* pull at viewers conflicting feelings of fascination and horror toward the female migrant body, rendering them marvelous. Similarly, Melliti conjures up a suspended body in Yousef, but one who is unjustly categorized as a terrorist through gradual stereotyping, leading to his final demise.

Unlike these films, productions such as Comencini's *Bianco e nero* and Munzi's *Il resto della notte* demonstrate a tendency to be unable to go beyond the realm of orientalist citation, thus stereotyping the migrant and Italian bodies into relatively fixed identities. I show how cinematic form is related to content by articulating how such films tend to not portray characters and the general cultural diegetic worlds they inhabit in the humoristic mode, often resorting to more realist modes of representation.

For many reasons a small gem of a film, Paola Randi's film *Into Paradiso* (*Inside Paradise*, 2010) can be taken as an example of the current end-point of new migrant cinema's twenty-year-long trajectory from primarily realist productions to films containing more genre experimentation and representations of cultural hybridity in the humoristic mode that actively question the Self/Other dichotomy. As seen through various examples in the previous chapters, filmmakers have undertaken this questioning of cultural stereotypes through deployment of marvelous bodies within the diegetic worlds and/or through meta-cinematic and self-reflexive stylistic choices that caused viewers to reflect upon their affective connections to the bodies on screen. *Into Paradiso* reveals one of the many creative paths that new migrant cinema is currently pursuing and might follow in the future years as immigration continues to roil Italian society's understanding of its chronically ambivalent position in a globalized world. For these reasons, I will employ this interesting film as our guide to this conclusion to the exploration of Italy's new migrant cinema.

Into Paradiso narrates the tale of an immigrant subject/protagonist, but equally divides our attention between two characters, a recently unemployed Neapolitan biologist, Alfonso D'Onofrio, and a Sri Lankan cricket champion, Gayan Pereira. This splitting of the film's interests into not one immigrant subject but two characters (one Italian and another immigrant) already shows how the initial neo-neorealistic tendency to meticulously understand immigration as a "social issue" through the recording of the immigrant experience (such as in *Pummarò*) has waned and diffused into a more multi-pronged humoristic questioning of a multiplicity of identities. Randi's premise creates not one, but two marvelous bodies. Thus, it is yet another thematic choice that amply demonstrates how new migrant cinema in Italy is "detourist." Such films utilize the arrival of the immigrants into Italian society as an occasion to reexamine the nation itself in addition to representing their intended objects or attractions of their gaze, the immigrant body, just as the other marvelous bodies in this book have done.

Conclusion

Alfonso and Gayan are not analogous to representations of the "colonizer" and "colonized" respectively. Randi's characterization of these two protagonists allows them to be Bhabha's "colonial subjects," since both are suspended by their unusual backgrounds and peculiar personalities; the unattractive and underwhelming Italian (and importantly, southern Italian Neapolitan) Alfonso is paradoxically the submissive cowardly character who lives inside a multi-story urban cemetery and pines for his dead mother. Alfonso is fired from his job as a university researcher without any warning or explanations and takes the blow without a single word or gesture of rebellion. Gayan, on the other hand, disrupts the stereotype of the immigrant as either underprivileged, poor, lazy, or a criminal; he is one of the most important sporting celebrities in his home country, and this important aspect frames his arrival to Italy. Indeed, in one of the first shots that depict him, a fellow Sri Lankan migrant recognizes Gayan and immediately takes a "selfie" with him, thus documenting and cementing his celebrity status on screen with a photographic image (Figure 33). Gayan is tall, athletic, serious, determined, and also used to a certain lifestyle that the rich and famous typically enjoy. His linguistic

Figure 33: Gayan as celebrity cricketer. *Into Paradiso*

hold on Italian is excellent, further reinforcing his hybridity. The viewer takes Gayan's Italian for granted even though no explanation is offered as to why a recent arrival in Italy should not have a stereotypically "migrant Italian" marker. His expectations of a materially comfortable and rewarding new life in Italy are dashed when he discovers that his cousin, who he has traveled to join, is in actuality not a rich immigrant as he was made to believe though photographs, but works as a *badante*—a caretaker for a rich elderly Italian woman. In a classic *commedia equivoco* (mix-up), the photographs that his cousin sent him were not of his own home, but of his employer's luxurious apartment.

Characters that switch or oscillate between Manichean Italian (Self) and Migrant (Other) identities occur frequently in films studied in this book. I have demonstrated how Gianni Amelio's *Lamerica* provides us one of the most elaborate of these suspended marvelous bodies—that of Gino and Spiro/Michele. Indeed, I show that due to the plot and stylistic choices, this film is epic and humoristic rather than neo-neorealistic in its understanding of Italy's colonial and postcolonial relationship with Albania. In the final sequence shot on the ferry taking migrants from Albania to Italy, Gino is stripped of his Italian-ness, while Spiro/Michele, already suspended beyond demarcated cultural histories and geographies, thinks that he is going to America as one of the many Italians that departed for the New World in the first half of the twentieth century. In this final scene, the Mediterranean Sea becomes a *locus amoenus* of suspension, a quintessential example of Bhabha's in-between "third space" of the interstices where culture "works."

The Mediterranean also becomes the location for other such suspensions, such as in Tullio Giordana's *Quando sei nato*. Sandro, the adolescent protagonist, does get stripped of his bourgeois Northern Italian identity when he is lost at sea and picked up by a boat full of migrants. His suspension is problematic, as it does not completely go beyond the duality of the immigrant/Italian. As soon as Sandro arrives on land, the filmmakers' "politics of sentimentality" create a calibrated and controlled di/vision in a multicultural vision of society rather than a hybrid one. Hybridity in the Bhabhian sense remains restricted to the world of childhood rather than also permeating the adult world. A film in which the Mediterranean becomes a more complex location of hybridity is Crialese's *Terraferma*. A far more intricate production than *Quando sei nato*, this film accomplishes suspension of rigid identities by providing an alternative conceptual dichotomy to the viewers: that of the LAND versus the SEA. Not unlike Antonioni's *L'avventura*, the sea in *Terraferma* is represented as a psychological, moral, and ideological "third space" which belongs to *both* the impoverished Sicilian fishermen and the desperate migrants that seek to cross it. Utilizing the haptic properties of the sea, Crialese provides the viewer with an innovative, literally immersive experience of suspension where the fluidity of the sea provides a humoristic "feeling of the other," and alternative method of thinking of bodies and identities in contrast to the violent institutional cruelty of the touristic and governmental (land-based) institutions in the film. The suspended marvelous marine bodies of *Terraferma*, in opposition to the rigid stereotyping of these institutions, represent the double possibilities present in hybridity: they offer subverted, translated, and transformed identities, but also identities that offer possibilities of new structures, identities, spaces, and hegemonies.

Political authority is scrutinized in *Into Paradiso* through the character of the supercilious, scheming, and self-serving Vincenzo Cacace. Alfonso has been tricked by this local slimeball politician to carry a "gift" to some unknown friends in return for the vague promise of being reinstated to this job through Cacace's influential connections. This gift turns out be a gun that has been used in the assassination of a rival gang member, and Cacace has been ordered to have it delivered to some men by a local Camorra boss. As Alfonso, unaware of the box's contents, tries to make the delivery of this "gift," a rival gang rides up in a Vespa and shoots the men who approach him to pick up the consignment. Alfonso makes a hasty escape, and accidently ends up in "Fondaco Paradiso" (Paradise Lane)—a magical Bhabhian third space where a well-established Sri Lankan community lives. Stuck with Cacace in Gayan's rooftop shack, Alfonso and Gayan find their destinies united for the rest of the film.

Filmmaker Randi was certain that she wanted to approach the question of Italian society's problems through the tradition of the *commedia all'italiana,* utilizing irony. In an interview, she attributes her sighting of one single incongruent scene in Piazza Dante in Naples that inspired her to write this particular story: "on one side, some scugnizzi [Neapolitan street urchins] were playing soccer, and on the other side a group of Sri Lankans, very elegantly dressed, were playing cricket, and right there, I told myself that it was the story I was looking for" (Randi). The contradiction witnessed in the very public stage of the Italian piazza arises from the fact that it is the supposedly subaltern migrant bodies that are elegantly dressed, playing the quintessential game of the colonial elite that they have appropriated, whereas the native population, the supposedly hegemonic Italians, are translated into *scugnizzi,* the famous Neapolitan subaltern icons of a perpetually poverty-stricken subproletariat. This incongruence provides the director with a manifest "discrepant experience," to use Edward Said's phrase. As described in Chapter 2, the *commedia all'italiana* tradition thrived on such discrepant experiences in the Sixties, as they provided a "feeling of the Other" within the Self that could be harnessed to expose hypocritical societal values as well as various inequalities and injustices. It is therefore not surprising that Randi should latch on to that arresting image full of contradictory meanings and liminal bodies in the piazza in order to develop a migrant film that represents fluid identities. The image that Randi saw is a moment of the marvelous—a moment of the *suspension of a cyclical repetition of identification*. The moment when Randi sees the non-white migrants in elegant cricket gear, and the white Italian boys in relatively poor conditions, they all become marvelous bodies, whose identities are suspended between these national categories. The marvelous, that unsaid eruption of an ambivalent feeling provoked by the marvelous body, coincides with Randi's moment of *stupor*—a feeling of being dazed but also astonished, where the spectacle becomes not one of pleasure in access to the stereotype but an experience of disorientation, of going *beyond*. The suspension offered by this incongruent image is opposed by the visibility of the stereotype-as-fetish of the racial/colonial Other, which is "at once the point of identity ("Look, a Negro") and at the same time a problem for the attempted closure with discourse" (Bhabha 116).

Experiences of stupor such as the discrepant scene witnessed by Randi characterize key scenes in most films in this book—indeed I disclose how stupor, whether felt by characters within the diegetic world or felt by the viewer as a result of a stylistic choice or plot twist, is a crucial visual/thematic symptom that reveals the precise cinematic moment of the humoristic suspension of bodies that render them marvelous. I therefore characterize the tradition of the *commedia all'italiana*—with its meticulous use of moments of stupor and its humoristic treatment of identities as "masks"—as a sophisticated and non-didactic "model" tradition that penetratingly represents Italy's in-between status as an "almost European—but not quite" nation. I undertake a rehabilitation of this relatively ignored and lesser-loved sibling to neorealism in this book both for its utility in helping scholars better understand the cultural functions of cinematic humor (as opposed to realism or the comic) as well as for its massively understated and understudied influence in Italian cinema.

The chapter on "Ambivalent Desires" contains several films that explore gender and sexuality by utilizing the humoristic mode with varying results. Stupor occurs in Cupellini's *Lezioni di cioccolato* through a classic *commedia* story of mistaken/swapped identities. In this case, Italian Mattia is forced to masquerade as Egyptian Kamal. The subversion of power that occurs in this film allows the filmmakers to provide the Italian audiences with a humoristic feeling of being the migrant Other. As I have tried to demonstrate in my analysis of this film, the oscillation between Mattia's Italian and Egyptian identities mirrors an almost more subversive oscillation in his masculinity. The romance in this romantic comedy only becomes possible due to this important oscillation, which allows a strong-willed Cecilia to accept Mattia/Kamal as her lover. *Lezioni di cioccolato* thus allows the Italian viewer to "daydream" the "Other" yet this fantasy is not a completely comfortable Orientalized one, but one that allows for a controlled game of libidinous possibilities, both enticing and menacing, to take place on the screen.

While *Lezioni di cioccolato* provides some possibilities of fantasizing the Other through the *commedia* tradition, *Bianco e nero* is an example of a film in the more generic rom-com genre that does not provide a Pirandellian "feeling of the Other." Rather than a humoristic representation of identities, Comencini's film unwittingly perpetuates hierarchies of race, social class, and most importantly, gender in order to preserve and maintain the image of the erotic immigrant body. *Bianco e nero* effectively perpetuates "separate but equal" multiculturalism rather than Bhabhian hybridity by continuous voyeurism and fetishistic scopophilia of Nadine's body. Essentially, her body is caught in a consumerist postcolonial stereotype with no possibilities of becoming a marvelous body.

In contrast to *Bianco e nero,* in *Into Paradiso* Pirandellian humor allows for several meta-cinematic moments of stupor, in a way that questions the construction of *all* identities, including that of the film itself. This moment of stupor is portrayed through three "daydream" sequences, which are filmed in a unique style. The entry into this meta-cinematic "paradise," a kind of cinematic third

Conclusion

space, or stupor if you will, occurs whenever Alfonso wants to escape from his reality and enter a daydreaming state. This is not simply a function that drives the plot, it is a way for the director to state her artistic intentions and situate as well as diffuse her agency as the author of the cinematic voice. Indeed, Randi declares that the capacity to daydream is what makes us *all* capable of being filmmakers in our mind's eye—our ability to *voluntarily* fantasize and meld the real and the imagined parallels the cinematic urge to be a desiring machine. She distinguishes between active daydreaming and dreaming, which "is involuntary to a large degree."

Alfonso enters his daydreaming state by inserting earplugs into his ears. When viewers watch him carry out this action of insertion, the sounds of the diegetic world are accordingly blocked out. We therefore enter an inner sanctum through a very self-reflexive use of sound. In the first of these dream episodes, Alfonso imagines he is in the police station as he tries to make his escape from the rooftop prison of Paradiso Apartments (Figure 34). In this sequence,

Figure 34: Daydream sequence 1. *Into Paradiso*

he discusses various escape strategies with the police officer, thus allowing the viewer to examine these options and almost play an active role in imagining how the plot should develop. The second daydream sequence continues to point toward the construction of the film via a sequence in which Alfonso re-imagines the scene in which the rival gang members shoot the Camorra men. Shot inside Gayan's dark shack resembling a photographic dark room much akin to a cinema hall, Alfonso (and the viewer who shares his point of view) projects his mind's images onto food cans and other objects set out by him on the table (Figure 35). The images re-screen the shootout scene and re-imagine it again and again, not as if the scene were a real event in the diegetic world of the film, but as it the images were different takes of a shot where Alfonso himself is the director.

Figure 35: Reimagining the past: Daydream Sequence 2.
Into Paradiso

Similar meta-cinematic moments of self-reflexivity occur in Matteo Garrone's *Terra di mezzo*. For example, in the scene where a socially challenged young lady wonders aloud at the possibilities of dating her plumber, Garrone exposes his own artistic *equivoco* (ambivalence) toward being the authoritative voice in stereotyping identities related to class, gender, race, and nationality, both Italian and non. Throughout the film, Garrone displays a humoristic and ironic touch in representing very difficult instances of migrant life, providing a stunningly innovative twist to the typical understanding of *cinema engagé* that blurs the thin red line between fiction and documentary, realism and fantasy.

The final daydreaming sequence in *Into Paradiso* occurs as Paradise Apartments is stormed by the Camorra boss's henchmen, who are still seeking the missing Alfonso, Vincenzo, and the missing gun. As the magical period of suspension in this Bhabhian third space is threatened by violence, Alfonso once again plugs his ears and willfully imagines a scene in which he is not on the verge of being killed, but is instead having a romantic Bollywood-style champagne date with Giacinta, his love interest—a Sri Lankan single mother who is Gayan's relative. Through an excellent sequence of parallel editing that builds up rhythmic tension, Alfonso projects his orientalist fantasies of the exotic woman on screen for the viewers to consume as a spectacle, while the gang members search the apartment complex for the missing men. Randi also deftly undercuts the problematic sexual and racial politics of this imaginative act with excellent irony—as Giacinta looks at her elaborate sari and jewelry, telling Alfonso,

Conclusion

"But ... I am dressed like an *Indian!*" As Edward Said points out in *Orientalism*, in probably his most important contention, the discursive practices of Orientalism have little bearing, if any at all, on its actual putative subject. Giacinta's single comment humoristically chides Alfonso's (and the Italian audience's) naïve projection of the desirable Oriental Other while allowing him to imagine this moment of fantasy as an escape from the harsh reality of the approaching gunmen and possible death (Figure 36). Giacinta's intervention also disrupts this hermeneutically sealed visual fantasy, thus co-opting his problematic agency within the desiring machine. The logic of male heterosexual scopophilia, which mirrors the logic of Orientalism, is thus upended. It is Giacinta who slaps Alfonso (literally) out of his fantasy world at the end of this last daydream sequence, and it is once again Giacinta who upbraids Gayan and points to the fact that he cannot live in his own financially comfortable paradise anymore—that in Italy "you need to work to put food on the table" (Randi).

Figure 36: Daydream Sequence 3. *Into Paradiso*

Desiring and desired bodies abound in the films discussed in this book. As Robert Young states, fantasies of desire abound in colonial discourse, as they are the location for the control and calibration of both biological and cultural hybridity:

> It was through the category of race that colonialism itself was theoretically focused, represented and justified in the nineteenth century, it was also through racial relations that much cultural interaction was practiced. The ideology of race, a semiotic system in the guise of ethnology, the "science of races," from the 1840s onwards necessarily worked according to a doubled logic, according to which it both enforced and policed the differences between the whites and the non-whites, but at the same time focused fetishistically upon the product of

the contacts between them. Colonialism was always locked into the machine of desire [...] Folded within the scientific accounts of race, a central assumption and paranoid fantasy was endlessly repeated: the uncontrollable sexual drive of the non-white races and their limitless fertility. (Young 180–81)

Italy's chronic ambivalence vis-à-vis the racial boundaries of its own nation allows for a complicated series of fantasies around Italian and migrant sexual desire and the encounter's reproductive possibilities. The theme of sexual and reproductive transgression across rigid national, racial, and cultural boundaries is all the more ironic in a nation whose birth rate, already the lowest in the European Union, is sustained only due to the growing number of immigrant children.[1] Even the very fact that the Italian nation's demographic health is being given a dose of much needed vitality by its new migrants, and the reality that immigrant children constitute one in five new births in Italy today, can be perversely interpreted to fuel the stereotype of the racial other possessing, to use Young's phrases, "uncontrollable sexual drive" and "limitless fertility." As I demonstrate in my analysis of the ordering of visuals in *Pummarò* and *Lettere dal Sahara*, viewers are provided with a "safe" space to negotiate their fascination and horror toward interracial desire and its biological and cultural consequences. As soon as romantic interest between Kwaku and Eleanora in *Pummarò* and between Assane and Caterina in *Lettere* seems to evolve into a stable point of equilibrium, a limit is reached. The possibility of transgression of racial boundaries, or a suspension of their racialized bodies through a stable union, is too much to display on screen. Violent racial stereotyping therefore occurs in both films at these points. Through my interpretation of the films, I show how these seemingly sudden violent irruptions of racial violence are cinematic procedures that not only represent the constant threat of physical and mental abuse faced by blacks in Italian society, but also safely contain and seal off the narrative possibility of any long-lived intimacy between the Italian woman and the black man.

Tracing my steps back to *Into Paradiso*, I would like to draw attention to the overarching metaphor present in the film, as it is quite an appropriate one to close a study of Italian/migrant cinematic bodies. Alfonso elaborates this metaphor in the final climactic sequence in the surreal abandoned supermarket that is the mob boss's stronghold. He has decided to be a master of his own destiny and after an escape from his confinement in Paradise Apartments by masquerading as a member of the Sri Lankan cricket team, decides to hand over the gun and Cacace back to the Camorra boss. Alfonso explains his innocence to the boss. He then goes on to tell him:

> Io sono uno scienziato. Io studio la migrazione delle cellule. Le cellule communicano tra di loro, parlano, e si dicono cose importanti. Per esempio, dicono cose come "Io esisto, io sono qui. Occupo questo spazio." Però ogni tanto certe cellule non ascoltano più, impazziscono. E io cerco di capire come comunicare con loro, queste cellule impazzite. Gli dico di fare apoptosi. Cioè, di autodistruggersi. Per far campare le altre. Perché altrimenti queste cellule impazzite si moltiplicano, si diffondono e distruggono tutto quello che c'è intorno. Diventano un cancro.
> Come questo stronzo qui.
> Come voi tutti.

> I am a scientist. I study cell migration. Cells communicate with each other, they talk, they say important things. For example, they say things like "I exist, I am here. I occupy this space." But once in a while, certain cells don't listen anymore, they go crazy. And I try to understand how to communicate with them, with these mad cells. I tell them to commit apoptosis. That is, to self-destruct. In order to let the other (cells) live. Because otherwise these mad cells multiply, they spread and destroy everything that surrounds them. They become a cancer.
> Like this shithead here.
> Like you all.

Randi's biological metaphor illustrates the central question in this book of communication between bodies and cultures in the context of migration. The metaphor underlines Randi's conscious reflexive act of thinking about how to represent fluid identities through cinema—she wonders how to represent and therefore communicate about personal and collective identities through visual, aural, and haptic cues. Her answer is to represent identities with a degree of irony, utilizing the humoristic mode to shake away Manichean notions of Self/Other in a wonderfully eccentric Neapolitan urban landscape.

The question of criminality and illegality, the focus of the final chapter, also arises in this final scene. *Into Paradiso* tackles the stereotype of the immigrant-as-criminal headlong and displays how it is the Italians themselves who are often responsible for undesirable violent activity. In this way, Randi elegantly diffuses/diverts stereotypes of the migrant-as-criminal. In addition to de-racializing and de-nationalizing the abject figure "criminal," the filmmaker uses humor to ridicule and thus subvert any potential glorification. She does so by portraying the *camorristi* as exaggerated grotesque masks in the *commedia* tradition: they are ugly and unkempt, and have very awkward adolescent wardrobe choices. Their boss binge eats Neapolitan sweets such as the *sfogliatella* and has a childish, effeminate giggle that subverts the iconic image of the crime boss as an enviable epitome of masculinity. If one must understand Orientalism as a "radical realism" as I have called it in my analysis of *Il resto della notte* in Chapter 5, then Randi's representation of the criminal world is its complete antithesis: the *camorra* here is an organization made up of infantile violent child-men without any ability to communicate and live in society in a productive and creative way. The true cancer of Neapolitan society.

Munzi's film does the opposite of Randi's operation of diffusion and substitution of the stereotype of the ugly migrant, presenting viewers with a fantasy-drama of building menace. *Il resto della notte* slowly and gradually builds audience expectation toward confirmation that Maria is indeed a thief. A vast collection of visual and thematic techniques serves to first frame and then confirm the encounter between Italians and migrants as a dangerous and destabilizing influence in society today. True to the citational quality of Orientalism, Munzi's film does not generalize openly, but presents viewers with one case study. However, as the stereotype-as-fetish must repeat itself *ad infinitum* to gain agency, this single representation in the realistic mode of migrant criminality only confirms the pattern for the Italian viewers who are faced with a media barrage of daily stories of crimes committed by immigrants. The Bossi-Fini law of 2009 mandated that mere presence in Italian territory without documentation is a crime. In a cinematic analogy, mere presence of the stolen pearl earrings damns that immigrant, and by consequence, all immigrants, as potentially double-faced undesirable elements of contemporary society.

Building menace also features prominently in Tornatore's masterfully wrought noir-thriller-splatter *La sconosciuta*. However, unlike Munzi, Tornatore never confirms the stereotype, but allows the audience to create a troubling set of contradictory feelings of both attraction and foreboding toward the central character, Irena, by playing carefully with audience affect. Split between these opposing feelings, the unknown woman thus becomes a marvelous body, whose biological and psychological ambivalence suspends her beyond the Mother/Whore, Caretaker/Murderer, Italian/Migrant dichotomies. Similarly, Capotondi's film *La doppia ora* features another fascinating ambivalent character, Sonia, who tugs the viewer's allegiance in opposite directions, thus effectively suspending her beyond stereotypes.

The diverse and sometimes problematic collection of cinematic first-responses to Italy's vital crisis of immigration studied in this book reflects the nation's cultural designation as Europe's internal Other. Every film discussed here represents a discrete cultural "coping strategy" that seeks to stabilize the nation's *oikos* via detourism. The study of these cinematic products is therefore all the more relevant and important as it can lead to the better understanding of the continuing hybridization of personal and collective identities in Europe and beyond. It is my hope that this thematically categorized analysis will encourage students and scholars to continue exploring the rich and unique nature of Italy's new migrant cinema due to its complex relationship with the nation's own fraught cultural history. I explicitly intended to create a dynamic link between Italy's new migrant cinema and historical genres of Italian cinema in order to inspire further discussion of the continued influence on Italian filmmakers of neorealism and the various humoristic genres that follow it. An unintended but welcome consequence of this contextualization has been my rehabilitation and placement of the *commedia all'italiana* on par with neorealism as a dominant genre in Italian cinema. Understanding humor (strictly understood in the Pirandellian use of the word) as a consistent major critical tool in Italian cinema allows for a weakening of some of the fetishistic importance placed upon neorealism by scholars of cinema.

In addition to contextualizing new migrant cinema in Italian cinematic history, I also seek to establish that the concepts of hybridity contained in postcolonial theory, particularly in Bhabha's notions of the stereotype-as-fetish and mimicry, can provide an urgent as well as detailed analysis of transnational cultures in a rapidly changing world by providing a critical counterpoint to popular as well as scholarly approaches that mischaracterize hybridity as a form of multiculturalism. Indeed, it is becoming all the more urgent for scholars to further Bhabha's understanding of the management of cultural discourse through stereotype and mimicry as Europe and the rest of the world become increasingly polarized between seemingly antagonistic identities.

Through an understanding of the various strategies employed by the filmmakers and highlighting the similarities and contrasts between the detourist films studied in this book, it becomes evident that Italy's chronic ambivalence and the historical tension between Neorealism and post-Neorealism haunt the nation's cinematic exploration of immigration in two ways. The first consequence of this tension, caused by unintended slips or by deliberate stylistic experimentation with various degrees of realism and humor, is the creation of marvelous bodies that are momentarily neither completely Italian nor immigrant. Second, these root tensions also cause a "generic ambivalence" in the films explored, i.e., the Italian films on immigration tend to be hybrids in terms of tone, style, and genre. In representing the human body, they often toe the fine line between realism and artifice, as well as documentary and fiction.[2] The repeated presence of marvelous bodies and a pervasive generic hybridity in turn are proof of Italy's own chronic ambivalence resulting from its history as a cultural crossroads of the Mediterranean.

Notes

Introduction

1. For a thorough analysis of the various forms of popular Italian cinema that reflect domestic filmmakers' tastes, see Bayman and Rigoletto, *Popular Italian Cinema*.

2. For an excellent analysis of the construction of whiteness and blackness in Italian popular imagination from colonial times to the present, see Giuliani and Lombardi-Diop.

3. For a diverse range of approaches being recently undertaken to understand cultural hybridity in the context of Italian colonial and postcolonial studies, see Andall and Duncan.

4. From this point forward, I will not place the term "chronic ambivalence" in quotation marks as it has been established as a new term here.

5. For an earlier formulation of this concept, see Vetri Nathan, "Mimic-Nation, Mimic-Men: Contextualizing Italy's Migration Culture through Bhabha."

6. For a complete listing of these films, please refer to Franca Pellegrini's excellent *Italian Cinema and Immigration Database*.

7. For example, in 2004, Italy recorded 1.9 million legal foreign residents, while the most recent census figures from 2013 indicate an increase to almost 4.4 million "Cittadini stranieri in Italia—2013". These figures can be compared to those at the beginning of the immigration phenomenon, but total numbers can be hard to pin down due to differing methodologies of institutions that have collected this data in the past. Yet, as a general indication, in 1990, after the Martelli law granting legal amnesty to foreign presences in the nation was applied, there were only 238,130 residents from African nations and only 145,182 from Asian countries, as compared to the 4.4 million legal immigrant residents in 2013 (*L'altro diritto* Ch.1).

8. Alemanno was appointed as provincial secretary for the Fronte della gioventù, the youth wing of the MSI (Movimento Sociale Italiano), a neo-fascist party, in 1982. Then in 1988 he took Gianfranco Fini's post as its national secretary.

9. "Under the new law, an immigrant who is stopped without a residence permit will be accompanied to the border and expelled immediately. Immigrants are also subject to arrest and detention of six to twelve months, to be followed by immediate deportation, if caught attempting to re-enter Italy before the expiry of a re-entry ban. A second offence is punishable by up to four years imprisonment. […] Also under the new law, the time limit for seclusion in detention centres whilst waiting for extradition has been extended from thirty days to sixty days and asylum seekers will be placed in detention while awaiting asylum review, in contravention of Article 5 of the European Convention on Human Rights ("Harsh Immigration Law Passed in Italy").

10. For an example of the debate on the ethics of showing the images of Kurdi's body in the media, see Mackey, "Brutal Images of Syrian Boy Drowned Off Turkey Must Be Seen, Activists Say."

11. As of September 1, 2015, the International Organization for Migration (IOM) estimates that a total of more than 350,000 migrants have arrived in Europe, principally from conflict regions such as Syria and Afghanistan. The dead bodies found in the Mediterranean number 2664 as of that date, most of them found in the waters between Libya and Italy ("International Organization for Migration").

12. See Graziella Parati, *Migration Italy: The Art of Talking Back in a Destination Culture*; Ian Chambers, *Mediterranean Crossings the Politics of an Interrupted Modernity*; Grace Russo Bullaro, *From Terrone to Extracomunitario*; Alessandro Dal Lago, *Non-persone: L'esclusione dei migranti in una società globale*.

13. See the chapter by Silvia Camilotti entitled "Continenti asiatici e popoli dimenticati" in Gnisci.

14. I am referring to Gnisci's criticism of Editrice Laterza's excellent collection *Pecore nere,* edited by F. Capitani and E. Coen. See footnote in Gnisci, p. 30.

15. For a complete breakdown and a list of the astonishing variety of immigrants in Italy from around the globe, see "Cittadini Stranieri."

16. *Screening of the Film: The Orchestra of Piazza Vittorio*. This description was first added to the official website of the film, but at the time of writing had been removed. You can access this blurb now at http://www.iictoronto.esteri.it.

17. See Caminati; Howie; Kiliçbay; and Prono.

Chapter One

1. For an outline of Italy's hesitant and belated inclusion as a subject of analysis in postcolonial studies, see Miguel Mellino, "Italy and Postcolonial Studies: A Difficult Encounter."

2. For an earlier formulation of my description of Bhabhian hybridity and Italy's immigration culture, please see my "Mimic-Nation, Mimic-Men."

3. The Southern Question has been the subject of extensive scholarship. Please refer to some of the following key works for more information: Antonio Gramsci and Pasquale Verdicchio, *The Southern Question;* Nelson Moe, *The View from Vesuvius;* John Dickie, *Darkest Italy.*

4. I believe that the study of *i*mmigration *to* Italy will be an excellent way to renew the study of *e*migration *from* Italy to places such as the Americas in the future. Indeed, a major voice in the field of Italian-American Studies, Anthony Tamburri, has been urging exactly this kind of dialogue in order to provide mutually enriching scholarship.

5. For a comprehensive analysis of Italy's representations of mixed-race subjects in Italian cinema from colonial times to present, see Shelleen Greene, *Equivocal Subjects.*

6. For details, see Stephen Greenblatt, *Marvelous Possessions.*

Chapter Two
1. See the "Tabelle riassuntive" in Umberto Rossi, "Appendice statistica," in Napolitano 229–33.
2. Napolitano 229–33.
3. For a succinct summary of the critical reception of the *commedie all'italiana*, see Claudio Camerini, "I critici e la commedia all'italiana: Le occasioni perdute," in Napolitano 179–92.
4. For an exploration of the hidden locations of ambivalence in Neorealist films, see Rocchio, *Cinema of Anxiety*.
5. For a similar call to define neorealism in cultural terms rather than in the context of a cinematic aesthetic, see Sergio J. Pacifici, "Notes toward a Definition of Neorealism.
6. See, for example, Moliterno 35.

Chapter Three
1. One such example is *The Guardian*'s first sentence of the film's review: "Matteo Garrone has created a gruelling species of neo-neorealist Italian cinema from Roberto Saviano's bestselling book *Gomorra* (or, in English, *Gomorrah*), about the power and reach of the Neapolitan mob: the camorra" (Bradshaw).
2. Maurizio Braucci, "Gomorra, il film: Conversazione con Matteo Garrone," in De Sanctis et al. All translations from the Italian are my own.

Chapter Four
1. Villa Literno was an emblematic location, chosen for its centrality in the discussion of Italy's immigration question in the early 1990s. It was in this town near Caserta that Jerry Masslo, a black South African tomato, was killed in 1989. Whether this killing was racially motivated or not was never established in the trial, but it became a symbol of the immigrants' often difficult and precarious situation in Italy.

Chapter Five
1. "L'uomo occidentale è riuscito ad ottenere tutte le ricchezze che l'umanità ha sempre sognato. L'occidente è riuscito a diventare materialmente ricco. Ma ora è stanco, appesantito. Il viaggio gli ha rubato l'anima. Questo uomo è sfinito. Tutto ciò che ha bisogno è a portata di mano, ma l'uomo in quanto tale non c'è più. Ora è il vostro momento. Avete la possibilità di diventare consapevoli. Consapevoli del fatto che dietro a tutte queste false verità ... c'è una volonta precisa. Cattiva. Quella di rendervi deboli e insicuri. Schiavi della paura. La soluzione è soltanto una. La resa. Arrendetevi! Io da tempo ho smesso di cercare di diventare qualcosa di diverso. Di ciò che sono. Oggi è un altro giorno prezioso sulla terra e quindi guardiamoci intorno, nell'amore. Tutti insieme—La gioa è con noi! Dentro di noi! Noi siamo! Sì, noi siamo! Noi viviamo! Noi siamo unici, insostituibili, perfetti!"
2. *Buonismo* is an Italian word used frequently in political discourse in contemporary Italy but is a difficult word to translate into English. The

Grandidizionari.it defines it as "Atteggiamento di benevola apertura e comprensione per tutte le posizioni, accusato di non andare al di là di generici appelli moralistici, capaci solo di produrre compromessi confusi e di basso livello" ("A manner of benevolent openness and understanding for all positions, accused of not going beyond general moralistic appeals, capable of only producing confusing compromises of a low standard").

Conclusion

1. 19% of births recorded in 2014 are from immigrant mothers in Italy. This is a significant number when compared to the general percentage of immigrant residents present in the country (approximately 7% of the general population) ("Demigrafia, Istat").

2. It is therefore unsurprising, given this context of generic hybridity, that a "documentary" film on immigration, Gianfranco Rosi's *Fuocoammare* (*Fire at Sea*, 2016) should win the Golden Bear for Best Picture at the 2016 Berlin film festival.

Bibliography

"Addio, Dolce Vita." *The Economist.* 24 November 2005. Web. http://www.economist.com/node/5164061.

Alemanno, Gianni. "Gianni Alemanno 2.0." *Gianni Alemanno 2.0.* Web. 16 May 2015. http://duepuntozero.alemanno.it/info/.

Althusser, Louis, and Etienne Balibar. *Reading Capital.* London: NLB, 1977. Print.

L'altro diritto. Centro di documentazione su carcere, devianza e marginalità. U of Florence. [2000?]. Web. 15 March 2017. http://www.altrodiritto.unifi.it/ricerche/devianza/dibello/cap1.htm.

Andall, Jacqueline, and Derek Duncan. *National Belongings: Hybridity in Italian Colonial and Postcolonial Cultures.* Oxford; New York: Peter Lang, 2010. Print.

Anderson, Benedict R. O'G. *Imagined Communities: Reflections on the Origin and Spread of Nationalism.* London; New York: Verso, 1991. Print.

Ashcroft, Bill, Gareth Griffiths, and Helen Tiffin. *The Empire Writes Back: Theory and Practice in Post-Colonial Literatures.* London; New York: Routledge, 2002. Print.

Autieri, Antonio. "Il resto della notte—recensione." *Sentieri del cinema.* 21 September 2008. Web. http://www.sentieridelcinema.it/il-resto-della-notte/.

Bayman, Louis, and Sergio Rigoletto, eds. *Popular Italian Cinema.* London: Palgrave Macmillan UK, 2013. Print.

Bazin, André. "From 'What Is Cinema?': The Ontology of the Photographic Image." *Film Theory and Criticism: Introductory Readings.* Ed. Leo Braudy and Marshall Cohen. New York: Oxford UP, 2004. 195–211. Print.

Beales, Derek, Edward Dawson, and Eugenio F. Biagini. *The Risorgimento and the Unification of Italy.* Harlow: Longman, 2002. Print.

Ben-Ghiat, Ruth. *Fascist Modernities: Italy, 1922–1945.* Berkeley and Los Angeles: U of California P, 2001. Print.

Benjamin, Walter. "The Work of Art in the Age of Mechanical Reproduction." *Film Theory and Criticism: Introductory Readings.* Ed. Leo Braudy and Marshall Cohen. New York: Oxford UP, 1999. 731–51. Print.

Bhabha, Homi K. *The Location of Culture.* London; New York: Routledge, 1994. Print.

Boni, Federico. "Il resto della notte: Recensione in anteprima." *Cineblog.it.* 6 October 2009. Web. http://www.cineblog.it/post/10915/il-resto-della-notte-recensione-in-anteprima.

Bibliography

Bossi, Umberto. "Intervento del segretario federale." *Leganord.org*. 1999. Web. http://www.leganord.org/phocadownload/ilmovimento/Presidente_Federale/discorsi_venezia/1999_12settembre.pdf.

Bradshaw, Peter. "Film Review: 'Gomorrah.'" *The Guardian*. 10 October 2008. Web. http://www.theguardian.com/film/2008/oct/10/crime.

Bullaro, Grace Russo, ed. *From Terrone to Extracomunitario: New Manifestations of Racism in Contemporary Italian Cinema: Shifting Demographics and Changing Images in a Multi-Cultural Globalized Society*. Troubadour Italian Studies. Leicester, UK: Troubadour, 2010. Print.

"Buonismo." *Grande Dizionario Hoepli Italiano*. 2015. Web. http://www.grandidizionari.it/Dizionario_Italiano/parola/b/buonismo.aspx?query=buonismo.

Calderoli, Roberto. "La questione Calderoli-Kyenge." *ilpost.it*. 16 April 2016. http://www.ilpost.it/2013/07/15/audio-calderoli-kyenge-orango/.

———. "Sicurezza, Calderoli: Rom, Rumeni, Terroristi Islamici." *Leganord.org*. 2013–15. Web. http://www.leganord.org/index.php/notizie2/6464-.

Caminati, Luca. "Filming Coming Communities: Ferzan Ozpetek's *Le Fate Ignoranti*." *Italica* 85.4 (2008): 455–64. Print.

Chambers, Iain. *Mediterranean Crossings: The Politics of an Interrupted Modernity*. Durham, NC and London, UK: Duke UP, 2008. Print.

"Cittadini stranieri in Italia—2013." *Tuttitalia.it*. 16 April 2015. Web. http://www.tuttitalia.it/statistiche/cittadini-stranieri-2013/.

Cossiga, Francesco, and Pasquale Chessa. *Italiani Sono Sempre Gli Altri: Controstoria D'Italia Da Cavour a Berlusconi*. Milano: Mondadori, 2007. Print.

Cowie, Elizabeth. *Representing the Woman: Cinema and Psychoanalysis*. Minneapolis: U of Minnesota P, 1997. Print.

Crespi, Alberto. "Tornatore Dal Bello Al Kitsch." *L'unità*, Paper ed., sec. In scena: 19. 2006. Print.

Crowdus, Gary, Deborah Young, and Dagnini Brey. "The Lack of Historical Memory: An Interview with Gianni Amelio." *Cineaste: America's Leading Magazine on the Art and Politics of the Cinema* 28.1 (2002): 14–18. Print.

Dal Lago, Alessandro. *Non-Persone: L'Esclusione Dei Migranti in Una Società Globale*. Milano: Feltrinelli, 1999. Print.

Dalle Vacche, Angela. *The Body in the Mirror: Shapes of History in Italian Cinema*. Princeton: Princeton UP, 1992. Print.

De Donno, Fabrizio, and Neelam Srivastava. "Colonial and Postcolonial Italy." *Interventions: International Journal of Postcolonial Studies* 8.3 (2006): 371–539. Print.

De Lauretis, Teresa. "Difference Embodied: Reflections on *Black Skin, White Masks*." *Parallax* 8.2 (2002): 54–68. Web. 7 March 2017. DOI: 10.1080/135346402 10130421.

Del Grande, Gabriele. "Fortress Europe." *Fortress Europe (Blog)*. 3 October 2013. Web. http://fortresseurope.blogspot.com/2006/02/nel-canale-di-sicilia.html.

"Demografia, Istat: nel 2014 nati 509 mil abambini, mai così pochi dall'Unità d'Italia." *Repubblica.it*. Cronaca. 12 February 2015. Web. http://www.repubblica.it/cronaca/2015/02/12/news/istat_nascite_morti_2015-107147481/.

De Sanctis, Pierpaolo, Domenico Monetti, and Luca Pallanch. *Non Solo Gomorra: Tutto Il Cinema Di Matteo Garrone*. Cantalupo in Sabina (RI) [i.e. Rieti, Italy]: Sabinæ, 2008. Print.

Dickie, John. *Darkest Italy: The Nation and Stereotypes of the Mezzogiorno, 1860–1900*. New York: St. Martin's, 1999. Print.

Duncan, Derek. "Italy's Postcolonial Cinema and Its Histories of Representation." *Italian Studies* 63.2 (2008): 195–211. Print.

Favero, Paolo. "The Spectacle of Multicultural Art and the Invisibility of Politics: A Review of the Documentary Film *L'orchestra Di Piazza Vittorio* (by Agostino Ferrente, Italy 2006)." *Social Anthropology* 17.3 (August 2009): 345–50. Print. Wiley Online Library. Web. DOI: 10.111/j. 1469–8676.2009.00074.x.

Forgacs, David. "*Pummarò* and the Limits of Vicarious Representation." *Media and Migration: Constructions of Mobility and Difference*. Ed. Russell King and Nancy Wood. London; New York: Routledge, 2001. 83–94. Print.

Foschi, P. "Rutelli-Alemanno: Match sulla legalità." 26 April 2008. Web. 8 March 2017. http://www.corriere.it/politica/08_aprile_26/rutelli_alemanno_a3bb1898-1358-11dd-a656-00144f02aabc.shtml.

Freud, Sigmund, and Peter Gay. *The Freud Reader*. New York: W.W. Norton, 1989. Print.

Gili, Jean A. *Arrivano i Mostri: I Volti Della Commedia Italiana*. Bologna [Italia]: Cappelli Editore, 1980. Print.

Giordana, Marco Tullio, Sandro Petraglia, Stefano Rulli and Lorenzo Codelli. *Quando Sei Nato Non Puoi Più Nasconderti*. Venezia: Marsilio, 2005. Print.

Giordano, Federico. *Le Parole Di Tornatore*. Reggio Calabria: Città del sole, 2007. Print.

Bibliography

Giuliani, Gaia, and Christina Lombardi-Diop. *Bianco E Nero: Storia Dell'Identità Razziale Degli Italiani*. Ed. Fulvio Cammarano. Quaderni di storia ed. Milano: Mondadori-Le Monnier, 2013. Print.

Gnisci, Armando. *Nuovo Planetario Italiano: Geografia E Antologia Della Letteratura Della Migrazione in Italia E in Europa*. Troina (Enna): Città aperta, 2006. Print.

Gramsci, Antonio, and Pasquale Verdicchio. *The Southern Question*. Toronto: Guernica, 2005. Print.

Greenblatt, Stephen. *Marvelous Possessions: The Wonder of the New World*. Chicago: U of Chicago P, 1992. Print.

Greene, Shelleen. *Equivocal Subjects: Between Italy and Africa—Constructions of Racial and National Identity in the Italian Cinema*. New York: Continuum, 2012. Print.

Grosz, Elizabeth. *Jacques Lacan: A Feminist Introduction*. London, England: Routledge, 1990. Print.

"Harsh Immigration Law Passed in Italy." *ERRC—European Roma Rights Center*. 7 November 2002. Web. http://www.errc.org/article/harsh-immigration-law-passed-in-italy/1598.

Hoepli Italian Dictionary. Grande Dizionario Italiano di Aldo Gabrielli. Milan: Hoepli, 2015. Print. Also online http://www.grandidizionari.it/Dizionario_Italiano.

Hooper, J. "Italian Woman's Murder Prompts Expulsion Threat to Romanians." *The Guardian*. 1 November 2007. Web. http://www.guardian.co.uk/world/2007/nov/02/italy.international.

Hope, William. *The Films of Giuseppe Tornatore*. Market Harborough: Troubador, 2001. Print.

Howie, Cary. "Wait and See: The Ignorant Fairies of Marie De France and Ferzan Özpetek." *Romanic Review* 101.4 (2010): 823–38. Print.

"International Organization for Migration." United Nations. 2015. Web. http://www.iom.int.

"Italy: The Sick Man of Europe." *The Telegraph*. 15 April 2008. Web. http://www.telegraph.co.uk/comment/3557277/Italy-The-sick-man-of-Europe.html.

Jazairy, El Hadi. "Cinematic Landscapes in Antonioni's *L'Avventura*." *Journal of Cultural Geography* 26.3 (2009): 349–67. Print.

Jones, Caroline A., Peter Galison, and Amy E. Slaton. *Picturing Science, Producing Art*. New York: Routledge, 1998. Print.

Keating, Abigail. "All Roads Lead to Piazza Vittorio: Transnational Spaces in Agostino Ferrente's Documusical." *Studies in Documentary Film* 5.2–3 (2011): 197–209. Print.

Kiliçbay, Baris. "Queer as Turk: A Journey to Three Queer Melodramas." *Queer Cinema in Europe*. Ed. Robin Griffiths. Bristol, England: Intellect, 2008. 117–28. Print.

Kingsley, Patrick. "Record Number of Migrants Expected to Drown in Mediterranean This Year." *The Guardian*. 1 April 2015. Web. http://www.theguardian.com/world/2015/apr/01/record-number-of-migrants-expected-to-drown-in-mediterranean-this-year.

Lerner, Giovanna Faleschini. "Ending 'Ventroloquistic Discourses' and Creating a Dialogue of Difference in De Seta's *Lettere Dal Sahara* and Moroni's *Le Ferie Di Licu*." *From Terrone to Extracomunitario: New Manifestations of Racism in Contemporary Italian Cinema: Shifting Demographics and Changing Images in a Multi-Cultural Globalized Society*. Ed. Grace Russo Bullaro. Troubadour Italian Studies. Leicester, UK: Troubador, 2010. 341–65. Print.

"Letta in Post." *The Economist*. 27 April 2013. Web. http://www.economist.com/news/europe/21576686-old-president-new-prime-minister-but-same-troubles-italy-letta-post.

Luciano, Bernadette, and Susanna Scarparo. *Reframing Italy: New Trends in Italian Women's Filmmaking*. PSRL 59. West Lafayette: Purdue UP, 2013. Print.

Mackey, Robert. "Brutal Images of Syrian Boy Drowned Off Turkey Must Be Seen, Activists Say." *New York Times*. 3 September 2015. Web. http://www.nytimes.com/2015/09/03/world/middleeast/brutal-images-of-syrian-boy-drowned-off-turkey-must-be-seen-activists-say.html?_r=0.

Marchetti, Silvia. "From *Extracomunitario* to *Terrone*: Towards a Discovery of Italy's Foreignness in Ferzan Özpetek's *Le Fate Ignoranti* (2001)." *From Terrone to Extracomunitario: New Manifestations of Racism in Contemporary Italian Cinema: Shifting Demographics and Changing Images in a Multi-Cultural Globalized Society*. Ed. Grace Russo Bullaro. Troubadour Italian Studies. Leicester, UK: Troubadour, 2010. 240–63. Print.

Marcus, Millicent. "Caro Diario and the Cinematic Body of Nanni Moretti." *Italica* 73.2 (1996): 233–47. Print.

"Marvelous." *Online Etymology Dictionary*. 2012. Web. http://www.etymonline.com/index.php?term=marvelous.

Mellino, Miguel. "Italy and Postcolonial Studies: A Difficult Encounter." *Interventions: International Journal of Postcolonial Studies* 8.3 (2006): 461–71. Print.

Moe, Nelson. *The View from Vesuvius: Italian Culture and the Southern Question*. Berkeley and Los Angeles: U of California P, 2002. Print.

Moliterno, Gino. *Historical Dictionary of Italian Cinema*. Lanham, MD: Scarecrow Press, 2008. Print.

Moroni, Vittorio. "Intervista—Le ferie di Licu." *YouTube*. Uploaded 7 November 2011: Redazione Babel. Web. https://www.youtube.com/watch?v=FEbLsymH9sI.

Mulvey, Laura. "Visual Pleasure and Narrative Cinema." *Feminist Film Theory: A Reader*. Ed. Sue Thornham. New York: New York UP, 1999. 58–69. Print.

Naficy, Hamid. *An Accented Cinema: Exilic and Diasporic Filmmaking*. Princeton: Princeton UP, 2001. Print.

Napolitano, Riccardo. *Commedia all'Italiana: Angolazioni Controcampi*. Roma: Gangemi, 1986. Print.

Nathan, Vetri. "Mimic-Nation, Mimic-Men: Contextualizing Italy's Migration Culture through Bhabha." *National Belongings: Hybridity in Italian Colonial and Postcolonial Studies*. Ed. Jacqueline Andall and Derek Duncan. Italian Modernities 7. Bern: Peter Lang, 2010. 41–62. Print.

———. "Nuovo Cinema Inferno: The Affect of Ambivalence in Giuseppe Tornatore's *La sconosciuta*." *From Terrone to Extracomunitario: New Manifestations of Racism in Contemporary Italian Cinema: Shifting Demographics and Changing Images in a Multi-Cultural Globalized Society*. Ed. Grace Russo Bullaro. Troubadour Italian Studies. Leicester, UK: Troubadour, 2010. 264–79. Print.

Ní Chonghaile, Clár. "UN Official Decries Toxic Backdrop as EU Debates New Migration Policies." *The Guardian*. 31 March 2015. Web. http://www.theguardian.com/global-development/2015/mar/31/un-official-eu-debates-migration-policies-peter-sutherland.

O'Healy, Áine. "Lamerica." *The Cinema of Italy*. Ed. Giorgio Bertellini and Gian Piero Brunetta. London, England: Wallflower, 2004. 245–53. Print.

———. "'[Non] È Una Somala': Deconstructing African Femininity in Italian Film." *The Italianist: Journal of the Department of Italian Studies, University of Reading and of the Department of Italian, University of Cambridge* 29.2 (2009): 175–98. Print.

Ottieri, Maria Pace. *Quando Sei Nato Non Puoi Più Nasconderti: Viaggio Nel Popolo Sommerso*. Roma: Nottetempo, 2003. Print.

Pacifici, Sergio J. "Notes toward a Definition of Neorealism." *Yale French Studies* 17 (1956): 44–53. Print.

Palumbo, Patrizia, ed. *A Place in the Sun: Africa in Italian Colonial Culture from Post-Unification to the Present*. Berkeley and Los Angeles: U of California P, 2003. Print.

Parati, Graziella. *Mediterranean Crossroads: Migration Literature in Italy.* Madison, NJ; London: Fairleigh Dickinson UP; Associated UP, 1999. Print.

———. *Migration Italy: The Art of Talking Back in a Destination Culture.* Toronto: U of Toronto P, 2005. Print.

Pastorino, Gloria. "Death by Water? Constructing the 'Other' in Melliti's *Io L'Altro.*" *From Terrone to Extracomunitario: New Manifestations of Racism in Contemporary Italian Cinema: Shifting Demographics and Changing Images in a Multi-Cultural Globalized Society.* Ed. Grace Russo Bullaro. Troubadour Italian Studies. Leicester, UK: Troubadour, 2010. 308–40. Print.

Pellegrini, Franca. *Italian Cinema and Immigration Database.* Italian Studies at Oxford. Web. 7 March 2017. http://www.mod-langs.ox.ac.uk/mml_apps/italian_movies/.

Perrin, Anne Gray. "*Guess Who's Coming to Dinner*: The Web of Racial, Class, and Gender Constructions in Late 1960s America." *Journal of Popular Culture* 45.4 (August 2012): 846–61. Print.

Pirandello, Luigi, Antonio Illiano, and Daniel P. Testa. *On Humor.* Chapel Hill: U of North Carolina P, 1974. Print.

Preziosi, Adelina, and Flavio Bernardis. "Splitsegno-Lamerica." *Segnocinema* 70. November-December (1994): 37–42. Print.

"Primissima: *Gomorra.*" *Primissima.it.* 2008. Web. http://www.primissima.it/film/-archivio/pagina13790.html.

Prono, Luca. "Gay Pride, Italian Style: Ferzan Ozpetek's *Le Fate Ignorati* (*Ignorant Fairies*)." *Bright Lights Film Journal* 34 (1 October 2001). Web. http://brightlightsfilm.com/gay-pride-italian-style-ferzan-ozpeteks-le-fate-ignoranti-ignorant-fairies/#.

Randi, Paola. "Paola Randi—Il Cinema Oggi: Il mestiere del regista." YouTube interview. 2 September 2011. Web. https://www.youtube.com/watch?v=5OlHHckSu3k.

Ricciardi, Alessia. "The Italian Redemption of Cinema: Neorealism from Bazin to Godard." *Romanic Review* 97.3–4 (2006): 483–500. Print.

Rocchio, Vincent F. *Cinema of Anxiety: A Psychoanalysis of Italian Neorealism.* Austin: U of Texas P, 1999. Print.

"Ronde anti-rom dopo le sevizie." *Corriere della Sera* [Milano]. 7 November 2007. Web. http://www.corriere.it/cronache/07_novembre_01/ronde_donna_seviziata.shtml. 2007.

Rossellini, Roberto. "A Few Words about Neo-Realism." *Springtime in Italy: A Reader on Neo-Realism.* Ed. David Overbey. Hamden, CT: Archon Books, 1979. 88–91. Print.

Bibliography

Rossellini, Roberto. "Ten Years of Cinema." *Springtime in Italy: A Reader on Neo-Realism*. Ed. David Overbey. Hamden, CT: Archon Books, 1979. 98–101. Print.

Said, Edward W. *Culture and Imperialism*. New York: Vintage Books, 1994. Print.

———. *Orientalism*. New York: Pantheon Books, 1978. Print.

Schrader, Sabine, and Daniel Winkler. *The Cinemas of Italian Migration: European and Transatlantic Narratives*. Cambridge, UK: Cambridge Scholars Publ., 2013. Print.

Scott, A. O. "Hollywood's Year of Heroine Worship." *New York Times*. 9 December 2012. Web. http://www.nytimes.com/2012/12/09/magazine/hollywoods-year-of-heroine-worship.html?ref=magazine.

Screening of the Film: The Orchestra of Piazza Vittorio. Documentary. Istituto Italiana de Cultura Toronto. 7 August 2010. Web. Accessed 13 February 2017. http://www.iictoronto.esteri.it

Sesti, Mario, interviewer. "La Straniera Invisibile—Viaggio Della Sconosciuta." Interview of Giuseppe Tornatore. *La Sconosciuta*. Medusa: Video, 2006. DVD.

Slemon, Stephen. "Post-Colonial Critical Theories." *New National and Post-Colonial Literatures: An Introduction*. Ed. Bruce King. Oxford: Clarendon, 1996. 178–97. Print.

Smith, Andrew. "Migrancy, Hybridity, and Postcolonial Literary Studies." *Cambridge Companion to Postcolonial Literary Studies*. Ed. Neil Lazarus. Cambridge, UK: Cambridge UP, 2004. 241–61. Print.

Spackman, Barbara. "Detourism: Orienting Italy in Amalia Nizzoli's Memorie Sull'Egitto." *Italianist: Journal of the Department of Italian Studies, University of Reading* 25.1 (2005): 35–54. Print.

"Spain Train Bombings Fast Facts." *CNN*. 11 March 2015. Web. http://www.cnn.com/2013/11/04/world/europe/spain-train-bombings-fast-facts/.

Steimatsky, Noa. *Italian Locations: Reinhabiting the Past in Postwar Cinema*. Minneapolis: U of Minnesota P, 2008. Print.

"La storia della cattedrale." *Eolie nel mondo*. n.d. Web. http://www.eolienelmondo.it/Biblioteca/Il%20Patrono%20San%20Bartolomeo/La%20Basilica%20Cattedrale-3.htm.

"Trope." *Merriam Webster Online Dictionary*. Merriam Webster. 2015. Web. Accessed 7 March 2017. http://www.merriam-webster.com/dictionary/trope.

Van den Abbeele, Georges. *Travel as Metaphor: From Montaigne to Rousseau*. Minneapolis: U of Minnesota P, 1992. Print.

Vecchi, Gian Guido. "Il suo motto era 'Nigrizia o morte': Comboni fu il Luther King del '800." *Corriere della sera—Archivio storico*. 6 October 2003. Web. http://archiviostorico.corriere.it/2003/ottobre/06/suo_motto_era_Nigrizia_morte_co_0_031006107.shtml.

Verdicchio, Pasquale. "The Preclusion of Postcolonial Discourse in Southern Italy." In *Revisioning Italy: National Identity and Global Culture*. Ed. Beverly Allen and Mary Russo. Minneapolis: U of Minnesota P, 1997. 191–212. Print.

Vitali, Alessandra. "Rutelli crolla contro Alemanno: Così finisce il 'laboratorio Roma.'" *La Repubblica.it*. 28 April 2008. Web. 7 March 2017. http://www.repubblica.it/2008/04/sezioni/politica/elezioni-2008-sei/sconfitta-rutelli/sconfitta-rutelli.html.

Young, Robert J. C. *Colonial Desire: Hybridity in Theory, Culture and Race*. London: Routledge, 1995. Print.

Zagarrio, Vito. "Before the (Neorealist) Revolution." *Global Neorealism: The Transnational History of a Film Style*. Ed. Saverio Giovacchini and Robert Sklar. Jackson: UP of Mississippi, 2011. Print.

Zavattini, Cesare. "A Thesis on Neorealism." *Springtime in Italy: A Reader on Neo-Realism*. Ed. David Overbey. Hamden, CT: Archon Books, 1979. 71–74. Print.

Filmography

Bianco e nero (White and Black). Dir. Cristina Comencini. Prod. Marco Chimenz. Cattleya, RAI Cinema, 2008. Film.

La doppia ora (The Double Hour). Dir. Gianni Amelio. Prod. Alia/Arena Films. Cecchi Gori Home Video, 1994. Film.

Le fate ignoranti (The Ignorant Fairies). Dir. Ferzan Özpetek. Medusa, 2001. Film.

Le ferie di Licu (Licu's Holidays). Dir. Vittorio Moroni. 50N, 2008. Film.

Gomorra (Gomorrah). Dir. Matteo Garrone. Prod. Domenico Procacci. Fandango, RAI Cinema, 2009. Film.

Into Paradiso (Inside Paradise). Dir. Paola Randi. Cinecittà Luce, 2010. Film.

Io, l'altro (I, the Other). Dir. Mohsen Melliti. 20th Century Fox Italia, 2006. Film.

Lamerica. Dir. Gianni Amelio. Prod. Alia/Arena Films. Cecchi Gori Home Video, 1994. Film.

Lettere dal Sahara (Letters From the Sahara). Dir. Vittorio de Seta. Prod. Metafilm. 20th Century Fox Home Entertainment, 2006. Film.

Lezioni di cioccolato (Chocolate Lessons). Dir. Vittorio de Seta. Prod. Metafilm. 20th Century Fox Home Entertainment, 2006. Film.

L'orchestra di piazza Vittorio (The Orchestra of Piazza Vittorio). Dir. Agostino Ferrente. Eurozoom, 2006. Film.

Pummarò (Tomato). Dir. Michele Placido. Prod. Claudio Bonivento. Cineeuropa 92, RAI, 1990. Film.

Quando sei nato non puoi più nasconderti (Once You're Born You Can No Longer Hide). Dir. Marco Tullio Giordana, Cattleya, 2005. Film.

Reality. Dir. Matteo Garrone. Fandango, 2012. Film.

Respiro. Dir. Emanuele Crialese. Fandando, Les Films des Tournelles, Roissy Films, Medusa. 2002. Film.

Il resto della notte (The Rest of the Night). Dir. Francesco Munzi. Bianca Film; RAI Cinema, 2008. Film.

La sconosciuta (The Unknown Woman). Dir. Guiseppe Tornatore. Prod. Medusa Films. Medusa, 2006. Film.

Terra di mezzo (In-Between Land). Dir. Matteo Garrone. Archimede, 1996. Film.

Terraferma (Terrafirma). Dir. Emmanuele Crialese. Prod. Cattleya. 01 Distribution, 2011. Film.

Index

Abbot, Paul, 40
Accattone, 176
"Addio, Dolce Vita," 36
After Fellini, 58–59
Albanians, 213. *See also Lamerica*
 represented in *Terra di mezzo,* 92, 96–98
 in *Terraferma,* 121
Alemanno, Gianni, 9, 229n8
Althusser, Louis, 51
ambivalence, chronic
 centrality of, 38–39
 of Italy, 32–37
 melancholy and, 183–84
 menace and, 179–80
 in post-neorealist film, 48–51, 71–79
Amelio, Gianni, 43–44, 69, 216. *See also Lamerica*
 concern with Italy's historical amnesia, 103
 on filming in Panavision, 107
anamorphic format, 114–15
Andall, Jacqueline, 4
Anderson, Benedict, 11
Antonioni, Michelangelo, 81, 122, 216
Arab Spring movements, 10
Argentero, Luca, 168
Ashcroft, Bill, 27–28
avventura, L', 81, 122, 216

Bazin, André, 66–67, 68–69, 73
Beales, Derek, 33
"belated" nation, Italy as, 33
Bengali marriage in *Le ferie di Licu,* 157–67
Ben-Ghiat, Ruth, 35
Berlusconi, Silvio, 9, 10, 55, 72
Bertolucci, Bernardo, 81–82
Bhabha, Homi, 5, 16, 27, 71, 226–27
 on colonial stereotypes, 39–42, 132, 134, 175, 197–98
 on cultural hybridity, 30–31, 38–39, 52, 175, 181
 embodied conception of culture and, 52–53
 on mimicry, 42–45, 49
 on regime of visibility, 41–42
Biagini, Eugenio, 33
Bianco e nero: storia dell'identità razziale degli italiani, 20, 148–57, 213, 219–20
 as mainstream, big-budget film, 149
Big Deal on Madonna Street (I soliti ignoti), 194
Black Skin, White Masks, 52, 205
bodies
 in neorealism, 65
 in post-neorealism, 74
body-as-nation, 57–60
Bossi, Umberto, 9, 10, 34
Bova, Raoul, 206
Brexit vote, 2
Bush, George W., 206
Buy, Margherita, 182

Cahiers du Cinema, 60, 66
Caillois, Roger, 108–09
Calderoli, Roberto, 45–48, 195
 use of the Marvelous in analyzing speech of, 50–51
Camorra organization, 87
camorrista, Il, 186
Capotondi, Giuseppe, 188, 226
Caro Diario, 111
Catholic Church, 137–38, 143–44
centrality of chronic ambivalence, 71–79
Cinema Paradiso, 1, 178
Colonial Desires, 17
colonial discourse
 analysis, 29
 fantasies of desire in, 131–32, 222–23
 mimicry in, 42–45, 47

Index

colonial legacy of Italy, 35
Colpire al cuore, 103
Comboni, Daniele, 137
Comencini, Cristina, 148–49, 150, 157, 213
    actors used by, 152
Commedia all'italiana, 57, 59, 60, 71, 217
    chronic ambivalence in, 71
    criminality depicted in, 176
    exaggerated physical traits and cultural stereotypes in, 169, 173
    iconic actors of, 78
    importance of, 61–62
    main stylistic characteristics of, 74
    masked performances in, 78–79
    as mix of comedy and tragedy, 73, 75–78
    origins of, 72–73
    use of geographies in, 86, 96
    visual distortions of bodies in, 74–75
commedia di costume, 74
controstoria, 37
Coppa Volpi, 188
Così ridevano, 103
Cossiga, Francesco, 32–33
Cowie, Elizabeth, 169–70
"Creative Writers and Daydreaming," 173
Crespi, Alberto, 181
Crialese, Emanuele, 121–29, 209, 216–17
criminality, 175–77, 224–25
    cronaca nera, 194
    La doppia ora and, 188–91
    one-dimensional stereotype of delinquency and, 198
    post–9/11 stereotypes, 194–95
    Il resto della notte and, 191–205
    La sconosciuta and, 8, 178–88
cronaca nera, 194
cultural discourse creation, 17
cultural economy of detourist films, 11–14
cultural hybridity, 7–8
    Bhabha's theory of, 30–31, 38–39, 52, 175
    fantasies of desire in biological and, 131–32
    fear(s) of, 4–5
    framing, 21–25
    located on screen, 48–51
    multiculturalism vs., 14–21
    postcolonial studies and, 14, 27–30
    third space of, 181, 190, 216
Culture and Imperialism, 29–30
Cupellini, Claudio, 168, 219

Dalle Vacche, Angela, 57–58, 61–62
D'Azeglio, Massimo, 33
"Deanimations: Maps and Portraits of Life Itself," 50
De Donno, Fabrizio, 36
De Lauretis, Teresa, 52
Deleuze, Gilles, 68–69
De Mauro, Tullio, 33
De Seta, Vittorio, 83, 136, 140
De Sica, Vittorio, 67–68, 175–76
desire, 131–35, 213, 219–23
    fantasies in colonial discourse, 131–32, 222–23
    immigrant-as-masquerade and sugar-coated fantasy in *Lezione di cioccolato,* 133, 167–74
    and marriage in *Le ferie di Licu,* 157–67
    the palatable immigrant in *Bianco e nero: storia dell'identità razziale degli italiani* and, 20, 148–57
    scopophilia and, 133–34, 153–54
    stereotype-as-fetish and, 132

volatile sexual politics of the gaze in *Pummarò* and *Lettere dal Sahara* and, 135–48
detourist films, 4, 56, 206, 226
  cultural economy of, 11–14
Dial M for Murder, 179
diaspora, Italian, 35
"Difference Embodied: Reflections on *Black Skin, White Masks,*" 52
Di Mazarelli, Carmelo, 105
Divorzio all'italiana, 78
dolce vita, La, 81
domesticity and sense of space, 141–42, 142–43, 146
doppia ora, La, 188–91, 198, 226
Dormiveglia, 92
Duncan, Derek, 4, 41

Eaton, Mick, 77
Economist, The, 36
embodied conception of culture, 52
Empire Writes Back, The, 27–28
Esposti, Piera Degli, 182
Euglen e Gertian (Terra di mezzo), 92, 96–98
European Union, 2
  fear of immigration in, 9
extracomunitario, 25

Fanon, Frantz, 52–53, 205
Fascism, 57, 58
fate ignoranti, Le, 23–24, 37
Favero, Paolo, 19
Favino, Pierfrancesco, 182
Fellini, Federico, 72, 75, 80, 81
ferie di Licu, Le, 157–67
Ferrente, Agostino, 19–20
fetishistic scopophilia, 134, 153–54, 162
Forgacs, David, 136–37
Forza, Roberto, 114
4 Months, 3 Weeks and 2 Days, 192
"fragmented" nation, Italy as, 33–34

framing of hybridity, 21–25
Freud, Sigmund, 39, 41, 42, 132, 134
  "Creative Writers and Daydreaming," 173

Garrone, Matteo, 1, 2, 69, 86, 166, 199, 213, 221
  actors used by, 88
  aestheticized humoristic style, 93
  interest in expressing rather than commenting, 90–91, 96
  as interpreter of reality, 89–90
  oneiric spaces used by, 86–102
  open-ended relationship to screenplays, 90
  stress on visual over textual, 91–92
  use of mise-en-scène, 88, 94–95
Gassman, Vittorio, 78, 177
gas station attendant represented in *Self Service,* 92, 98–102
gaze, 161–62
  dominant, 168–74
  glazed look and, 166–67
  scopophilia and, 133–34
  volatile sexual politics of, 135–48
gender roles, 128–29, 145
geographies and landscapes, 85–86, 213
  haptical Mediterranean in *Terraferma,* 120–29
  oneiric spaces in *Terra di mezzo,* 86–102
  politics of sentimentality and, 111–20
  politics of sentimentality in *Quando sei nato non puoi più nasconderti,* 83, 112–20
  recuperation of embodied history in *Lamerica,* 103–11
Germania Anno Zero, 64, 65
Germi, Claudia, 182

247

Index

Giordana, Marco Tullio, 83, 112, 114, 216
  on the "innocent" gaze and points of view, 115–18
Giuliani, Gaia, 20
Gnisci, Armando, 14, 15–16
Godard, Jean-Luc, 68–69
Golino, Valeria, 127
Gomorra, 1, 87–88, 99, 102, 199
  Italian subtitles used in, 88–89
  social commentary in, 90
Gramsci, Antonio, 36–37
grande bellezza, La, 1
grande guerra, La, 73
Greenblatt, Stephen, 48–49
Greene, Shelleen, 154–56
Grosz, Elizabeth, 49, 108
Guess Who's Coming to Dinner?, 156

Haber, Alessandro, 182
Haraway, Donna, 50
Hope, William, 180, 183
humor, 73, 75–78
  Bianco e nero as, 150–51
  criminality and, 177–78
  in *Lamerica,* 105
  in *Lettere dal Sahara,* 142–43
  realist and humoristic modes of representation, 79–83, 218–19
hybridity. *See* cultural hybridity

Imaginary, the (Lacan), 41–42
immigration into Italy
  current crisis, 14–15
  detourism and, 4
  fear of hybridity and, 4–5
  global response to immigration and, 1–2, 229n9
  populations, 16–17, 229n7
  question, 8–11, 200–201
  by refugees, 10
  Self/Other dichotomies and, 3, 11, 21
  statistics, 229n7, 230n11, 232n1

impegno sociale, 66, 69–70, 79
International Organization for Migration (IOM), 230n11
interracial relationships. *See Lettere dal Sahara; Pummarò*
Into Paradiso, 214–25
Io, l'altro, 1, 205–11
Isole (section of *Caro Diario*), 111
Italian cinema, 1
  cultural hybridity located in, 48–51
  depictions of criminality in, 175–76
  geographies and landscapes (*See* geographies and landscapes)
  Mediterranean as trope in, 111–12, 121
  as national art form, 58
Italian Cinema in the Light of Neorealism, 59
Italy
  as "belated" nation, 33
  as both center and periphery of imagined Western Civilization, 30
  chronic ambivalence, 32–37
  as Europe's internal, hybrid Other, 33, 52
  failed colonial legacy of, 35
  as "fragmented" nation, 33–34
  global diaspora, 35
  immigration into (*See* immigration into Italy)
  paths forward for postcolonial studies in, 52–53
  recuperation of embodied history of, 103–11
  as "sick man" of Europe, 36–37
  "Southern Question," 34–35
  trasformismo, 36, 72
"Italy: The Sick Man of Europe," 36

Jameson, Fredric, 183–84
JanMohammed, Abdul, 17
Jazairy, El Hadi, 122

Index

Keating, Abigail, 19
Kurdi, Aylan, 10
Kyenge, Cécile, 10, 45–48, 50

Lacan, Jacques, 41–42, 108
ladro di bambini, Il, 103
Lamerica, 2, 43–44, 48, 69, 114, 122, 216
   as both epic and humoristic, 105
   filmed in Panavision, 107
   recuperation of embodied history and, 103–11
   use of the Marvelous in analyzing, 50–51
legendary psychasthenia, 108
Lerner, Giovanna Faleschini, 140
Letta, Enrico, 72
Letta, Gianni, 10, 45
Lettere dal Sahara, 83, 213, 223
   volatile sexual politics of the gaze in, 140–48
Lezione di cioccolato, 133, 167–74, 213, 219
Lloyd, David, 17
Location of Culture, The, 5, 31, 53
Lombardi-Diop, Cristina, 20
Luciano, Bernadette, 77

Mahgoub, Ahmed, 98–102
Mailat, Nicolae Romulus, 17
Malena, 181, 185
Manfredi, Nino, 78
map-fetishism, 50
Marchetti, Silvia, 24
Marcus, Millicent, 58–59
Mare Nostrum, 10
marriage, Bengali, 157–67
Martorana, Giuseppe, 206
Marvelous bodies, concept of, 5–6, 13, 24, 227
Marvelous Possessions: The Wonder of the New World, 48–49
Marx, Karl, 51
Masoni, Tullio, 72
Masslo, Jerry, 231Ch4n1
Mastroianni, Marcello, 78

Mazzini, Giuseppe, 36
Mediterranean, the
   haptical, 120–29
   as trope, 111–12, 121
Mediterraneo, 111
meglio gioventù, La, 115
melancholy, 183–84
Melliti, Mohsen, 13, 205–11, 210, 213
Methnani, Salah, 15
metonym, 42
metonymy of presence, 175
mimic-men, 78, 172
mimicry, 39, 42–45, 49, 134
   affective, 180–81
   menace of, 45–48, 175, 181–82, 187
mise-en-scène, 88, 94–95, 142, 166–67
Monicelli, Mario, 71–72, 73, 176
Monti, Mario, 10
moralities, 213
   depictions of criminality and, 175–77
   double-visions in *La sconosciuta* and *La doppia ora* and, 177–91
   latent Orientalism in *Il resto della notte* and, 191–205
   War on Terror in *Io, l'altro*, 1, 205–11
Moretti, Nanni, 92, 111
Moroni, Vittorio, 157, 159–60, 213
Morricone, Ennio, 184
mostri, I, 176
Mount Vesuvius, 85–86
Moussa-Ba, Saidou, 15
multiculturalism vs. hybridity, 14–21
Mulvey, Laura, 133–34, 135, 157, 169
Munzi, Francesco, 191–95, 196–97, 202, 204, 213, 225–26
Mussolini, Benito, 4, 35, 104

249

neorealism, 2–3, 6–7, 56–57. *See also* post-neorealism
   body-as-nation and, 57–60
   containing, 62–71
   criminal-minded citizen in, 175–76
   criteria in style of, 65
   defining, 60–62
   immigration films as not, 70
   impegno sociale, 66, 69–70
   major meanings attributed to, 63
   neo-neorealism, 2–3, 56, 59, 70, 104, 214, 216, 231Ch3n1
   as proponents of true realism, 66–67
   realist and humoristic modes of representation in, 79–83
   use of geographies in, 86
new migrant cinema, 226–27. *See also* Italian cinema
   centrality of chronic ambivalence in post-neorealist, 71–79
   as detourist, 4, 11–14, 56, 206, 226
   examples of, 1–2
   marvelous bodies of, 5–6
   tradition of neorealism in, 2–3, 6–7, 56–57
Nizzoli, Amalia, 12
Nuovo Cinema Paradiso, 178, 183–84

O'Healy, Ainé, 104–05, 151, 154, 206–07
oikos, 12, 13, 14, 16, 24, 25, 82
   hybrid, 79
   split between West and East, 55
   vehicle-as-, 141–42
   of the viewer, 117
On Humor, 73
orchestra di Piazza Vittorio, L', 19–20, 23, 24, 25
Orientalism, 29–30, 135, 222
   black females and, 149, 154, 156–57
   importance of "fact" in creation of discourse of, 209–10
   stereotypes post–9/11, 194–95
   radical realism as, 196
   in *Il resto della notte,* 191–205
   unequal logic of, 158
Other/Otherness. *See also* desire
   Arab, 169–74, 205–11
   black, 45–47, 96, 119–20, 138–39
   Italy as Europe's internal, hybrid, 33, 52
   Italy's south as, 34–35
   as point of entry into identity, 132–33
   /Self dichotomies, 3, 11, 19–22, 187, 214
   in *Silhouette (Terra di mezzo),* 96
   volatile sexual politics of the gaze and, 135
Ottieri, Maria Pace, 113–14
Özpetek, Ferzan, 23–24, 37

Panavision, 107
Parati, Graziella, 14, 32, 58, 131, 141
Pasolini, Pier Paolo, 82, 176
Perrin, Anne Gray, 156
Petraglia, Sandro, 115–16
photography, 66–67, 73–74
Pintus, Pietro, 73
Pirandello, Luigi, 57, 73, 75–77, 151, 219–20
Placido, Michele, 136, 179, 182, 185, 186
Plantinga, Carl, 180–81
Poitier, Sidney, 156
politics of sentimentality, 111–20
polygamy, 171–72
Porte aperte, 103
postcolonial studies, 14, 27–30
   paths forward for Italian, 52–53
postino, Il, 1

post-neorealism, 70. *See also* neorealism
  body-as-nation in, 57–60
  centrality of chronic ambivalence in, 71–79
  defining, 60–62
  Gomorra, 87
  main stylistic characteristics of, 74
  realist and humoristic modes of representation in, 79–83
Prodi, Romano, 17
prostitutes represented in *Silhouette*, 92, 93–96, 213
psychosis, 108–09
Pummarò, 2, 3, 133, 151, 213, 223
  volatile sexual politics of the gaze in, 135–40

Quando sei nato non puoi più nasconderti, 83, 112–20, 122, 128, 186, 213, 216

race, performativity of, 155–56
radical realism, Orientalism as, 196
Randi, Paola, 214–25
Rappoport, Ksenia, 182, 188, 197
realist and humoristic modes of representation, 79–83
Reality, 86, 87–88, 102
Rear Window, 179
Red Desert, 122
Reggiani, Giovanna, 17–18, 193
Renzi, Matteo, 10
repetition, importance of, 40–42
Representing the Woman, 169
Respiro, 127–28
resto della notte, Il, 191–205, 213
Ricciardi, Alessia, 63
Risi, Dino, 176
Risorgimento, 33, 36, 37
Rocco e i suoi fratelli, 176
Roma, 17–18
Roma città aperta, 63–64
Romeo and Juliet, 139

Rossellini, Roberto, 63–64, 68
  on art of "waiting," 91
Rulli, Stefano, 115–16, 119–20
Rushdie, Salman, 15
Rutelli, Francesco, 9

Sacher d'Oro, 92
Said, Edward, 29–30, 192, 195, 209–10, 218, 222
Salvatore, Gabriele, 111
Saviano, Roberto, 87
Scarparo, Susanna, 77
Sciascia, Leonardo, 103
Scola, Ettore, 176
sconosciuta, La, 8, 178–88, 198, 225–26
scopophilia, 133–34, 153–54, 162
Scott, A. O., 150
sea, film representations of the, 121–29
Self/Other dichotomies, 3, 11, 19–22, 187, 214
self-reflexivity, 60–62, 79–80
Self Service (Terra di mezzo), 92, 98–102
Senegalese immigrants. *See Bianco e nero: storia dell'identità razziale degli italiani*; *Lettere dal Sahara*
sentimentality, politics of, 111–20
Servino, Luca, 199
Sesti, Mario, 182
"Sick man" of Europe, Italy as, 36–37
Silhouette (Terra di mezzo), 92, 93–96, 102
Slemon, Stephen, 38
Smith, Adam, 51
soliti ignoti, I, 78–79, 176
Sordi, Alberto, 78
Sorrentino, Paolo, 1, 91
Southern Question, The, 37
"Southern Question" and Italy, 34–35

Index

space/landscapes
  in neorealism, 65
  in post-neorealism, 74
Spackman, Barbara, 12
Srivastava, Neelam, 36
Steimatsky, Noa, 86
stella che non c'è, La, 103
stereotype-as-fetish, 39, 49, 175
  desire and, 132
  importance of the visible and of repetition in, 40–42
  reinscription of, 45–48
  structure of, 39–40
  in *Terra di mezzo,* 100–01
stupor, 6, 213
  as being dazed and astonished, 50–51, 218
  classificatory confusion and, 77
  as disorientation, 144
  suspension of identity and, 82, 219–20
  in tradition of *commedia all'italiana,* 218, 219
suspension
  of allegiance, 191
  of gender roles, 128, 133, 162–63
  Gomorra's moral tension and stylistic, 88–89
  humoristic, 218
  of identities, 6, 44, 45, 82, 111, 122, 197, 218
  interplay of gazes and, 162
  as momentary confusion, 109
  moment of the marvelous as moment of, 50
  partial, 117, 120, 162
  of racial caricatures, 147–48, 223
  in the sea, 117, 120–21, 217
  temporary, 111, 145
  threatened by violence, 221
  in time and space, disruption of, 101
Sutherland, Peter, 1

Telegraph, The, 36
Terra di mezzo, 1, 3, 6, 69, 166, 221
  as detourist film, 13
  Euglen e Gertian, 92, 96–98
  lack of dramatic events in, 91–92
  oneiric spaces in, 86–102
  as response to polarized global reaction to immigration, 2
  Self Service, 92, 98–102
  Silhouette, 92, 93–96, 102
  three distinct episodes of, 91–92
terra trema, La, 122
Terraferma, 120–29, 209, 216–17
time
  in neorealism, 65
  in post-neorealism, 74
  in *Terra di mezzo,* 99
Timi, Filippo, 188
Tognazzi, Ugo, 78, 177
Tornatore, Giuseppe, 8, 178–88, 225–26
torpor, 82
trasformismo, 36, 72
Travolti da un insolito destino nell'azzurro mare d'agosto, 111
trope
  defined, 49–50
  map-fetishism as, 50
  Mediterranean as, 111–12
Trump, Donald, 2

Umberto D, 67–68
Un Americano a Roma, 78
Una pura formalità, 186
Unità, L', 181

Van Den Abbeele, Georges, 12
Vasiliu, Laura, 192, 196
Vecchi, Paolo, 72
Venice Film Festival, 103
Viaggio nel popolo sommerso, 113–14
Visconti, Luchino, 122, 176

visible, the
    in *Le ferie di Licu,* 158–59
    importance in stereotype-as-fetish of, 40–42
    scopophilia and, 133–34
    volatile sexual politics of the gaze and, 135–48
"Visual Pleasure and Narrative Cinema," 133
Vitti, Monica, 192
Volo, Fabio, 151–52
voyeurism, 134

War on Terror, 205–11
working class represented in *Euglen e Gertian,* 92, 96–98

Young, Robert, 17, 21–22, 38, 53
    on fantasies of desire in colonial discourse, 131–32, 222–23

Zagarrio, Vito, 56
Zavattini, Cesare, 64–65

About the book

Vetri Nathan
Marvelous Bodies: Italy's New Migrant Cinema
PSRL 70

Historically a source of emigrants to Northern Europe and the New World, Italy has rapidly become a preferred destination for immigrants from the global South. Life in the land of *la dolce vita* has not seemed so sweet recently, as Italy struggles with the cultural challenges caused by this surge in immigration. *Marvelous Bodies* explores thirteen key full-length Italian films released between 1990 and 2010 that treat this remarkable moment of cultural role reversal through a plurality of styles. In this landmark study Nathan argues that Italy sees itself as the quintessential internal Other of Western Europe, and that this subalternity directly influences its cinematic response to immigrants, Europe's external Others. In framing his case to understand Italy's cinematic response to immigrants, Nathan first explores some basic questions: Who exactly is the Other in Italy? Does Italy's own past partial alterity affect its present response to its newest subalterns? Drawing on Homi Bhabha's writings and Italian cinematic history, Nathan then posits the existence of marvelous bodies that are momentarily neither completely Italian nor completely immigrant. This ambivalence of forms extends to the films themselves, which tend to be generic hybrids. The persistent curious presence of marvelous bodies and a pervasive generic hybridity enact Italy's own chronic ambivalence that results from its presence at the cultural crossroads of the Mediterranean.

About the author

Vetri Nathan is an Assistant Professor of Italian Studies in the Department of Modern Languages, Literatures and Cultures at the University of Massachusetts Boston. He received his BA in Italian from Connecticut College, and an MA and PhD in Italian from Stanford University in 2009. Vetri's research interests include immigrant cultures and globalization in contemporary Italy, colonialism and postcoloniality, Italian cinema and food studies. He has published various articles on these topics.

"A very well written and researched contribution to the field of world cinema, *Marvelous Bodies* is also tremendously timely. A testimony to the complex nature and prolificacy of Italy's immigration cinema, *Marvelous Bodies* is a pioneering work whose blend of originality and academic rigor will help scholars and student alike understand the continuing hybridization of identities and imaginaries in Italy (and in Europe)."

—Fulvio Orsitto
California State University Chico